The Second Liberal Art

A Guide to Traditional Logic

Michael W. Tkacz

Gonzaga University

Cover Illustration:

A medieval master and his students from the frontispiece of the
Regulae grammaticales of Guarino da Verona, printed at Florence
in 1494 probably by Bartolommeo di Libri. Guarino da Verona
(1370–1460) was appointed master of arts at the University of
Ferrara in 1436 where he taught rhetoric as well as
Greek and Latin grammar.

Kendall Hunt
publishing company

www.kendallhunt.com
Send all inquiries to:
4050 Westmark Drive
Dubuque, IA 52004-1840

Copyright © 2011 by Kendall Hunt Publishing Company

ISBN 978-0-7575-8574-6

Printed in the United States of America
10 9 8 7 6 5 4 3

Dedication

Guillelmo Augustino Wallace
Ordinis Praedicatorum
Doctori Eruditissimi
Scientiae Logicae Materialis

Contents

Dedication   iii
Preface to the Student   vii
Acknowledgments   ix

§1   Liberating Arts   1
§2   Giving Reasons   3
§3   The True, the False, and the Neither   17
§4   Picturing Propositions   37
§5   From One Proposition to Another   45
§6   Categorically Arguing   65
§7   Picturing Arguments   71
§8   Being Elliptical   91
§9   Being Complex   111
§10   The Simple and the Complex   129
§11   Either/Or and Therefore   141
§12   If/Then and Therefore   157
§13   It Is Absurd and Therefore   171
§14   Therefore It Is Probable   197
§15   To Err Is Human   217
§16   The Same, the Different, and the Like   223
§17   In Common and In Particular   237
§18   Waiting for an Answer   243
§19   What Is the Alternative?   249
§20   Personal Attack   259

Appendix I: Schemata of Standard Deductive Forms   271
Appendix II: Catalogue of Common Fallacies   273
Appendix III: Additional Exercise Sets   277

Glossary of Logical Terms   287
Glossary of Latin Terms   298

Preface to the Student

Higher education is very ancient, going back more than two thousand years to the time of the ancient Greeks and ancient Chinese. Institutions of higher education, however, are a medieval invention. The earliest universities were founded in the last few decades of the twelfth century. Right from the start, the study of logic was central to the university curriculum and every university student was expected to have some knowledge of the forms of argument and common fallacies. It was recognized that progress in all the sciences and the professions depended on skill in reasoning. This remains just as much the case in modern universities where any kind of scientific research and all professional training presuppose the ability to think in a rigorous and critical manner.

Because a good place to begin learning any skill is to start at the beginning, the art of logic will be introduced in this book in the way it was in the medieval universities. In those days, the professor would introduce students to the methods of logical argument by lecturing on some classical logical textbook and providing examples. He would then orally question his students to learn whether they understood the examples. This book takes a similar approach. The methods of logic and examples of arguments and fallacies are presented in twenty sections. After each section is an exercise or series of exercises that provide the student the opportunity to respond in writing to the given examples, demonstrating understanding of the methods. This practical method of learning logic was very successful in the medieval university and provides the modern student with a useful technique for developing logical skill. By reading the text sections of this book and writing out the exercises, the student will attain the same abilities that prepared medieval university students for more advanced studies in the sciences and the professions. In addition to the text sections and exercises in this book, additional exercises and reference materials are included at the back of the book as a further aid to the student.

Acknowledgments

Like my previous book *The Art of Reasoning*, this book is intended as a contribution to a long tradition that has its roots in antiquity. Mostly it owes its form and content to the many generations of masters who labored in the medieval universities teaching the logical tradition as the foundation for all knowledge. My more recent debts include Maria Bermudez and the other editors and staff at KendallHunt Publishing for their assistance and encouragement. I also wish to thank Sandy Hank of Gonzaga University Faculty Services and my graduate student assistant Ricardo Davila for their technical assistance. Finally, I wish to express my gratitude to Professors Douglas Kries and Thomas McLaughlin for their advice on the development of the dialectical approach taken in this book.

§1 Liberating Arts

The first universities were established in Western Europe during the Middle Ages. In those days, university students did not "declare a major" in one or another discipline, but instead studied with the Faculty of Arts or one of three professional faculties in law, medicine, or theology. Naturally, the task of the three professional faculties was to prepare their students for a career in their respective professions. The job of the Faculty of Arts, however, was not to prepare students for a particular profession, but to teach a certain set of basic intellectual skills known as the seven liberal arts. These liberal arts are the skills needed to practice any profession and successfully pursue any goal in life.

In Latin, the language of the medieval university, the word *artes* indicates a set of skills or abilities. Our modern English word "arts" still retains something of this ancient meaning. There are, of course, many different sorts of skills, many arts. Technical skills aimed at producing some sort of artifact are one sort. Carpenters, for example, possess skill in producing useful things out of wood. Sculptors have the various skills required for the construction of beautiful or expressive objects that are carved from stone or wood or cast in bronze or made in some other way. Electrical engineers apply their special skills to making useful electrical products or systems. Another kind of technical skill aims not so much at producing an artifact but at producing a sort of well-ordered state of affairs, such as the physician who employs medical skills to restore health to the body. Not all skills, however, are technical. Some skills are not abilities for making a product or a state of affairs, but are skills aimed at attaining knowledge. Such intellectual skills are abilities to do what is necessary for learning and knowing. The natural scientist, for example, will seek mathematical skills in order to be able to rigorously and accurately measure and describe natural objects. So, some skills are technical arts aimed at producing useful, beautiful, or expressive objects. Other skills are intellectual arts aimed at attaining knowledge.

People have always realized that, if a person wants to learn something, then that person must have the ability to do so. Abilities of these kinds are those intellectual arts that enable one to gain knowledge. Without such skills, one cannot come to actually know what there is to know. So, what exactly are these skills? What are these intellectual arts? In the medieval university, seven of these intellectual arts were taught as the foundation of all knowledge. Three of these arts concern skill in using language and four concern basic mathematical skills.

It is clear that learning or coming to knowledge will somehow involve language, for what is known must be articulated, even if only to oneself. So, the knower must possess the *art of grammar*: skill in using the parts of language to produce articulations, to say things. Once one is able to say things, then one needs skill in relating the various things that are said—what is said today with what was said yesterday, what one person says with what another says, and so on. Thus, the knower must also possess the *art of logic*: skill in recognizing and using the actual and possible relationships among things that can be said in language. Having attained skill in using the grammatical structure of language and its logical relationships, then one will want to use language to articulate reality accurately and respond to it in various ways according to one's needs. Thus, the knower must also possess the *art of rhetoric*: skill in using language for many and varied purposes. The person with grammatical skill knows the parts of language and how to put them together in various ways to say different things clearly and properly. The person with logical skill knows when what is said is compatible with something else said, when it excludes something else said, and when it supports or establishes something else said. The person with rhetorical skill knows how to use language with all of its grammatical and logical possibilities to effectively describe, inform, persuade, warn, discourage, instruct, and do all those other things people do with language in the course of their lives.

It is clear that learning also requires some basic skill in recognizing and using various formal relationships involving quantities. So, the knower must possess the *art of arithmetic*: skill in recognizing and using discrete quantities (numbers). Likewise, the knower must possess the *art of geometry*: skill in recognizing and using continuous quantities (figures). In addition, the knower must possess the *art of proportions*: skill in recognizing and using the proportional relationships among discrete quantities. Finally, the knower must possess the *art of astronomy*: skill in recognizing and describing the various continuous patterns traced by the regular movements of the heavenly bodies.

In the medieval university, the Faculty of Arts taught these basic skills as the foundation of all education. They realized that without at least some level of skill in each of these areas, one cannot hope to learn and understand the advanced sciences that constitute knowledge of reality. Thus, all professional studies and all the theoretical sciences are grounded in these basic intellectual skills. Any sort of intellectual progress, any sort of scientific research, and any sort of professional ability requires basic training in the seven liberal arts. Over the past 800 years, human knowledge has grown tremendously. Yet it remains as true today as it was in the early universities of medieval times that all progress in learning depends on facility in the three language arts and the four mathematical arts.

The second of the liberal arts, the art of logic, is the subject of this book. As already mentioned, one can describe this art as skill in recognizing, understanding, and making use of the various logical relationships between what can be articulated in language. Sometimes this sort of skill is called "the art of reasoning" or "the art of critical thinking." Yet this is a very general way to think about the subject of logic and a more precise definition would be helpful. If one were to ask a medieval professor for a definition of logic, he would say something like this: *logic is the art of recognizing, analyzing, and evaluating arguments and their parts*. Why the focus on argument? It is not because argument is the only logical relationship in language. Rather, it is because, with respect to learning, argument is the most important and fundamental logical relationship. It is through argument that our knowledge is advanced. Beginning with what we already know, we proceed through argument to what we did not yet know but come to know by means of the argument. Thus, our medieval professor will characterize argument as the process by which we *proceed in knowing from the known to the unknown*. All the other logical relationships in language are important insofar as they are part of or help us understand this most basic relationship of argument.

§2 Giving Reasons

Just how does the activity of argumentation bring us from the previously known to knowledge of the previously unknown? How does one recognize an argument? These are apt questions, because not everything we do in language is the expression of arguments. Thus, we need to be able to recognize when language is argumentative and when it is not. Given that argument is a process of moving from the known to new knowledge, all arguments must have at least two parts: one part expressing what is already known and another expressing what comes to be known through the argument. What comes to be known by means of the argument is called the *conclusion* of the argument. So, in argument we draw a conclusion from what is already known to be true. This means that we consider what is already known to be true to be a good reason for knowing the conclusion is true. An argument, then, can be thought of as a process of giving reasons in support of a conclusion. The reasons we provide in argument to show that the conclusion is true are called the *premises* of the argument. All arguments have at least two parts: a conclusion representing what comes to be known through the argument and at least one premise representing a reason offered in support of the conclusion. Every argument has only one conclusion, but may have more than one premise. Each argument, however, always has more than one part, because there is a big difference between simply making a claim about what is true and showing the reasons for claiming it is true. Every argument, then, is composed of a conclusion and at least one premise and possibly more than one premise.

The recognition of arguments is a matter of determining when language is being used in such a way that reasons are being offered in support of a conclusion. Yet, the recognition of arguments is just the first step in understanding arguments, for one cannot fully recognize and understand an argument unless one can clearly articulate the conclusion of the argument and the reasons being offered in support of it. Thus, the analysis of arguments begins with the identification of the conclusion and premises of the argument. Unless one can clearly identify the parts of an argument, one does not truly recognize or understand the argument. Consider the following passage:

[1]   We know from observation that the earth casts a curved shadow on the surface of the moon during a lunar eclipse and that anything casting a curved shadow on the surface of the moon during a lunar eclipse must have a curved surface. That is why we know that the earth has a curved surface.

A careful reading of this passage indicates that there is an argument being expressed because reasons are being offered in support of a conclusion. Recognition of the presence of an argument here depends on being able to identify the conclusion as *the earth has a curved surface*. Recognition that reasons are being offered in support of this conclusion depends on the identification of at least one of the premises. In fact, this argument has two premises: *the earth casts a curved shadow on the surface of the moon during a lunar eclipse* and *anything that casts a curved shadow on the surface of the moon during a lunar eclipse has a curved surface*. Once the conclusion is identified and the premises offered in its support are clearly recognized, then it is clear that this passage

3

does indeed contain an argument. It is also clear just what the argument is, for the identification of the parts of the argument indicate just what reasons are being offered for the truth of the conclusion.

Not everything expressed in language is argument. On account of this, one must read carefully to see if reasons are being offered for a conclusion in order to determine whether an argument is present or not. Often in the expression of arguments, certain logical words and phrases are used to indicate when reasons are being offered for a conclusion. Some words and phrases are *conclusion indicators* and introduce a conclusion. Typical conclusion indicators include: "therefore," "thus," "it follows that," "hence," "we can conclude that," "we have shown that," and many other words and phrases. Some words and phrases are *premise indicators* and introduce a premise or series of premises. Typical premise indicators include: "because," "since," "the reason is that," "on account of the fact that," and many other words and phrases. Premise and conclusion indicators need not be used to express arguments, but they often are used as an aid to the reader. A good practice, when reading, is to ask yourself whether reasons are being offered in support of a conclusion. If so, then argument is present, even if there are no special logical words or phrases indicating the presence of conclusions and premises. Where such indicators are present, that is a clue to the presence of argument.

Outlining Arguments

In order to study the logical structure of arguments, it is useful to have a method of outlining an argument that makes clear what its parts are. One way of doing this is to draw a line and below the line write out the conclusion of the argument and above the line write out the premises. The line can be thought to represent a conclusion indicator and can be called the "therefore line." For example, the argument contained in the passage [1] may be outlined like this:

[2]   The earth casts a curved shadow on the surface of the moon during a lunar eclipse.
Anything casting a curved shadow on the surface of the moon during a lunar eclipse has a curved surface.

_____

The earth has a curved surface.

Consider another example. Suppose that one comes across this passage in one's reading:

[3]   Master Odo of Orleans held that virtue is a habit conducive to happiness on the grounds that it is a stable way of acting according to right reasoning.

A careful reading of this passage [3] indicates that a reason is being given for Master Odo's view of what virtue is. Helpful here is noticing the premise indicator "on the grounds that" which introduces the reasons why Odo considers his conclusion true.

Master Odo's argument can then be rewritten in outline form making it clear just what the argument is:

[4] Virtue is a stable way of acting according to right reasoning.
Any stable way of acting according to right reasoning is a habit conducive to happiness.

Virtue is a habit conducive to happiness.

Consider one more example:

[5] The University Charter mandates that the regent master of theology be either appointed by the chancellor or elected by the other masters. As the office of chancellor is currently vacant, the new master of theology will be elected by the other masters.

The argument in this passage [5] may be outlined as:

[6] The new master of theology is to be either appointed by the chancellor or elected by the masters.
The new master of theology is not to be appointed by the chancellor.

The new master of theology is to be elected by the masters.

Evaluating Arguments

The giving of reasons in support of a conclusion is an activity. Like any activity, it can be done well or poorly. A successful argument is one that provides good reasons for believing that the conclusion is true. An unsuccessful argument, by contrast, is one that fails to provide good reasons for the truth of the conclusion. The success or failure of an argument depends on whether or not the premises constitute good reasons for accepting the conclusion as true. When the premises are good reasons for the truth of the conclusion, then the argument is successful in leading the arguer from the premises he knows to be true to the truth of something new: namely, the conclusion.

There are two ways in which an argument can fail to adequately support the conclusion. It might be that the premises are related to the conclusion in the argument in such a way that they do not support the conclusion. This can happen when the premises are irrelevant to the conclusion or when the premises fail to lead the arguer to the truth of the conclusion with absolute certainty. This kind of argument failure is due to a faulty argument structure. Regardless of the subject matter of the argument, it cannot show that the conclusion is true unless it has the right kind of argument structure or *logical form*.

An argument that has the kind of logical form by which the premises provide good reasons for the truth of the conclusion is called a *valid argument*. A valid argument shows that, if one accepts the premises as true, then one logically must accept the conclusion as true as well. Anyone who accepts the premises of a valid argument as true but denies the truth of the conclusion is simply being unreasonable. An argument in which the premises are related to the conclusion in such a way that they do not support the truth of the conclusion is an *invalid argument*. An invalid argument is one in which the premises may all be true, but the conclusion may still be false. Thus, one way in which an argument may fail to be successful is to have an invalid form.

Consider the following argument examples. The first [7] is valid, because if one accepts all the premises as true, one is logically committed to accepting the conclusion as true. The second [8] is invalid, because the premises may all be true while the conclusion may still turn out to be false.

[7]   Anyone eligible to be appointed a provincial governor has previously served at
          least one year as a magistrate.
       All those who have previously served at least one year as a magistrate have some
          judicial experience.
       Therefore, anyone eligible to be appointed a provincial governor has some
          judicial experience.

This is a valid argument, because the premises are related to the conclusion in such a way that their truth necessitates the truth of the conclusion. If it is true that any eligible candidate for governor must have served as magistrate and anyone who has served as magistrate attains some judicial experience, then it absolutely must be true that all those eligible for a governorship have some judicial experience. It is logically impossible that this conclusion be false, if both of these premises are true.

[8]   Some provincial governors receive their appointments from the senate.
       Some provincial governors receive their appointments from the emperor.
       Therefore, some provincial governors do not receive their appointments from the
          senate.

This is an invalid argument, because even if both premises are true, that does not necessitate the truth of the conclusion. It may seem as though the truth of these two premises shows that there must be some provincial governors who are not appointed by the senate—namely, those appointed by the emperor instead. But the information contained in the premises, even if true, does not guarantee that conclusion is true. It could be, for instance, that appointment as a provincial governor requires both senatorial and imperial approval. In that case both premises would be true while the conclusion is false. There is nothing said in these premises that rules out the possibility that both senate and emperor must appoint a governor. As a result, the truth of those two premises alone is not enough to guarantee the truth of the conclusion and the argument fails to show that the conclusion absolutely must be true given the truth of the premises.

Another way in which premises can fail in supporting a conclusion is when the premises are false. It might be that a certain set of premises leads to a certain conclusion in a valid argument. If these premises are false, however, they will not show that the conclusion must be true even in a valid argument. A valid argument is one in which the truth of the premises necessitates the truth of the conclusion. Yet, the relation of necessity between the premises and the conclusion is not enough to guarantee the truth of the conclusion. In order to show that the conclusion is necessarily true, a valid argument must also have true premises. A valid argument that has true premises is called a *sound argument*. A sound argument *both* shows a relation of necessity between the premises and the conclusion *and also* has true premises. It is possible that a certain set of premises necessitates a certain conclusion in a valid argument. If these premises are false, however, the conclusion has not been shown to be necessarily true, only necessarily following from the premises. If, on the other hand, the premises of a valid argument are true, then the fact that the conclusion validly follows from the premises shows that the conclusion must also be true. An *unsound argument* is one which may be valid, but has false premises.

Consider the following example. It is a valid argument, because it has a valid logical form by which the premises necessitate the conclusion. But it is unsound, because it has a false premise.

[9]   Any fundamental material part of a ponderable body that is capable of
            stable existence is an element.
        Water is a fundamental material part of a ponderable body that is capable of
            stable existence.
        Therefore, water is an element.

This argument is valid, but unsound. The premises state that being an element always goes with being a fundamental material part of a stable and ponderable body and that being such a fundamental part goes with being water. Were both of these premises true, then it would necessarily be true that water is an element. Yet, the second premise is false, for water is not fundamental material part of a ponderable body capable of stable existence because it is composed of hydrogen and oxygen which are themselves capable of stable existence and can chemically compose other non-elemental bodies, such as air. The logical form of this argument is valid, but its premises are not all true. As a result, this argument is unsound and fails to guarantee the truth of the conclusion.

For arguments to be useful in providing reliable reasons for the truth of conclusions, they must be both valid and sound. The validity of an argument depends on its logical form. Studying the various forms of argument and distinguishing those that are valid is the task of the discipline of logic. Determining the truth of possible premises is the task of the various sciences that study the way reality exists, such as the sciences of nature, the sciences of human behavior and society, and the science of divine things. The art of logic provides the method by which the various sciences of reality accomplish their research and draw their conclusions about the way the reality exists. The primary tool of logic is argument: the means by which we proceed from what we already know to be true about the subjects of the various sciences to new knowledge in these sciences.

Exercise 1

Student: _____

For each of the following passages, indicate whether or not it contains an argument. If it does, write out the premises and conclusion in the space provided.

1.   Master Robert explained that the argument for God's existence given by the blessed Bishop Anselm was based on the diversity of goods. Given that there are many good things and that each good cannot be good through itself, but only through another, it follows that there is some one good thing which is goodness itself. As Master Robert said, it is obvious that this one thing that is goodness itself is God.

☐ This passage does not contain an argument.
☐ This passage contains the following argument:

Premise 1: _____

_____

Premise 2: _____

_____

Conclusion: _____

_____

2.   Master Odo came to the University of Paris five years ago from his native town of Orleans. When he arrived, he was asked to lecture on Aristotle's book on virtues. Odo gave a series of seven lectures in which he explained Aristotle's difficult arguments. Odo remained at Paris lecturing and disputing until the year 1296 when he was called to Rome to serve as an advisor to the Papal cabinet.

☐ This passage does not contain an argument.
☐ This passage contains the following argument:

Premise 1: _____

_____

Premise 2: _____

_____

Conclusion: _____

_____

3.   During that hard winter of 1301, many students went hungry and had to leave Oxford, returning to their native places. By Christmas of that year, the town was nearly deserted.

☐ This passage does not contain an argument.
☐ This passage contains the following argument:

Premise 1: _____

_____

Premise 2: _____

_____

Conclusion: _____

_____

4.   Lacking sufficient funds, Jordan of Saxony faces a dilemma. Either he must leave the university before he completes his examinations or he must immediately take his theology examinations. If he leaves the university, he will fail to take his degree this year. Yet that will also happen if he immediately takes his examinations for he is not prepared. Therefore, he will fail to take his degree this year.

☐ This passage does not contain an argument.
☐ This passage contains the following argument:

Premise 1: _____

_____

Premise 2: _____

_____

Premise 3: _____

_____

Conclusion: _____

_____

5. No master will be allowed to attend the chancellor's dinner without a gown, because all masters are subject to the university regulations.

☐ This passage does not contain an argument.
☐ This passage contains the following argument:

Premise 1: _____

_____

Premise 2: _____

_____

Conclusion: _____

_____

6. If all masters are subject to university regulations, then they can be disciplined for violating them. All masters are, of course, subject to university regulations. Therefore, masters can be disciplined for violating university regulations.

☐ This passage does not contain an argument.
☐ This passage contains the following argument:

Premise 1: _____

_____

Premise 2: _____

_____

Conclusion: _____

_____

Exercise 2

Student: _____

For each of the following passages, indicate whether or not it contains an argument. If it does, write out the premises and conclusion in the space provided.

1. I read in Aristotle's book that all ruminants lack molars, because any animal that chews the cud lacks molars and all ruminants chew the cud.

    ☐ This passage does not contain an argument.
    ☐ This passage contains the following argument:

    Premise 1: _____

    _____

    Premise 2: _____

    _____

    Conclusion: _____

    _____

2. I read in Aristotle's book that all ruminants lack molars.

    ☐ This passage does not contain an argument.
    ☐ This passage contains the following argument:

    Premise 1: _____

    _____

    Premise 2: _____

    _____

    Conclusion: _____

    _____

13

3. In order to demonstrate that a triangle must have three internal angles, begin by assuming that a triangle does not. Now, a triangle is a closed plane figure with three straight sides. If a triangle is a closed plane figure with three straight sides, then the sides must meet at an angle in three places. If the sides of a triangle meet at an angle in three places, then a triangle must have three internal angles. From this it follows that a triangle must have three internal angles. But this contradicts the assumption that a triangle does not have three internal angles. Therefore, triangles must have three internal angles.

☐ This passage does not contain an argument.
☐ This passage contains the following argument:

Premise 1: _____

_____

Premise 2: _____

_____

Premise 3: _____

_____

Premise 4: _____

_____

Conclusion: _____

_____

4. Every student reporter of Master Gilbert's lectures is required to submit his reports to the master for editing. Stephen is a reporter of Master Gilbert's lectures and, therefore, he is required to submit his reports to the master for editing.

☐ This passage does not contain an argument.
☐ This passage contains the following argument:

Premise 1: _____

_____

Premise 2: _____

_____

Conclusion: _____

_____

5.　　All university students who have completed examinations become senior members of college and any senior member of college may enter the senior common room. This is why university students who have completed examinations may enter the senior common room.

☐ This passage does not contain an argument.
☐ This passage contains the following argument:

Premise 1: _____

_____

Premise 2: _____

_____

Conclusion: _____

_____

6.　　All university students are expected to show respect to university masters.

☐ This passage does not contain an argument.
☐ This passage contains the following argument:

Premise 1: _____

_____

Premise 2: _____

_____

Conclusion: _____

_____

§3 The True, the False, and the Neither

Before one can begin recognizing and evaluating arguments, one must know something about the ingredients of arguments. Arguments are composed of parts: a conclusion and at least one premise, maybe more. Exactly what are premises and conclusions? Just what sort of things are they? Clearly, they are something said in language: either spoken language, written language, or thought language. Yet, this is not enough to clearly identify and characterize premises and conclusions, because there are many things we do in life with language that have nothing to do with the drawing of conclusions and the giving of reasons in support of conclusions. We use language to give orders, make requests, ask questions, impart warnings, make wishes, express desires, perform rituals, express hopes, and give greetings. None of these uses of language function as premises or conclusions of arguments. There is, however, one use of language that is capable of serving as a conclusion or as a premise. This is language that expresses what is true or false about reality. Not every use of language is true or false, but language that is capable of truth or falsity is called *propositional language*. A *proposition*, then, is a use of language that is capable of being either true or false. The premises and conclusions of arguments are propositions.

In order to understand the parts of arguments, two things are necessary. First, one must be able to recognize a proposition and distinguish propositions from non-propositional uses of language. Second, one must know how propositions work—that is, one must understand how propositions can express what is true or false of reality. The truth or falsity of a proposition is its *truth value*. There are two possible truth values: *true* and *false*. All propositions have truth value. In fact, a use of language cannot be propositional unless it is capable of having truth value. Recognizing that propositions possess truth value is not the same as knowing what the specific truth value of a proposition is. We know that all propositions have truth value, but we do not know the truth or falsity of all propositions. Consider the following example:

[1]   There are large deposits of iron ore under the Martian surface.

Sentence [1] clearly expresses a proposition, for what it says is either true or false. It therefore has truth value. Yet, there may be no one who actually knows whether the truth value of this proposition is true or false. Clearly, it must be one or the other and we can know this, even if we do not know what the actual truth value is.

While every proposition has truth value, it cannot actually have both truth values. A proposition cannot be both true and false at the same time and in the same respect. Yet, every proposition is either true or false. This is the case even if no one actually knows what the truth value is. The following sentence expresses a proposition:

[2]   All university masters are skilled in the language arts.

What this sentence expresses has one of the two possible truth values, so it clearly expresses a proposition. Yet, what it says cannot be both true and false at the same time and in the same respect.

Identifying Propositions

Consider the following sentences:

[3]   The soldiers are standing at attention.

[4]   His father is a knight of the Order of St. George.

[5]   Knights of St. George are brave men.

Each of these sentences expresses a proposition. The first [3] truly or falsely reports that the soldiers are standing at attention. The second [4] and third [5] truly or falsely say something about certain persons. All three sentences have truth value and each is a propositional use of language. Each expresses what is true or false of reality.

Many uses of language do not involve truth or falsity at all. Imperatives, for example, do not say what is true or say what is false, but give orders or make requests. Consider the following examples:

[6]   Please close the window.

[7]   Stand at attention!

The first [6] does not say anything true or false about the window or anything else. It requests that something be done. Neither does the second [7] say what is true or false. It imparts a command to which obedience is expected. Imperatives like this may be effective or ineffective, possible or impossible to perform, reasonable or unreasonable. What they cannot be is true or false.

Performative expressions are another use of language that is non-propositional. Consider the following examples:

[8]   I promise to return the book.

[9]   I hereby make you a knight of the Order of St. George.

Neither of these examples has truth value. The first [8] is not truly or falsely reporting that one is making a promise. Rather, the saying of these words in the right circumstances *is* the making of a promise. Likewise, the second [9] is not saying truly or falsely that a certain person is a knight, but it is the ritual performance of actually making the person a knight. Performative language like this is effective or ineffective, legal or illegal, beneficial or harmful. Yet, it is not true or false. This becomes clear when these two examples [8] and [9] are compared to the following:

[10]   I gave him my sincere promise to return the book.

[11]   Yesterday, I invested him as a knight in the Order of St. George.

The first of these examples [10] is a proposition, because it is either true or false that one made the promise. The second [11] is also a proposition, because it truly or falsely reports what one has done.

There is one type of expression that does concern truth or falsity, but is not propositional. Interrogative expressions do not say what is true or false, but ask what is true or false. Consider these examples:

[12]   Did he promise to return the book?

[13]   Is he a knight of the Order of St. George?

The first of these [12] does not claim that he did make such a promise nor does it claim that he did not. Rather, it seeks to find out what is true. Similarly, the second [13] does not say that he is a knight nor does it say that he is not, but it is an expression used to discover the truth of the matter. Questions, then, are not propositions and do not have truth value. This is because they do not express truth or falsity—they do not say what is true or say what is false. Questions do, however, concern truth and falsity insofar as they seek the truth or falsity about some subject. The answers to questions, therefore, are propositions, even though the questions themselves are not. Consider the following:

[14]   Are the knights of St. George brave?

[15]   Yes, the knights of St. George are very brave.

While the first of these examples [14] lacks truth value, the second [15] possesses it. The first [14] seeks the truth about the knights of St. George and the second [15] actually makes a true or false claim about the knights of St. George.

Because an argument is a process of giving reasons in support of the truth of a conclusion, the conclusion of an argument must be capable of having truth value—that is, it must be a proposition. Premises offered in support of the conclusion actually support the truth of the conclusion when they are all true. Thus, premises must also have truth value and be propositions. The clear identification and understanding of arguments, then, depends on the ability to recognize propositions and distinguish them from the various non-propositional uses of language.

The Structure of Propositions

The function of propositions is to express what is true or false about reality. In order to do this, a proposition must have certain features or characteristics. These features or characteristics are called *the parts of the proposition*. Because propositions are not physical things, but rather the meanings of certain uses of language, their parts are not physical parts but abstract parts. They are those characteristics that make it possible for the proposition to say what is true of reality or to say what is false of reality.

The most fundamental characteristic of a proposition is that it must have a subject matter. All propositions are about something; they express something true or false about some subject matter. For a proposition to function like this, it must have parts that convey the subject matter about which the proposition is expressing truth or falsity. The parts of a proposition that express the subject matter of a proposition are the *terms* of the proposition. Consider this example of a proposition:

[16]   All university students speak Latin.

If this sentence [16] expresses a proposition saying something true or false, then it must be expressing something about some subject. Another way of saying this is that the proposition must have a part that picks out or refers to a subject about which it is saying something truly or falsely. To whom or what is this proposition referring? What subject is picked out by this proposition? The proposition is referring to university students about whom it says something. Thus, the *subject term* of this proposition is:

[17]   People who are university students.

Notice that the subject term [17] is not itself a proposition. It cannot have truth value. It is, instead, a name or description of a subject about which some proposition can say something. There is no single way of expressing a subject term. If I am asked what this proposition [16] is all about, I can intelligibly answer: "People who are university students" or "being a university student" or even simply "university students." Each of these expressions names, describes, or refers to the same subject.

All propositions have subject terms. Yet, the subject matter of a proposition cannot be conveyed by the subject term alone. This is because picking out something with a name or description cannot have truth value. This means that propositions must always have more than one term. Any subject term of a proposition must be linked with another term that predicates or says something of the subject. Thus, the *predicate term* of proposition [16] is:

[18]   People who speak Latin.

Notice that, as with the subject term, the predicate term by itself lacks truth value and is not itself a proposition. Rather, the predicate term attributes something to the subject term of the proposition. These two terms, taken together, provide the complete subject matter of the proposition. As with the subject term, there is no one way to express a predicate term. Instead of the expression [18], the same predicate can be expressed as "being a person who speaks Latin" or more simply "Latin speakers." Each of these expressions predicates the same thing of a subject.

All propositions must have two terms: a subject term and a predicate term. Yet, this is not quite all there is to the structure of propositions. This is because any pair of subject and predicate terms can be related within the proposition in different ways. Given some subject, one can predicate something of it in two different ways: one can affirm the predicate of the subject or one can negate the predicate of the subject. Consider the following examples:

20

[19]   All university masters have read Aristotle's new book.

[20]   No university masters have read Aristotle's new book.

Both of these propositions [19] and [20] have the same subject term "people who are university masters" and both have the same predicate term "people who have read Aristotle's new book." Yet, the first proposition [19] says something very different from the second proposition [20]; the situation in the real world that would make the first [19] true is very different from the situation that would make the second [20] true. In fact, both of these propositions cannot be true together. Even though they share the same terms, these examples are very different. What makes them different is the way the terms are related with respect to affirmation and negation. In the first [19] the predicate is affirmed of the subject: the predicate is said to go with being the subject. In the second [20] the predicate is negated of the subject: the predicate is said to not go with being the subject. The relation between the terms in a proposition with respect to affirmation and negation is called the *logical quality* of the proposition. All propositions have quality and there are two possible qualities for any given proposition: *affirmative quality* or *negative quality*.

All propositions, then, have two terms and one of two possible qualities. Yet, this is not all there is to propositions. This is because one can affirm or negate a predicate of a subject with respect to every case of the subject or with respect to at least some cases of the subject. The relation of the terms with respect to the extent of the affirmation or negation of the predicate to the subject is called the *logical quantity* of the proposition. So, in addition to terms and quality, every proposition must have quantity. Consider the following examples:

[21]   All university students respect Master Robert.

[22]   Some university students respect Master Robert.

Both of these examples [21] and [22] have the same subject term *people who are university students* and the same predicate term *people who respect Master Robert*. Also both have affirmative quality. Yet, they say something quite different. The first proposition [21] is true only when being a person who respects Master Robert is affirmed of being a university student in every case of being a university student. This is called *universal quantity*. The second proposition [22] is true when being a person who respects Master Robert is affirmed of being a university student in at least one and maybe more cases of being a university student. This is called *existential quantity*. Negative propositions also must have quantity:

[23]   No university students respect Master Robert.

[24]   Some university students do not respect Master Robert.

What makes it possible for a proposition to say something truly or falsely about reality is that it has these different types of parts. Every proposition has two terms that convey the subject matter of the proposition. These terms are always related in the proposition with respect to quantity and quality. Understanding a proposition depends on being able to recognize and clearly express its parts. One who cannot clearly pick out the subject and predicate terms of a proposition or who cannot determine whether the predicate is affirmed or negated of the subject or who cannot determine whether the affirmation or negation is universal or existential does not understand what the proposition is saying. If one does not clearly understand what the proposition is saying about reality, one cannot determine its truth or falsity.

Basic Forms of Propositions

Once the parts of the proposition are understood, then it is clear that one can form different types of propositions. Given that every proposition must have a subject term and a predicate term and one of two possible quantities and two possible qualities, four basic types of propositions are possible. The predicate of a proposition can be universally affirmed of the subject or universally negated of the subject. Similarly, the predicate can be existentially affirmed of the subject or existentially negated. This provides the four basic forms that a simple proposition can take:

Universal Affirmative Proposition: the predicate is affirmed of the subject in all cases of being the subject.

Universal Negative Proposition: the predicate is negated of the subject in all cases of being the subject.

Existential Affirmative Proposition: the predicate is affirmed of the subject in at least one or more cases of being the subject.

Existential Negative Proposition: the predicate is negated of the subject in at least one or more cases of being the subject.

The expression of propositions in language varies widely. This means that there are different ways in which the quantity and quality of propositions are expressed. There are, for example, distinctive words and phrases that indicate quantity and quality. Yet, there is no uniformity of these indicators and one must be alert to the structure of propositions as well as the meanings of logical words and phrases that appear in propositions. Consider the following examples:

[25] All university students must take oral exams in Latin.

[26] Every university student must take oral exams in Latin.

[27] Each university student must take oral exams in Latin.

[28] University students must take oral exams in Latin.

All of these examples have the same subject matter, because they share the same terms; each one is about being a university student and each one predicates, in some way, being a person who must take oral exams in Latin. Yet, these examples are alike in quantity and quality as well: they are all universal affirmatives. Notice the different ways in which universality and affirmativeness are expressed. The first three examples, [25], [26], and [27], are expressed by sentences beginning with distinctive universal quantifier words. Yet, the last example [28] lacks a special quantifier word, but is clearly still universal. In each case the predicate is affirmed of the subject in all cases of being the subject. These represent typical ways in which we express universal affirmative propositions. Other ways of expressing universal affirmation include use of the words "any," "anybody," "anything," "everybody," "everything," and "only." Phrases such as "every man," "every woman," "every person," and "none but" also indicate the universal affirmative. There is no one way in which this type of proposition is expressed and one must always be ready to ask oneself whether the proposition is affirmative and whether the affirmation is being made universally.

Consider the following examples:

[29] No masters can read Arabic.

[30] None of the masters can read Arabic.

[31] Not one of the masters can read Arabic.

All of these examples [29]–[31] have the same terms and so share the same subject matter. Each of them is also universal in quantity and negative in quality. Notice the different words and phrases that can indicate universal negative propositions. One also finds universal negative quantifiers such as "there is no," "there are no," "not any," and "nothing." Sometimes universal negative propositions are expressed with a negation of the predicate term, as in this example:

[32] Masters cannot read Arabic.

This example [32] is another way of saying that none of the masters can read Arabic. This sort of example will be discussed further later in the book.

Consider the following examples:

[33] Some Oxford masters have studied at the University of Paris.

[34] Certain Oxford masters have studied at the University of Paris.

[35] There are Oxford masters who have studied at the University of Paris.

[36] At least one Oxford master has studied at the University of Paris.

In addition to sharing the same terms, each of these examples [33]–[36] is an existential affirmative. As with universal propositions, there is no one way to express existential affirmatives. In ordinary conversation, the word "some" is typically used to refer to more than one, but not necessarily all. Logically speaking, however, there is no distinction between one and some, so existential propositions refer to at least one, maybe more, but not necessarily all.

Consider these examples:

[37]   Some Oxford masters have not visited Rome.

[38]   There are Oxford masters who have not visited Rome.

[39]   Certain Oxford masters have not visited Rome.

[40]   At least one Oxford master has not visited Rome.

Each of these examples [37]–[40] has the same terms, existential quantity, and negative quality. As with existential affirmatives, there are many ways in which existential negative propositions are expressed.

General and Particular Propositions

A universal proposition is one in which the predicate is affirmed or negated of the subject in all cases of the subject. Thus, all of the following examples are universal affirmative propositions:

[41]   All arts masters have read Porphyry's book.

[42]   Theology masters are required to lecture on the scriptures.

[43]   Master Alan has written a new book on geometry.

[44]   The earth is a sphere.

In each example [41]–[44], the predicate term is affirmed of the subject in all cases of being the subject. The first example [41] will be true, if being a person who has read Porphyry's book is rightly attributed to being a master of arts in each and every case of being such a master. The second example [42] is similar—it will be true when being required to lecture on the scriptures is correctly affirmed of every master of theology. Notice, however, that the other examples [43] and [44] are also universal. The first of these [43] is true when having written a new book on geometry is affirmed of being Master Alan in every case of being Master Alan. Because Master Alan is a particular person there is only one case of being that Master Alan, but that is all the cases there are. So, [43] is universal. The same is true of the last example [44] which affirms being a sphere of the earth in all cases of being the earth of which there is only one. This shows that there are two different types of universal propositions depending on the scope of the subject term. Some universal propositions have subject terms that refer to a collection of things or a kind of thing, such as the first two examples [41] and [42]. These are called *universal generalizations*. Some universal propositions have subject terms that refer to a unique person or thing, as in the last two examples [43] and [44]. These are called *universal particularizations*. This can be the case with universal negatives as well:

[45]   None of the masters at Paris read Arabic.

[46]   Master Alan does not read Arabic.

The subject term of the first example [45] is general because it refers to a group of people. So, this is a universal generalization. The subject term of the second example [46] refers to a particular person. So, this is a universal particularization.

To say that a proposition is universal is to specify the logical quantity of the proposition. It is to say that the predicate is affirmed or negated of every case of the subject. Yet, the subject can be either a group of people or things, a species or kind of person or thing, or an individual person or thing. To say that a proposition is general is to indicate that the subject term refers either to a group or collection of persons or things or to a kind or species of persons or things. To say that a proposition is particular is to indicate that the subject term refers either to an individual person or a unique object. Be careful not to confuse universal quantity with generality. The first concerns the logical form of the proposition and the second concerns the scope of the subject term.

Exercise 3

Student: _____

For each of the following sentences, determine whether or not it expresses a proposition and mark accordingly.

1.   Master Siger is a member of the Faculty of Arts.

   ☐ proposition   ☐ non-proposition

2.   Is Master Siger a member of the Faculty of Arts?

   ☐ proposition   ☐ non-proposition

3.   Tell him that Master Siger is a member of the Faculty of Arts.

   ☐ proposition   ☐ non-proposition

4.   Master Siger is lecturing on Aristotle's book on syllogisms today.

   ☐ proposition   ☐ non-proposition

5.   Please, Master Siger, lecture on Aristotle's book on syllogisms today.

   ☐ proposition   ☐ non-proposition

6.   Master Siger received his degree in arts from the University of Paris.

   ☐ proposition   ☐ non-proposition

7.   Master Siger promised to lecture on physics next term.

   ☐ proposition   ☐ non-proposition

8.   Many students respect Master Siger's great learning.

   ☐ proposition   ☐ non-proposition

9. Master Siger is able to read Arabic.

    ☐ proposition   ☐ non-proposition

10. Is Master Siger able to read Arabic?

    ☐ proposition   ☐ non-proposition

11. I wish Master Siger were able to read Arabic.

    ☐ proposition   ☐ non-proposition

12. If Master Siger were able to read Arabic, then he could lecture on the new book.

    ☐ proposition   ☐ non-proposition

13. Both Master Siger and Master William have spoken with the chancellor.

    ☐ proposition   ☐ non-proposition

14. Did Master Siger speak with the chancellor?

    ☐ proposition   ☐ non-proposition

15. Inform Master Siger that he is to speak with the chancellor.

    ☐ proposition   ☐ non-proposition

Exercise 4

Student: _____

For each of the following sentences, determine whether or not it expresses a proposition and mark accordingly.

1. Does Master Robert wish to be the new chancellor?

    ☐ proposition   ☐ non-proposition

2. Master Robert wishes to be the new chancellor.

    ☐ proposition   ☐ non-proposition

3. I wish Master Robert were the new chancellor.

    ☐ proposition   ☐ non-proposition

4. Master Robert is a good chancellor.

    ☐ proposition   ☐ non-proposition

5. Either Master Robert or Master William is our new chancellor.

    ☐ proposition   ☐ non-proposition

6. Master William is not qualified to be the new chancellor.

    ☐ proposition   ☐ non-proposition

7. Master Robert has been elected the new chancellor.

    ☐ proposition   ☐ non-proposition

8.   Inform Master William that Master Robert has been elected the new chancellor.

☐ proposition   ☐ non-proposition

9.   Would that Master Robert could be our new chancellor!

☐ proposition   ☐ non-proposition

10. Master Robert is now chancellor at the University of Oxford.

☐ proposition   ☐ non-proposition

11. When Master Robert becomes the new chancellor, Master William will resign.

☐ proposition   ☐ non-proposition

12. O, Master Robert, accept the appointment as chancellor!

☐ proposition   ☐ non-proposition

13. Master Robert accepts the appointment as chancellor.

☐ proposition   ☐ non-proposition

14. Master Robert is serving a five-year term as chancellor.

☐ proposition   ☐ non-proposition

15. If Master Robert is serving as chancellor, he is not lecturing this year.

☐ proposition   ☐ non-proposition

Exercise 5

Student: _____

Identify and write out the terms for each of the following propositions.

1.   Master Robert is doing light-reflection experiments with mirrors.

subject term: _____

predicate term: _____

2.   All mirrors reflect light at an angle of refraction.

subject term: _____

predicate term: _____

3.   Master Robert is writing an important book on the science of perspective.

subject term: _____

predicate term: _____

4.   No scholar knows the optical explanation of color differentiation in rainbows.

subject term: _____

predicate term: _____

5.   Some masters have read Master Robert's book on the science of perspective.

subject term: _____

predicate term: _____

6.   There are masters who know of Master Robert's experiments with mirrors.

subject term: _____

predicate term: _____

7.   Master Robert has completed his light-reflection experiments with mirrors.

subject term: _____

predicate term: _____

8.   At least one student is reporting on Master Robert's lecture on perspective.

subject term: _____

predicate term: _____

9.   Every student of Master Robert is expected to have studied geometry.

subject term: _____

predicate term: _____

10. Master Robert is famous for his experiments on light reflection.

subject term: _____

predicate term: _____

§4 Picturing Propositions

The function of a proposition is to say what is true or false of reality. This function is carried out by two terms expressing some subject matter being related within the proposition with respect to quality and quantity. So, every proposition can be considered as a set of relationships between two terms. In a proposition, a certain predicate term is qualitatively and quantitatively related to a certain subject term. Typically, the terms of a proposition and their relationships are expressed in spoken, written, or thought sentences or some other form of language. They can also be graphically represented in the form of a diagram. A propositional diagram (or Venn diagram) is simply an alternative way of expressing a proposition. When studying logic, the diagrammatic expression of propositions can be useful making clear how the terms are related to each other in the proposition.

The technique of diagraming propositions works like this. Two circles are drawn in such a way that they overlap each other, creating three spaces or regions within the circles: one region is within the circle on the left but outside the circle on the right, another region is within both circles at the same time, and one region is within the circle on the right but outside the circle on the left. Each circle stands for a term and the regions within the circles stand for three of the possible relationships that can exist between two terms. In order to illustrate the technique, consider a diagram in which one circle stands for the term *people who are masters* and the other circle stands for the term *people who wear academic gowns*. The following diagram shows that there are four possible ways in which these two terms can be related to each other:

People who are masters

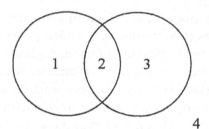

People who wear academic gowns

Region 1, which is within the *people who are masters* circle but outside the *people who wear academic gowns* circle, represents the possibility of being a master who does not wear an academic gown. Region 2, which is within both circles, represents the possibility of being a master who wears an academic gown. Region 3, which is within the *people who wear academic gowns* circle but outside of the *people who are masters* circle, represents the possibility of being a person who wears an academic gown who is not a master. Region 4, which is outside of both circles, represents being a person who is not a master and does not wear an academic gown. The four regions of this diagram represent all the logically possible ways in which these two terms can be related to each other.

Because any two terms can only be related to each other in four possible ways, this diagram technique can represent any actual relation of a pair of terms. Consider

37

another pair of terms: *the person who is Master William* and *being a master of arts at Oxford*. These two terms can be related to each other in four possible ways:

Master William 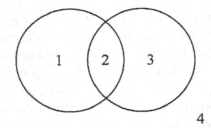 Being a Master of Arts at Oxford

It is possible that Master William is not a master of arts at Oxford (Region 1). It is possible that Master William is a master of arts at Oxford (Region 2). It is possible to be a master of arts at Oxford who is not Master William (Region 3). It is possible to be a person who is not Master William and not a master of arts at Oxford (Region 4).

Drawing a diagram for any two terms in this way allows the diagram to display any logically possible relationship that might exist regarding these two terms. In a proposition, the two terms are related in two ways: with respect to quality (they are either affirmed or negated of each other) and quantity (they are affirmed or negated of each other universally or existentially). Once we have set up a diagram capable of showing any possible relationship between two particular terms, then we can mark the diagram to show the specific relationship of quality and quantity that the terms have in the proposition we are diagraming.

For universal propositions, marking the diagrams to show the quantitative and qualitative relationship will always involve showing which possible relationship is excluded. This is shown by shading or drawing lines through the region on the diagram representing the logical possibility being ruled out. Consider the universal negative proposition *No masters wear academic gowns*. The possible relationship between the two terms *people who are masters* and *people who wear academic gowns* that this proposition excludes is the possibility of being both at the same time. So, the diagram of this universal negative proposition looks like this:

People who are masters 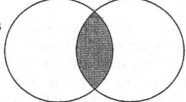 People who wear academic gowns

Notice that the region of the diagram that is within both circles at the same time is shaded (Region 2) showing that the possibility of being both a master and a person who wears an academic gown is completely excluded. The regions representing the other possibilities are left open, because even if there are no masters who wear academic gowns, there might be other people who do (Region 3), there might be masters who do not (Region 1), and there might be people who are neither masters nor people who wear academic gowns (Region 4).

Consider the universal affirmative proposition *All masters wear academic gowns*. This is shown by shading or drawing lines through the region on the diagram representing the logical possibility of being a master who does not wear an academic gown (Region 1). If all masters wear academic gowns, then there cannot be any who do not. Again, the region representing the possibility being excluded is shaded.

People who are masters 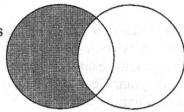 People who wear academic gowns

For existential propositions, marking the diagrams to show the quantitative and qualitative relationship will always involve showing which possible relationship is affirmed for at least one case, maybe more. This is shown by drawing the affirmation mark + in the region of the diagram representing the logical possibility being affirmed. Consider the existential affirmative proposition *Some masters wear academic gowns*. The possible relationship between the two terms *people who are masters* and *people who wear academic gowns* that this proposition affirms is the possibility of being both at the same time. So, the diagram of this existential affirmative proposition looks like this:

People who are masters 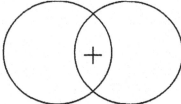 People who wear academic gowns

Notice that the affirmation mark is drawn in the region of the diagram that is within both circles at the same time (Region 2) showing that the possibility of being both a master and a person who wears an academic gown is affirmed in at least one case, maybe more. The regions representing the other possibilities are left open, because even if there are some masters who definitely wear academic gowns, there might or might not be other people who do too (Region 3), there might or might not be masters who do not (Region 1), and there might or might not be people who are neither masters nor people who wear academic gowns (Region 4).

Consider the existential negative proposition *Some masters do not wear academic gowns*. This is shown by drawing the affirmation mark in the region on the diagram representing the logical possibility of being a master who does not wear an academic gown (Region 1). The other regions are left open because, given what the proposition says, there might or might not be any people who fulfill those other possibilities.

People who are masters 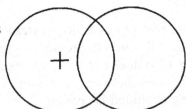 People who wear academic gowns

Any proposition can be expressed in diagram form. This means that any proposition that can be expressed in a spoken, written, or thought sentence can be expressed in the form of a diagram. Doing so makes it easy to analyze a proposition into its parts. This is because a propositional diagram clearly shows both terms in the way each circle is labeled and clearly shows the quantity and quality of the proposition in the way the circles are marked with exclusion or affirmation marks.

Exercise 9

Student: _____

For each of the following propositions, use a propositional diagram to show its logical form.

1.   Every master of medicine has read Avicenna's *Canon of Medicine*.

2.   Some masters of medicine have not read Avicenna's *Canon of Medicine*.

3.   No masters of medicine have consulted Avicenna's *Canon of Medicine*.

4.   There are masters of medicine who have studied at the Arabic School of Salerno.

5.   Every master of medicine at the University of Naples has studied at the Arabic School of Salerno.

6.   Masters of medicine must lecture on anatomy.

7.   At least one master at Oxford has studied anatomy at the Arabic School of Salerno.

8.   Every master of medicine at Naples has studied at the Arabic school of medicine at Salerno.

§5 From One Proposition to Another

Propositional diagrams give us a way to study and analyze individual propositions in order to understand what makes it possible for propositions to say what is true or false of reality. Once we have an idea of how propositions work, then we can consider how one proposition fits, or fails to fit, with another proposition. Because there are many things to say about reality, there are many possible propositions—perhaps infinitely many. Another way in which we can study propositions is to consider them in relation to each other. Given that a certain proposition is true, can a certain other also be true at the same time and in the same way? Are there propositions that exclude each other? Are there propositions that include each other? Most importantly, are there propositions that are related to certain other propositions such that they provide good reasons for believing those other propositions to be true?

Many propositions are distinguished from each other by their differing subject matter. Given any two propositions about completely different subject matters, it is not surprising that one could be true while the other is false. Nor is it surprising that the two could be true at the same time or false at the same time. Consider, for example, the following two propositions:

[1]   Earth is spherical.

[2]   Water is solid at certain temperatures.

Both of these propositions certainly can be true at the same time—in fact, they are both true now. Not only that, they both share the same logical form: they are both universal affirmatives. Yet, they are different propositions. What makes them different is their very different subject matters. They have differing terms. The first [1] is about the earth and its shape and the second [2] is about water and its physical characteristics under certain conditions.

It is possible, however, to have two different propositions about the same subject matter—that is, propositions with the same terms—that say something very different. Consider these examples:

[3]   All university masters wear academic gowns when lecturing.

[4]   No university masters wear academic gowns when lecturing.

These two propositions [3] and [4] have the same terms and, therefore, share a common subject matter. Yet, they are very different propositions. Assume, for example, that the first [3] is true. If it is true, then clearly the second [4] must be false. This is because reality is such that it cannot be that all masters wear academic gowns when lecturing while at the same time none do. If both propositions share the same subject matter because they have the same terms, then the difference between them must be due to their logical form. This is precisely the case. The first [3] says something about its subject matter in a universal affirmative way while the second [4] says something about the very same subject matter in a universal negative way. So, their difference in truth value is due to a difference in logical form.

The truth-value difference between propositions, then, can be due to a difference in subject matter indicated by a difference in terms. Another reason for a difference in truth value, however, is due to a difference in logical form. Some of these logical-form differences are very important to know if one wants to clearly understand propositional relations. Some of the more important propositional relations based on logical form are discussed below.

Propositional Equivalence

Language is rich in variation. Even when we are speaking, writing, or thinking about the same thing, we do not always express it in exactly the same way. Yet, what we are speaking, writing, or thinking of is the same with respect to truth or falsity. It is important, therefore, to be able to determine when we are expressing the same truth or falsity in different ways. Consider the following two propositions:

[5]   None of the masters are able to use the astrolabe.

[6]   All of the masters are unable to use the astrolabe.

These propositions [5] and [6] share the same terms and, therefore, concern the same subject matter. Yet, they are different in their logical form: the first [5] is a universal negative while the second [6] is a universal affirmative with a negated predicate term. Despite this difference in form, they say the same thing with respect to truth and falsity. If the first [5] is true, then the second [6] must be true. If the second [6] is true, then the first [5] must be true. In fact, this pair of propositions will always have precisely the same truth value. Assume, for instance, that it is true that there is a master who is able to use the astrolabe. Given this, the first proposition [5] is clearly false, but so is the second [6]. Propositions of the same subject matter whose truth values are always alike are *equivalent propositions*. So, two propositions are equivalent when they must always have the same truth value. Consider another pair of propositions:

[7]   No Oxford masters have ever visited China.

[8]   No one who has ever visited China is an Oxford master.

These propositions [7] and [8] are equivalent, because they will always have the same truth value.

Propositional equivalence is clearly indicated by the identity of the propositional diagrams for the two equivalent propositions. A diagram for examples [5] and [6] will be absolutely identical: each diagram will have the left circle labeled for the term *people who are masters* and the right circle labeled for the term *people able to use the astrolabe*; also each diagram will have lines drawn through the middle region that is within both circles showing that the possibility of existing in the way described by both terms is universally excluded. One can use propositional diagrams to show the equivalence of examples [7] and [8] in the same way. In the diagram for the universal negative proposition [7], the left circle is labeled *Oxford masters* and the right circle is labeled *people who have visited China*, and the middle region within both circles is ruled out to show that being both is universally excluded. In the diagram for the universal negative proposition [8], the circles are labeled in the same way and, again, the middle region within both circles has lines drawn through it to show universal exclusion. So, both diagrams look alike. Identity in propositional diagrams shows logical equivalence.

Propositional Exclusion

Clearly, many propositions can be true together, either because they have differing subject matter and just happen to have the same truth value or because they are equivalent. Yet, there may be propositions that cannot be true when another proposition is true. There are two ways in which propositions can exclude each other with respect to truth value. One way is when two propositions cannot be true together. Another way is when two propositions exclude each other because they must always have opposite truth values. Consider the following propositions:

[9]   All Oxford masters have studied Aristotle's book on topics.

[10]   No Oxford masters have studied Aristotle's book on topics.

Clearly, both of these examples [9] and [10] are about the same subject, for they share the same terms. Yet, if the first [9] is true, the second [10] cannot be true. Both, however, could be false, if some Oxford masters have studied Aristotle's book and some have not. Propositions that are never true together, but might be false together are called *contrary propositions*.

A more radical way in which propositions can exclude each other is when they always have opposite truth values. Consider these examples:

[11]   All university masters speak Latin.

[12]   Some university masters do not speak Latin.

These propositions [11] and [12] share the same terms, but must differ in truth value. If every university master speaks Latin, then clearly there cannot be some who do not. Yet, if some do not, clearly it cannot be true that all do. Propositions that must always have differing truth values like this are called *contradictory propositions*.

It is important not to confuse contrariety and contradiction. Let us say that two university masters, Master William and Master Giles, are having a debate on some subject. If the position taken by Master William is the contrary to the position taken by Master Giles, then they both cannot be right, but they both might be wrong. Yet, if Master William defends a position that is the contradictory to that defended by Master Giles, then one of them is right and the other is wrong. Contradictory propositions, in a sense, absolutely exclude each other because they always are opposite in truth value. So, Master William being right makes Master Giles, who holds the contradictory position, wrong. Likewise, Master Giles being right makes Master William's contradictory position wrong.

Contradiction of propositions is clearly indicated by propositional diagrams that are marked in incompatible ways. The diagrams for the contradictory propositions [11] and [12] are marked incompatibly in this way. Both diagrams will have the left circle labeled for the term *university masters* and both will have the right circle labeled for the term *people who speak Latin*. In the diagram for proposition [11], the region on the left that is within the *university masters* circle, but outside the *people who speak Latin* circle will have lines drawn through it to show universal exclusion. In the diagram for proposition [12], the same region on the left that is within the *university masters* circle, but outside the *people who speak Latin* circle will have an affirmation mark in it showing that being a university master without being a Latin speaker is affirmed for at least some cases. Looking at these diagrams, it is clear that they are incompatible, because one [11] universally excludes what the other [12] affirms. They are incompatible because there cannot be absolutely nothing that is a non-Latin speaking university master and something that is a non-Latin speaking university master at the same time.

Propositional Inclusion

Some propositions have a logical form that allows them to, in a sense, include other propositions having the same terms but a different logical form. Consider the following examples:

[13]   All Oxford masters have studied Aristotle's book on topics.

[14]   There are Oxford masters who have studied Aristotle's book on topics.

These two propositions [13] and [14] have the same terms, but very different logical forms: the first [13] is universal affirmative and the second [14] existential affirmative. Yet, if the first [13] is true, then the second [14] must be true. Propositions related like this are called *implications*. Generally, a universal proposition implies an existential proposition of the same quality and terms. The following propositions are also related as an implication:

[15]   No Oxford masters read Armenian.

[16]   There are Oxford masters who do not read Armenian.

Clearly, if none of the masters at Oxford read Armenian, then there exist Oxford masters who do not.

While a universal proposition implies a corresponding existential proposition with the same quality and terms, the relation of implication does not proceed from existential to universal. The fact that there are Oxford masters who do not read Armenian does not absolutely guarantee that none do. Likewise, if it is true that some Oxford masters have studied Aristotle's book on topics, that does not mean that it must be true that all Oxford masters have. In propositions, implication always proceeds from more universal to less universal and never from less universal to more universal.

Aristotle's Square

In medieval universities, the books of the ancient Greek philosopher Aristotle were used as textbooks for the teaching of logic. In one of these books, Aristotle presents the four basic types of proposition on a sort of chart formed as a square of opposed propositional forms. This square of opposition illustrates the basic relationships between propositions:

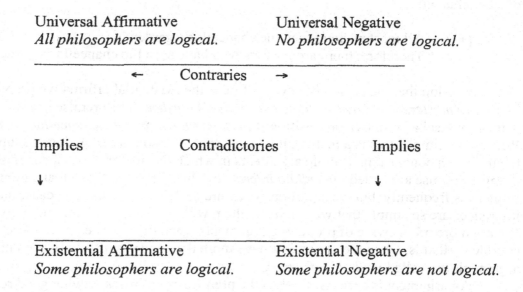

At each corner of the square is placed one of the four basic forms of proposition: at the upper left corner is the universal affirmative, at the upper right corner is the universal negative, at the lower left corner is the existential affirmative, and at the lower right corner is the existential negative. Across the top of the square are forms opposed as contraries (universal affirmatives and universal negatives are contraries). Down the two sides of the square are forms opposed as implications (universal affirmatives imply existential affirmatives; universal negatives imply existential negatives). At the obliquely opposite corners of the square are forms opposed as contradictories (universal affirmatives contradict existential negatives; universal negatives contradict existential affirmatives). This square of opposition provides a graphic display of these important propositional relations.

Propositional Inference

An inference is an argument, for one infers a conclusion from premises when one offers reasons in the premises in support of the conclusion. Argument, therefore, is a propositional relation: it is a relationship between a certain proposition that the arguer believes is true, the conclusion, and other propositions, the premises, that the arguer believes demonstrate the truth of the conclusion. The simplest form of argument is one in which there is only one premise supporting the conclusion. Let us say, for example, that a certain person is asked the question: Are there masters who have seen the chancellor's garden? And suppose that person answers: Yes, there are masters who have seen the chancellor's garden. Now, further suppose that the person is asked why he believes it is true that there are masters who have seen the chancellor's garden and the person answers that it is because all the masters have seen the chancellor's garden. This person has essentially performed a simple argument, because he has given a single reason in support of a conclusion:

[17]   All masters have seen the chancellor's garden.
        Therefore, there are masters who have seen the chancellor's garden.

The conclusion that the person believes is true is the existential affirmative proposition *There are masters who have seen the chancellor's garden*. The premise of his argument is the universal affirmative proposition *All masters have seen the chancellor's garden*. While very simple, this is a real argument, because a reason is being given in support of the truth of a conclusion. Simple arguments in which the arguer draws a conclusion from a single premise are called *immediate inferences*. In everyday life we make immediate inferences frequently, but we are often not aware of doing so. This is because such inferences are so simple that we can make them without much deliberation or awareness. We are more often aware of producing arguments when the arguments are more complex—that is, when the arguments have more than one premise. Multi-premise arguments are called *mediate inferences*.

An argument is successful when the premise or premises provide good reasons for believing the conclusion to be true. The best possible reason for believing a conclusion is true is when the arguer is able to show that the premises necessitate the truth of the conclusion. When an arguer is able to show that accepting all the premises as true logically commits one to accepting the conclusion as true, then one has a successful argument of the strongest possible form. This strongest form of argument is called a *valid argument*. An argument is valid when it has a logical form such that, when all the premises are true, the conclusion absolutely must be true. An argument which has true premises but a conclusion that still may be false is an *invalid argument*.

Consider argument [17]. Notice that it truly is an argument, for it has a conclusion *There are masters who have seen the chancellor's garden* for which a reason is given in its premise *All masters have seen the chancellor's garden*. Notice also that it is an immediate inference, because there is only one premise offered in support of the conclusion. It is also a valid argument, because if it is true that *All masters have seen the chancellor's garden*, then it absolutely must be true that *There are masters who have seen the chancellor's garden*. It is logically impossible that the existential affirmative proposition *There are masters who have seen the chancellor's garden* is false when the universal affirmative proposition *All masters have seen the chancellor's garden* is true. Now what makes this argument [17] valid is not the fact that is it about masters and people who have seen the chancellor's garden, but its logical form. In fact, it is a proper implication, as can be seen by looking at the propositional relations illustrated by Aristotle's square. Any other argument of the same logical form, any other immediate inference in which the premise implies the conclusion, is also valid. Consider this example:

[18]   Every university master lectures in Latin.
        Therefore, there are university masters who lecture in Latin.

Although it is a different argument from the one given at [17] on account of its different subject matter, it shares the same logical form as argument [17]. Like [17], the argument at [18] is valid and for the same reason [17] is valid: its logical form is a proper implication. For comparison, consider this example:

[19]   There are masters who have seen the chancellor's garden.
        Therefore, all masters have seen the chancellor's garden.

This argument [19] is an invalid immediate inference. It is invalid, not because of its subject matter, but because of its logical form: it is an improper attempt at implication. Just because there are masters who have seen the chancellor's garden does not imply that all masters have. The premise could be true while the conclusion is false. This could be the case if, for example, three out of one hundred masters have seen the chancellor's garden.

Argument is always the process of giving reasons in support of a conclusion. Arguments are valid when the reasons in the premises necessitate the truth of the conclusion—that is, when all the premises are true the conclusion absolutely must be true. Arguments are invalid when the reasons in the premises do not necessitate the truth of the conclusion—that is, when all the premises are true and the conclusion might still be false. What makes an argument valid or invalid is the logical form of the argument, not the subject matter of the argument.

Exercise 11

Student: _____

Part I

Assume that the proposition *all university masters lecture in Latin* is true, and determine the truth value of the following propositions. In each case, name the propositional relation that justifies your assignment of truth value.

1. Some university masters lecture in Latin.

    ☐ true   ☐ false   propositional relationship: _____

2. No university masters lecture in Latin.

    ☐ true   ☐ false   propositional relationship: _____

3. Some university masters do not lecture in Latin.

    ☐ true   ☐ false   propositional relationship: _____

4. There are university masters who lecture in Latin.

    ☐ true   ☐ false   propositional relationship: _____

5. University masters lecture in Latin.

    ☐ true   ☐ false   propositional relationship: _____

6. Nobody who lectures in Latin is a university master.

    ☐ true   ☐ false   propositional relationship: _____

Part II

Assume that the proposition *no university masters lecture in Latin* is true, and determine the truth value of the following propositions. In each case, name the propositional relation that justifies your assignment of truth value.

1.   Some university masters lecture in Latin.

        ☐ true   ☐ false   propositional relationship: _____

2.   No one who lectures in Latin is a university master.

        ☐ true   ☐ false   propositional relationship: _____

3.   Some university masters do not lecture in Latin.

        ☐ true   ☐ false   propositional relationship: _____

4.   There are university masters who lecture in Latin.

        ☐ true   ☐ false   propositional relationship: _____

5.   University masters lecture in Latin.

        ☐ true   ☐ false   propositional relationship: _____

6.   Anyone who lectures in Latin is not a university master.

        ☐ true   ☐ false   propositional relationship: _____

§6 Categorically Arguing

The simplest type of argument is immediate inference: an argument in which the arguer draws a conclusion from a single premise. Many arguments, however, are more complex, because they involve more than one premise. One can, for example, draw a conclusion from two premises, as in the following example:

[1]   Every university master receives an appointment from the chancellor.
        Anyone who receives an appointment from the chancellor has the
            chancellor's approval.
        Therefore, every university master has the chancellor's approval.

This is an example of a very common type of argument with two premises. It is called *categorical syllogism*. The word "syllogism" is the ancient Greek word for argument. Because the ancient Greeks were the first people to systematically study this type of argument, their name for it came to be used by many other people throughout the ages and is still used today. The reason why this form of argument received so much attention from ancient Greek logicians and their medieval and modern followers is that this is the most basic form of scientific reasoning. There are many forms of argument, but all scientific explanations can be set out in the form of a categorical syllogism or a series of categorical syllogisms. Because this form of argument is so basic and fundamental to learning, it is sometimes simply called "syllogism."

The logical form shared by all categorical syllogisms has two important features. The first, as is evident in example [1], is that the conclusion is drawn from two premises. Thus, categorical syllogisms are not immediate inferences. The second feature is that, in the conclusion and the two premises, there is some distribution of exactly three distinct terms. This is also clear from example [1]. Notice that the two terms of the first premise are *people who are university masters* and *people who receive an appointment from the chancellor*. The second premise has for its subject term the same term that served as the predicate term of the first premise. The predicate term of the second premise is *people who have the chancellor's approval*. The subject term of the conclusion is the same term as the subject term of the first premise and the predicate term of the conclusion is the same term as the predicate term of the second premise. Thus, the whole argument has only three distinct terms: *people who are university masters, people who receive an appointment from the chancellor*, and *people who have the chancellor's approval*. These terms are arranged in the two premises and the conclusion in a certain pattern of repetition. This arrangement or pattern of term repetition in the premises and conclusion of a categorical syllogism is called the *distribution of terms*.

These two elements of logical form provide the definition of this type of argument: a categorical syllogism is an argument with two premises and some distribution of exactly (no more than and no fewer than) three distinct terms. Any argument that fits this definition is a categorical syllogism. There are many ways in which three terms can be distributed in three propositions. The example of categorical syllogism given at [1] is only one possible distribution. For example, another form of categorical syllogism might have this distribution of terms:

[2]　All theology masters have read the *Book of Sentences*.
　　Anyone who has received an appointment to the theology faculty is a
　　　theology master.
　　Therefore, anyone who has received an appointment to the theology
　　　faculty has read the *Book of Sentences*.

This argument [2] is a categorical syllogism, because it fits the definition: it is an argument with two premises and in the two premises and the conclusion there is some distribution of exactly three distinct terms: *people who are theology masters, people who have read the Book of Sentences*, and *people who have received an appointment to the theology faculty*. Yet, this argument [2] is a different form of categorical syllogism from argument [1], because the distribution of terms is different. In categorical syllogism [1], the same terms appear in the subject of the first premise and the subject of the conclusion and the same terms appear in the predicate of the first premise and the subject of the second premise and the same terms appear in the predicate of the second premise and the predicate of the conclusion. Categorical syllogism [2] has a very different form: the same terms appear in the subject of the first premise and the predicate of the second premise and the same term appears in the predicate of the first premise and the predicate of the conclusion and the same term appears in the subject of the second premise and the subject of the conclusion.

　　Both categorical syllogisms [1] and [2], however, have one formal feature in common: they are both composed entirely of universal affirmative propositions. It is possible that categorical syllogisms might be composed of other types of propositions or combinations of types of propositions. A categorical syllogism might draw a universal negative conclusion from a universal affirmative first premise and a universal negative second premise. Alternatively, a categorical syllogism might draw an existential affirmative or negative conclusion from existential premises or some combination of universal and existential premises. So, there are many possible forms of categorical syllogism. In fact, if one considers that there are two possible qualities that the premises and conclusion can have and that there are two possible quantities that the premises and conclusion can have and that there are just so many possible distributions of three terms in two premises and a conclusion, then one can figure out that there are exactly 256 distinct forms of categorical syllogism. Thus, in addition to the two forms exemplified in [1] and [2], the following examples represent other patterns of categorical syllogism:

[3]　All theology masters have read the *Book of Sentences*.
　　No one who has read the *Book of Sentences* is ignorant of the theological
　　　opinions of Peter Lombard.
　　Therefore, no theology masters are ignorant of the theological opinions
　　　of Peter Lombard.

[4]　All university masters speak Latin.
　　Some university masters speak Greek.
　　Therefore, some Latin speakers are Greek speakers.

[5]   No Oxford master has ever visited China.
Some Arabic merchants have visited China.
Some Arabic merchants are not Oxford masters.

[6]   All university masters speak Latin.
Anyone who speaks Latin is familiar with the first declension.
Therefore, all people familiar with the first declension are university
        masters.

[7]   All university masters read Latin.
Some people who read Latin have read St. Augustine's *Confessions*.
Therefore, some university masters have read St. Augustine's *Confessions*.

§7 Picturing Arguments

While the categorical syllogism is not the only form of argument, it is a fundamentally important form. This is because, as already mentioned, all scientific explanations can be articulated in the form of this type of argument. Of course, only a valid categorical syllogism can successfully articulate a true scientific explanation. It is, therefore, most important to determine when a categorical syllogism is valid and when it is invalid. As already noted, there are 256 possible forms of categorical syllogism. Of these forms, only a few constitute valid arguments. The other possible forms are invalid. There are several methods of determining which syllogistic forms are valid, but one of the most effective is to use a form of argument diagram that is similar to the propositional diagrams discussed in §4.

Propositional diagrams are capable of displaying any possible relationship between the two terms of a proposition. When marked for the proposition's quantity and quality, the diagram displays the precise relationship in a particular proposition. The form of categorical syllogisms also depends on the relationship of terms in propositions. In this kind of argument, however, there are three terms to consider and they are related in three propositions: the conclusion and the two premises. The relationship of the three terms of a categorical syllogism, therefore, can be displayed on a three-term diagram.

Instead of just two circles, as in a propositional diagram, an *argument diagram* has three circles: one for each of the three terms of the categorical syllogism being diagramed. These circles are drawn so that they overlap each other creating seven spaces or regions within the circles. These seven regions, along with the region outside all three circles, represent the eight possible ways in which three terms can be related to each other. Consider a diagram capable of showing all possible relationships between the three terms *people who are university masters*, *people who wear academic gowns when lecturing*, and *people who often feel hot during the summer*:

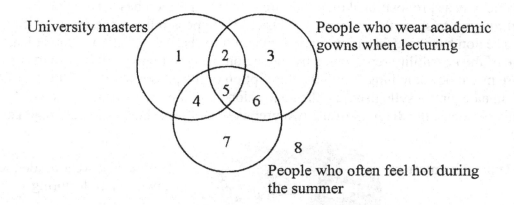

The region of the diagram that is inside the *university master* circle but outside the other two (Region 1) represents the possibility of being a university master who does not wear an academic gown when lecturing and does not often feel hot during the summer. The region inside both the *university master* and *people who wear academic gowns* circles but outside the *people who feel hot in summer* circle (Region 2) represents the possibility of being a university master who wears a gown when lecturing but who does not often feel hot during the summer. The region inside the *people who wear academic gowns when lecturing* circle but outside the other two (Region 3) represents the possibility of being a person who wears an academic gown when lecturing who is not a university master and does not feel hot in summer. The region inside both the *university master* and *people who often feel hot in summer* circles but outside the *people who wear academic gowns when lecturing* circle (Region 4) represents the possibility of being a university master who often feels hot in summer but does not wear an academic gown when lecturing. The region in the center inside all three circles (Region 5) represents the possibility of being a university master who wears an academic gown when lecturing and often feels hot in summer. The region within both the *people who wear academic gowns when lecturing* and *people who feel hot in summer* circles but outside of the *university master* circle (Region 6) represents the possibility of being a person who wears a gown when lecturing and feels hot in summer but is not a university master. The region inside the *people who feel hot in summer* circle but outside the other two (Region 7) represents the possibility of being a person who feels hot in the summer but who is neither a university master nor one who wears an academic gown when lecturing. Finally, the region outside all three circles (Region 8) represents the possibility of being a person who is not a university master, does not wear an academic gown when lecturing, and does not feel hot in summer.

Now consider a categorical syllogism composed of these three terms:

[1]   University masters wear academic gowns when lecturing.
       People who wear academic gowns when lecturing often feel hot during the summer.
       Therefore, university masters often feel hot during the summer.

The diagram of this argument will be marked for the quality and quantity of the premises in the same way as propositional diagrams are marked: a region has shading or lines drawn through it to show the universal exclusion of the possibility represented by the region, a region has the affirmation mark drawn in it to show the affirmation in at least one case of the possibility represented by the region, and the region is left open to show that there might be something fitting the description of the possibility represented by the region. In categorical syllogism [1], the conclusion and both premises are universal affirmatives. Thus, the diagram of the two premises will have the appropriate regions shaded:

University masters   People who wear academic gowns when lecturing

People who feel hot in summer

Notice that when one draws a diagram of an argument, one draws a diagram of the two premises of the argument. Now, if this is a valid argument, then the truth of the premises necessitates the truth of the conclusion. Graphically, this is shown when a diagram drawn to display the forms of the two premises also displays the conclusion. This shows that the two premises cannot both be true unless the conclusion is true as well. It might be said that, in a sense, when one has both premises (both premises are true), one also must have the conclusion (the conclusion must be true). To put this yet another way, if one diagrams a valid categorical syllogism properly, then in drawing a diagram of the two premises, one cannot help but have drawn a diagram of the conclusion as well. This is precisely what the diagram shows—it shows that the categorical syllogism [1] is a valid argument: if it is true that university masters wear academic gowns when lecturing and it is also true that anyone who does often feels hot during summer, it absolutely must be true that all university masters often feel hot during summer.

Consider some further examples of categorical syllogisms with universal premises and conclusions.

[2]   Earth casts a curved shadow on the moon during a lunar eclipse.
Anything casting a curved shadow on the moon during a lunar eclipse must have a curved surface.
Therefore, earth must have a curved surface.

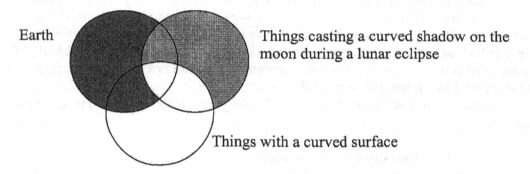

[3]   All university masters are appointed by the chancellor.
No one appointed by the chancellor is unknown to the bursar.
Therefore, no university masters are unknown to the bursar.

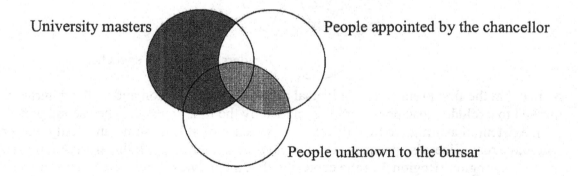

Notice that in both of these arguments [2] and [3] the diagram of the premises also is a diagram of the conclusion. That means that both of these arguments are valid. Now, consider this argument:

[4]   All university masters are paid by the bursar.
       Anyone who receives money from the university is paid by the bursar.
       Therefore, anyone who receives money from the university is a university
       master.

University masters   People paid by the Bursar

                                   People who receive money from the
                                   university

Notice that in this argument [4] the diagram of the two premises *all university masters are paid by the bursar* and *all people receiving money from the university are paid by the bursar* does not also constitute a diagram of the conclusion *all people receiving money from the university are university masters*. For this diagram to say what the conclusion says every region of the *people who receive money from the university* circle that is outside of the *people who are university masters* circle would have to be ruled out. Yet, this is not the case, because Region 6 remains open showing that it is possible that there are people who receive money from the university who are not university masters. Thus, this categorical syllogism [4] is invalid.

Consider some additional categorical syllogisms with existential propositions in them:

[5]   All university masters read Latin.
       Some university masters have read Cicero's speeches.
       Therefore, some readers of Cicero's speeches read Latin.

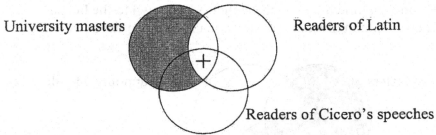

University masters   Readers of Latin

                                   Readers of Cicero's speeches

Notice that the first premise is a universal affirmative proposition and so the diagram is marked to exclude those possibilities excluded by the first premise. The second premise is an existential affirmative that affirms the existence of at least some university masters who have read Cicero's speeches. So, the diagram is marked with the affirmation mark in the only region (Region 5 in the center) within the university masters' circle that is also in the readers of Cicero circle that is left open by the first premise. This region (Region

5) is also within the Latin readers circle and so represents the possibility of being a reader of Cicero who also reads Latin. This is what is affirmed for some cases by the conclusion and, therefore, the argument is valid.

[6]   No Oxford masters traveled to China.
        Some people who have traveled to China have sailed the South China Sea.
        Therefore, some people who have sailed the South China Sea are not
            Oxford masters.

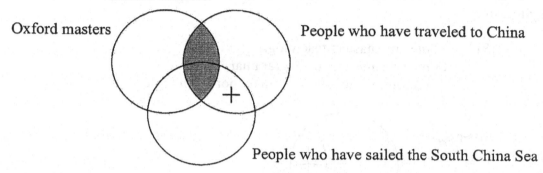

Notice that the first premise is a universal negative proposition and excludes any possible way of being both an Oxford master and a traveler to China. The second premise is an existential affirmative proposition that affirms that there are travelers to China who have sailed the South China Sea. This affirmation is also an affirmation that there are people who have sailed the South China Sea who are not Oxford masters, because the affirmation mark is within the South China Sea sailor circle but outside the Oxford master circle. Thus, this diagram of the two premises of this argument [6] is also a diagram of the conclusion showing that the argument is valid.

[7]   All Oxford masters are invited to the chancellor's dinner.
        There are Oxford masters who did not attend the chancellor's dinner.
        Therefore, some people who attended the chancellor's dinner were not
            Oxford masters.

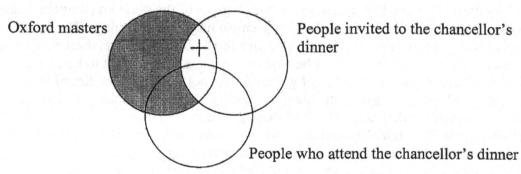

In this argument [7], the first premise universally excludes being an Oxford master who was not invited to the chancellor's dinner and the diagram is marked to show this. The second premise affirms that there are some Oxford masters who did not attend and the diagram is marked with an affirmation mark in the only region of the Oxford masters circle that is also outside of the dinner attendance circle that is left open by the first premise. The existential conclusion claims that there are people who attended the dinner who are not Oxford masters, but the diagram does not show this because there is no affirmation mark in any of the regions of the dinner attendance circle outside of the Oxford master circle. The diagram, therefore, shows that this argument is invalid.

Some categorical syllogisms have existential premises that do not definitely affirm something with respect to a third term, but could be true in more than one way. Such arguments are always invalid. Consider, for example, the following categorical syllogism:

[8]   Some arts masters teach logic.
      Some arts masters teach grammar.
      Therefore, some arts masters do not teach logic.

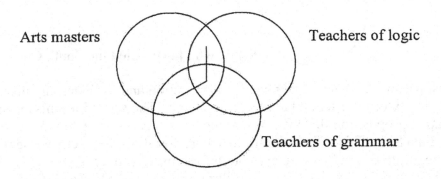

The first premise of this argument [8] is an existential affirmative proposition affirming that there exist arts masters who teach logic. This proposition can be true in two ways with respect to the third term *teachers of grammar*: an arts master can be a teacher of logic and not also a teacher of grammar (a possibility represented by Region 2) or an arts master can be a teacher of logic who also teaches grammar (a possibility represented by Region 5). The first premise does not give us enough information to determine which of these two ways this premise is true. Thus, we mark the diagram with the *indetermination mark* by drawing a line that extends into both regions of the diagram (Regions 2 and 5) representing the possibilities that the first premise might be affirming. The second premise is also an existential affirmative affirming that there are arts masters who teach grammar. This premise also might be true in two ways with respect to being a teacher of logic: a master might be a teacher of grammar and not logic or a teacher of both grammar and logic. So, again, the diagram must be marked with the indetermination mark. As a result, a diagram of both of these premises together has no definite affirmation marked on it. Thus, it does not also constitute a diagram of the existential negative conclusion, for there is no affirmation mark in any region representing the possibility of being an arts master without being a teacher of logic. Thus, the argument is invalid.

Exercise 15

Student: _____

Draw an argument diagram for each of the following categorical syllogisms.

1.   All arts masters at Oxford lecture on Boethius' logical treatises.
      Anyone who lectures on Boethius' logical treatises understands hypotheticals.
      Therefore, all arts masters at Oxford understand hypotheticals.

2.   All arts masters at Oxford are required to present an inaugural lecture.
      There are arts masters at Oxford who lecture exclusively on Aristotle.
      Therefore, some required to present an inaugural lecture lecture exclusively on Aristotle.

3.   All arts masters at Oxford are required to present an inaugural lecture.
      No law master at Oxford is also an arts master at Oxford.
      Therefore, no law master at Oxford is required to present an inaugural lecture.

4.   All arts masters at Oxford are required to present an inaugural lecture.
Nobody required to present an inaugural lecture reads Old Scythian.
Therefore, no art master at Oxford reads Old Scythian.

5.   All arts masters at Oxford are interested in Aristotle's book on animal motion.
Everyone interested in Aristotle's book on animal motion agrees to lecture on it.
Therefore, all arts masters agree to lecture on Aristotle's book on animal motion.

6.   No theology masters at Oxford agree with Master Alan's teaching.
Some who agree with Master Alan's teaching are arts masters at Oxford.
Therefore, some who agree with Master Alan's teaching are not theology masters
       at Oxford.

Exercise 16

Student: _____

Draw an argument diagram for each of the following categorical syllogisms and use your diagram to determine the validity of the argument.

1. All arts masters at Padua lecture on Aristotle's physics.
   Anyone who lectures on Aristotle's physics knows of hylomorphism.
   Therefore, all arts masters at Padua know of hylomorphism.

   ☐ valid categorical syllogism   ☐ invalid categorical syllogism

2. All arts masters at Padua lecture on Aristotle's physics.
   Some masters who use the new calculatory methods are arts masters at Padua.
   Therefore, some masters who use the new calculatory methods lecture on
       Aristotle's physics.

   ☐ valid categorical syllogism   ☐ invalid categorical syllogism

3.   Arts masters at Padua lecture on Aristotle's physics.
No one who lectures on Aristotle's physics is ignorant of final cause.
Therefore, no arts masters at Padua are ignorant of final cause.

□ valid categorical syllogism   □ invalid categorical syllogism

4.   Some arts masters at Padua lecture on Aristotle's logic.
Some arts masters at Padua lecture on Boethius' logic.
Therefore, some arts masters at Padua do not lecture on Aristotle's logic.

□ valid categorical syllogism   □ invalid categorical syllogism

5.   No arts masters at Padua accept an actual infinity as intelligible.
Some who accept an actual infinity as intelligible are mathematicians.
Therefore, some arts masters at Padua are mathematicians.

□ valid categorical syllogism   □ invalid categorical syllogism

Exercise 18

Student: _____

Read the following dialogue and answer the questions that follow.

The Lunar Eclipse

After four years working as an advisor to the pope in Rome, Master Augustino was eager to return to teaching at the university. He considered Padua his home and he felt he had been away too long. So it was with some satisfaction that he moved back into his rooms at the Convent of St. Xenia in the heart of the university district. As he was unpacking he heard a knock on his door and upon opening it he found his old student Marco of Venice standing before him.

Marco of Venice:	Welcome back to Padua, Master! I heard that you had returned.
Master Augustino:	Marco, my boy, I thought that you were with your father in Rhodes or some other far-away island. What are you doing here in Padua?
Marco of Venice:	Like you, Master, I have returned to my academic home. My father has finally released me from his service so that I can come back to the university to finish my degree. You will recall, Master, that you always said that I would one day return.
Master Augustino:	So, I did. So, I did. Well, it seems that we are both returned to university life. Come in, my boy, and tell me of all your adventures in the mysterious east. Please, sit here and let me pour you a cup of this fine Falernian. It is from the pope's own cellars. I am sure that you had nothing this good onboard ship.
Marco of Venice:	You are right there—nothing but the sort of foul stuff that all sailors drink. But my life of sailing for my father is finished. I made him a deal: I would give him three of my best years working on his ships and then he must allow me to return to my studies. As you know, he had his heart set on my taking over the family shipping business and he pressed me hard about staying, but in the end he relented and here I am. I say, this is very good wine!
Master Augustino:	Well, your merchant father's loss is our gain. It is good to see you again. As for that wine—yes, it is good. It was one of my few comforts in Rome.
Marco of Venice:	Come, do not tell me, Master, that you did not enjoy being around that elegant crowd at the papal court, to say nothing of being at the center of power. Did you not enjoy having the ear of His Holiness and, through him, influencing the affairs of the world?

83

Master Augustino:	No, no. Too much politicking and too little learning. Oh, the glamour of the court was exciting at first, but I soon missed serious conversation and philosophical research. His Holiness is a good man, I think, and he gave me important work. Yet, Rome is not Padua and I missed my books, my fellow masters, and my students. What good fortune to be back in Padua just as you are returning!
Marco of Venice:	I see, Master, that you are not in the mood for some of the salty stories I brought home from the east, so I will regale you with an intellectual tale from my travels. As it happens, I dazzled my shipmates with my great learning, for which I have you to thank, of course.
Master Augustino:	Come now, Marco, do you want me to believe that you and your young companions spent your time in intellectual pursuits while traveling through the bawdy districts of the Levant? I know those young fellows your father hires to run his ships as well as I know you and I am sure that all of you spent far more time searching out wine and women than you did searching out philosophical truths.
Marco of Venice:	Master, I am cut to the quick! You do me an injustice. As it happens, I turned some neat syllogisms while traveling through those bawdy districts, as you call them. Here, pour me another cup of the pope's wine and I will tell you the story.
Master Augustino:	Very well, impress me with your scientific investigations made while sailing the blue seas—and I do not mean those investigations you made into the fare offered by the dock-side taverns where you, no doubt, spent most of your time ashore.
Marco of Venice:	It happened while we were unloading a load of amber and tin at Tyre. We intended to take on a load of Arabian spices bound for Venice, but the spice dealer from Damascus had not yet arrived in Tyre with the goods. So, we had to kick around the port for a few days. One evening, my companions and I had just entered a tavern common room for a bit of refreshment, when we heard a cry from the street outside. Looking out to see what all the commotion was about, we found that it was quite dark which surprised me because our pilot told us to expect a bright full moon that night. Women were screaming and running through the streets. Men were falling on their knees calling to God in Greek, Arabic, Latin, and languages I had never heard before. I was wondering what this could be all about when I looked up just in time to see the moon stolen away by a dark shadow that moved across its face.
Master Augustino:	A lunar eclipse.
Marco of Venice:	Just so. I began to laugh and my companions, who were just as fearful as the people in the streets, looked at me as if I were mad. I reassured them on that point and invited them down into the tavern common room for a drink on me.
Master Augustino:	A costly piece of reassurance, no doubt.

Marco of Venice:	As it happens, I had just made a tidy sum playing . . . Well, leave that story for another time. Let us just say that I had the means to treat my friends. Once we were settled with our drinks and some of the tavernkeeper's tasty stew, served by an equally tasty wench, I got down to the business of scientifically explaining the eclipse. I explained that the moon is a spherical body that is illuminated by an external source and the proof of this was that the moon is a body that waxes and wanes through crescent phases and any such body is spherical and illuminated by an external source.
Master Augustino:	A simple syllogism.
Marco of Venice:	Yes, but now I had their attention. So, we established that the moon is externally illuminated. I continued: any spherical body illuminated by an external source can have that source of illumination blocked by an interposing body. I then concluded that the moon can have its source of illumination blocked by an interposing body. Of course, I identified that body as the earth.
Master Augustino:	Nicely done. Did they accept your arguments?
Marco of Venice:	Of course. They are valid, are they not?
Master Augustino:	Yes, they are, but whether you and your companions still had the wit to see that after what I assume were several pots of ale . . .
Marco of Venice:	Which only improved my logical skills and increased my companions' scientific curiosity, for our philosophical investigation did not end there.
Master Augustino:	What more?
Marco of Venice:	What more? Just this: I went on to prove the earth's sphericity!
Master Augustino:	Well, it seems that you learned something from your time at the university after all. Apparently, you did not sleep through my lectures on natural philosophy—at least, not all of them. Pray, tell me how your reasoning proceeded.
Marco of Venice:	I asked my friends about the shape of the shadow that moved across the face of the moon during the eclipse. They agreed that it was curved. I then reminded them that we had just identified the cause of the shadow as the earth's imposition between the moon and its source of illumination, the sun. They then realized that the shadow on the moon's face must be that of the earth.
Master Augustino:	So, you got them to agree that the earth casts a curved shadow on the surface of the moon during a lunar eclipse.

Marco of Venice:	Right. I then gave them a bit of geometry, just as you used to in your lectures: anything casting a curved shadow on the surface of the moon during a lunar eclipse must have a curved surface.
Master Augustino:	They then drew the conclusion that the earth has a curved surface.
Marco of Venice:	Well, I had to prompt them a bit, but they got the point. But then one of the fellows, emboldened by his ale, piped up, "But that only proves that the earth has one curved surface, not that it must be a sphere. I, of course, could not deny this.
Master Augustino:	Aha! He had you there. So, Marco, how did you answer him?
Marco of Venice:	I placed before him this neat syllogism: earth is a uniform solid body casting a curved shadow and any uniform solid body casting a curved shadow must be a sphere. Therefore, the earth must be a sphere.
Master Augustino:	My boy, I am proud of you. Even in your cups you prove yourself to be an accomplished natural philosopher. Besides, you allow me to tease you. Indeed, Marco, I truly missed you and I am happy that we are together again in Padua. Enough of this papal wine! Let us head down the street to the Blue Boar and share a pot of Paduan ale. I will tell you of the new book of Aristotle's I found when I was in Rome. I am thinking of lecturing on it in the coming term.

1. Master Augustino, a professor of natural philosophy at the University of Padua, has returned to his teaching post after a four-year leave of absence. What was he doing during those four years?

   _____

   _____

   _____

2. Just as he is settling into his old rooms in Padua, Master Augustino is visited by his old student Marco the Venetian who is also just returning to the university after an absence of some years. What was Marco doing while he was away from the university?

   _____

   _____

   _____

   _____

3.   What is Falernian?

   ☐   The name of the pope's residence in Rome.

   ☐   A fine wine from central Italy.

   ☐   The name of the pope's favorite dog.

   ☐   A form of syllogistic reasoning.

4.   Marco tells the story of an event that occurred while he was visiting the port city of Tyre in Lebanon. Just as he and his friends were about to sit down to dinner at a dock-side tavern, they heard a commotion in the street. Going out they saw that people were in a panic because of fear. Of what were the people afraid?

   ☐   An approaching tsunami.

   ☐   An eclipse of the moon.

   ☐   An attack by Saracen troops.

   ☐   An onslaught of syllogistic reasoning.

5.   In the course of scientifically explaining the lunar eclipse for his friends, Marco presents an argument intended to prove the conclusion that the moon is a spherical body that is illuminated by an external source. What are the premises of Marco's argument?

   Premise 1:   _____

   _____

   Premise 2:   _____

   _____

6.   Master Augustino correctly identifies the form of Marco's argument as

   ☐   an immediate inference by equivalence.

   ☐   an immediate inference by implication.

   ☐   a categorical syllogism.

   ☐   an onslaught of syllogistic reasoning.

7. Is Marco's argument that the moon is externally illuminated valid? Support your answer with an argument diagram.

☐ Yes, it is valid. ☐ No, it is invalid.

8. Marco goes on to give another argument using the conclusion of his first argument *the moon is a spherical body that is illuminated by an external source* as a premise of a new argument. What is his new argument?

Premise 1: _____

_____

Premise 2: _____

_____

Conclusion: _____

_____

9. What form of argument is Marco's second argument?

☐ An immediate inference by equivalence.

☐ An immediate inference by implication.

☐ A categorical syllogism.

10.   Is Marco's second argument valid? Support your answer with an argument diagram.

☐ Yes, it is valid.   ☐ No, it is invalid.

11.   Having used argument to show what causes a lunar eclipse, Marco goes on to prove that the earth is spherical in shape. He uses two separate categorical syllogisms to prove this. What is the first argument?

Premise 1:   _____

_____

Premise 2:   _____

_____

Conclusion: _____

_____

12.   Is the first of Marco's categorical syllogisms about the shape of the earth valid?   Support your answer with an argument diagram.

☐ Yes, it is valid.   ☐ No, it is invalid.

13. Why is Marco's first categorical syllogism about the earth's shape insufficient to prove that the earth must be a sphere?

_____

_____

_____

14. The second of Marco's arguments about the earth's shape is also a categorical syllogism. What is this second argument?

Premise 1: _____

_____

Premise 2: _____

_____

Conclusion: _____

_____

15. Is this second of Marco's categorical syllogisms about the shape of the earth valid? Support your answer with an argument diagram.

☐ Yes, it is valid.   ☐ No, it is invalid.

§8 Being Elliptical

It has already been pointed out that scientific explanations can be articulated in the form of categorical syllogisms. This does not mean that this kind of argument is reserved for technical scientific discussions and written research reports. The examples given in §6 and §7 show that categorical syllogisms are also frequently used in everyday speech and writing. When used in this ordinary everyday way, these arguments are often expressed elliptically. This means that they are expressed in an abbreviated way with a part left unexpressed. Consider the following categorical syllogism:

[1]   All arts masters have studied Boethius's logical treatises.
       Anyone who has studied Boethius's logical treatises is well-educated in
            the art of logic.
       Therefore, all arts masters are well-educated in the art of logic.

In an everyday conversation, this argument [1] might be expressed elliptically by leaving one of the premises unspoken:

[2]   All arts masters have studied Boethius' logical treatises and that is why
            they are well-educated in the art of logic.

Notice that [1] and [2] are different expressions of the very same categorical syllogism. Like all categorical syllogisms, this argument has two premises and a certain distribution of three distinct terms. This is just as true for the elliptical expression at [2] as it is for the fully expressed argument at [1]. In the elliptical argument [2], one of the premises is expressed and the conclusion is expressed. Yet, this argument [2] is a complete categorical syllogism with two premises and a conclusion. One of the premises is left unexpressed and the listener or reader is expected to supply the unexpressed premise in his mind in order to understand what the argument is.

In everyday speech and writing, categorical syllogisms are more often than not expressed elliptically. Yet, why would an arguer who intends a full categorical syllogism leave some part of the argument unexpressed? There are two primary reasons why this is often done. The first is for the sake of economy of speech or written expression. If we do not need to speak or write everything we mean in order to be understood, then we often do not bother to do so. Often elliptical expression makes for a smoother and more interesting style of speech or a more readable style of writing. The second reason is that, if an arguer knows that his audience is already familiar with the subject matter of his argument, then he will often decide to respect that knowledge and leave unexpressed what his audience already knows. Consider, for example, the following elliptical categorical syllogism:

[3] Because all dolphins are mammals, no dolphins are fish.

If the arguer knows his audience is already familiar with the difference between mammals and fish, then he does not have to express this difference explicitly in his argument and he might decide to leave it unexpressed for convenience. Another reason he might leave unexpressed the premise *No mammals are fish* is to respect the knowledge of his audience. If his audience is well-educated and knows all about the major kinds of animal life, then it might be pedantic or even insulting to instruct his audience about what he very well knows they all know. When analyzing a categorical syllogism, of course, it is necessary to be able to express fully all the parts of the argument. Argument [3] cannot be tested for validity using an argument diagram unless both premises are clearly known:

[4] All dolphins are mammals.
No mammals are fish.
Therefore, no dolphins are fish.

The elliptical expression of arguments also allows for variation in their expression. For example, it is common to express the premises first and follow that by drawing a conclusion. Yet, in everyday speech and writing, it is just as common to express a conclusion first and follow that by the premises that support it. So, the argument at [4] may be elliptically expressed by the example at [3] or by:

[5] No dolphins are fish, since all dolphins are mammals.

This might be even more elliptically expressed like this:

[6] Dolphins are not fish, since they are mammals.

Each of these examples [3], [5], and [6] are elliptical ways of expressing the fully expressed categorical syllogism at [4].

Notice also that elliptical expression of arguments makes it possible that a full categorical syllogism of two premises and a conclusion containing a distribution of three distinct terms be expressed in a single sentence. Most frequently in elliptical categorical syllogisms one of the premises is left unexpressed, leaving the audience to supply it in their minds. Yet, it is possible to elliptically express an argument by expressing both premises and leaving the conclusion unexpressed. This often happens when, for example, a public speaker expresses the premises of his argument and then says, "I will let you draw the obvious conclusion for yourselves." Whatever part of the argument is left unexpressed, it is necessary for analysis that all parts be explicitly stated. When reconstructing elliptically expressed categorical syllogisms, it is important to pay close attention to the various premise and conclusion indicators. These provide clues to which parts of the argument are being expressed and, therefore, what needs to be supplied. It is also important to give careful attention to the quantity and quality of the propositions expressed in the elliptical categorical syllogism, because these can also serve as guides to the reconstruction of the argument. Consider, for example, the following:

[7] Happiness is man's highest good because it is the attainment and enjoyment of the sovereign good.

This is an elliptical expression of a categorical syllogism. In reconstructing the full argument, one must first determine which parts of the argument are given in the elliptical expression. The premise indicator *because* shows that *Happiness is the attainment and enjoyment of the sovereign good* is a premise—that is, it is a reason given by the arguer for the truth of some conclusion. For what conclusion is this premise a reason? A careful look at the sentence [7] reveals that it is a reason being given to show why *Happiness is man's highest good*. This, then, is the conclusion. So far, the analysis provides the conclusion and one of the premises. Because all categorical syllogisms have two premises, there must be another premise in the argument that is left unexpressed. Another careful look at the expressed parts of the argument reveals that three distinct terms have been expressed: *being happiness*, *being the attainment and enjoyment of the sovereign good*, and *being man's highest good*. Because all categorical syllogisms have exactly three distinct terms, it is clear that the elliptical argument [7] provides all three of the terms that will show up in the fully expressed argument. The unexpressed premise, then, will be composed of two of these three terms. Noticing that the term *being happiness* has already shown up twice—as the subject term of the conclusion and the subject term of the expressed premise—it is not likely to be used again in the unexpressed premise. This means that the unexpressed premise will be composed of the two terms *being the attainment and enjoyment of the sovereign good* and *being man's highest good*. Next, the quantity and quality of the unexpressed premise must be determined. Both of the expressed parts of the argument are universal affirmatives, so it is a good guess that the unexpressed part is also universal and affirmative: *All attainment and enjoyment of the sovereign good is man's highest good.* This provides all the parts of the argument and, putting all these parts together, the fully expressed categorical syllogism can be reconstructed:

[8] Happiness is the attainment and enjoyment of the sovereign good.
Anything that is the attainment and enjoyment of the sovereign good is man's highest good.
Therefore, happiness is man's highest good.

The argument can now be diagramed to show its logical form and to test it for validity in the usual way.

Exercise 19

Student: _____

Read the following dialogue and answer the questions that follow.

On Being a Vegetable

The feast day of the Holy Apostle James in 1317 was a miserable day in Paris. A raw October wind blew down from the northwest and it was raining heavily. Two young men wrapped in hooded cloaks hurried across the bridge near the great Cathedral of Notre Dame. When they reached the left bank of the river, they turned up the Rue des Augustins and quickly made their way to the tavern known as the Ours d'Or. Entering the tavern's common room, they removed their cloaks and shook them out. Instead of immediately ordering wine, as they usually did, they ascended the stairs and entered a private room on the second floor. Closing the door shut out the loud singing and talk of the common room below. They found themselves in the presence of a group of other young men talking quietly with Master Gerard, a famous professor at the university. The newcomers addressed themselves to the master with a bow.

Scholar Marc:	Many apologies, Master, this miserable weather delayed us.
Scholar Malphus:	The wind drives the rain right through one's cloak like so many darts. We are cold and soaked through.
Master Gerard:	Welcome, young scholars! Come warm yourselves by the fire and take a cup of wine. Once you have refreshed yourselves, you can join our discussion concerning vegetative life.
Scholar Malphus:	You are discussing vegetables? I thought, Master, that we were to discuss Aristotle's treatise on the soul.
Master Gerard:	We are indeed discussing the soul and to do so we must begin with the vegetative soul.
Scholar Marc:	My head must still be soaked by that rainstorm. Do you mean to suggest, Master, that Aristotle says that plants have souls?
Master Gerard:	That is *precisely* what I mean to suggest.
Scholar Marc:	But how can that be? Vegetables do not think!
Scholar Matthew:	Master, could it be that our newly arrived friends here have too narrow an understanding of what a soul is?
Master Gerard:	That could very well be the case. Let us review Aristotle's definition of the soul. Perhaps that will help. Scholar Georges, please give Aristotle's argument that explains the nature of the soul.

Scholar Georges:	First let me have another piece of that fine Auvergne cheese. After all, one cannot do philosophy on an empty stomach!
Scholar Marc:	Nor with an empty head! Get on with the argument, Georges!
Scholar Georges:	[speaking with his mouth full] Here is what the great Aristotle has to say: The soul is that capacity by which a living thing performs its distinctive functions. Now, any capacity by which a living thing performs the functions distinctive to it is the living actuality of its organic body. Now, my friend Marc, I will let you draw the conclusion for yourself while I have another piece of this wonderful cheese from my home province of Auvergne.
Scholar Malphus:	This just goes to show that you can take the scholar out of Auvergne, but you cannot keep the Auvergne out of the scholar! [Laughter all around.]
Scholar Marc:	How can I follow this argument when you speak it with all that munching? Let me see if I have this right: Aristotle holds that the soul is the living actuality of an organic material body. Is that right?
Scholar Georges:	[speaking with his mouth full betwen munching noises] Thas [munch] correk.
Scholar Matthew:	I think he means "That is correct."
Master Gerard:	Yes, this conclusion is Aristotle's definition of soul. Notice that being the living actuality of an organic material body is not limited to thinking things.
Scholar Marc:	It follows that the soul is not limited to thinking things. Yes, I see now. By the word "soul" Aristotle means the source of life in living things.
Scholar Matthew:	Quite right. Just as each human being has a soul, so does each and every plant and animal. Each kind of living thing has the type of soul appropriate to its way of life.
Scholar Marc:	I see. And every type of soul appropriate to the living thing's way of life is designated by that living thing's highest and most distinctive function. Therefore, each kind of living thing is designated by its highest and most distinctive function.
Scholar Malphus:	But what is the distinctive function of a plant?
Scholar Matthew:	Well, it is to perform those basic functions that make a thing alive in the simplest way—a vegetative sort of way.
Scholar Malphus:	I see that this shows that a living body must have sufficient organization to grow and reproduce. But what has this to do with the souls of vegetables?

Scholar Marc: I am beginning to understand. The best way to answer your question, Malphus, is to formulate an argument that results in the definition of the vegetative soul. Let me try. A vegetative soul is what is generative of other things similar to it in species. This is why it is endowed with a nutritive potentiality to conserve its own being, to grow and to reproduce through the assimilation of food.

Master Gerard: Very good, Scholar Marc! This does indeed provide us with an accurate definition of the vegetative soul. In summary, plant souls are the capacities plants have to use food to grow and reproduce. This is the most basic form of life. Every form of life has at least these powers and without them there is no life.

Scholar Georges: I must say that all of this would be more obvious to you scholars, if you would nourish your minds with the best cheese in all creation: that wonderful cheese that comes from my home province of Auvergne!

1. What is the general topic of discussion between Master Gerard and his students?

_____

_____

_____

2. Scholar Georges comes from what province in southern France?

_____

3. Master Gerard asks Scholar Georges to present Aristotle's argument that explains the nature of the soul. What is the conclusion of the argument?

Conclusion: _____

_____

4. The conclusion of Aristotle's argument explaining the soul as set out by Scholar Georges is not actually spoken by Georges. Which of the students speaks the conclusion of Aristotle's argument?

_____

5. What is the logical form of Aristotle's conclusion explaining the nature of the soul?

    Quantity: _____

    Quality: _____

6. What are the premises of Aristotle's argument explaining the nature of the soul?

    Premise 1: _____

    _____

    Premise 2: _____

    _____

7. Draw a diagram of Aristotle's argument explaining the nature of the soul.

8. Is Aristotle's argument explaining the nature of the soul valid?

    ☐   Yes, it is a valid immediate inference by equivalence.

    ☐   Yes, it is a valid immediate inference by implication.

    ☐   Yes, it is a valid categorical syllogism.

    ☐   No, it is an invalid categorical syllogism.

9. Master Gerard points out that the conclusion of Aristotle's argument explaining the nature of the soul provides a definition of soul. He then notes that being the living actuality of an organic body is not limited to being a thinking thing. Scholar Marc immediately draws a conclusion. What is Scholar Marc's conclusion?

    Conclusion: _____

    _____

10.   What are the two premises of the argument supporting Scholar Marc's conclusion?

Premise 1:   _____

_____

Premise 2:   _____

_____

11.   Draw a diagram of Scholar Marc's argument.

12.   Is Scholar Marc's argument valid?

☐   Yes, it is a valid immediate inference by equivalence.

☐   Yes, it is a valid immediate inference by implication.

☐   Yes, it is a valid categorical syllogism.

☐   No, it is an invalid categorical syllogism.

13.   After drawing a conclusion, Scholar Marc explains what Aristotle means by the word "soul" and Scholar Matthew agrees with him. What, according to Aristotle, does the word "soul" mean?

_____

_____

_____

_____

14. Scholar Marc draws another conclusion that each kind of living thing is designated by its highest and most distinctive function. What are his reasons for believing that this is true?

Premise 1: _____

_____

Premise 2: _____

_____

15. Draw a diagram of Scholar Marc's second argument.

16. Is Scholar Marc's second argument valid?

☐   Yes, it is a valid immediate inference by equivalence.

☐   Yes, it is a valid immediate inference by implication.

☐   Yes, it is a valid categorical syllogism.

☐   No, it is an invalid categorical syllogism.

17. When Scholar Malphus asks what the most basic life functions are, Scholar Matthew answers by asking him to consider an argument. What is this argument?

Premise 1: _____

_____

Premise 2: _____

_____

Conclusion: _____

_____

18.   How do you know that Scholar Matthew's argument is a categorical syllogism?

_____

_____

19.   Draw a diagram of Scholar Matthew's argument.

20.   Is Scholar Matthew's argument valid?

☐   Yes, it is a valid categorical syllogism.

☐   No, it is an invalid categorical syllogism.

21.   Scholar Malphus again asks a question: What does the fact that living bodies must have sufficient organization to grow and reproduce have to do with vegetable souls? Scholar Marc answers this question with an argument that results in a definition of the vegetative soul. What is this argument?

Premise 1:   _____

_____

Premise 2:   _____

_____

Conclusion: _____

_____

22.   Draw a diagram of Scholar Marc's third argument.

23.   Is Scholar Marc's third argument valid?

☐   Yes, it is a valid immediate inference by implication.

☐   Yes, it is a valid categorical syllogism.

☐   No, it is an invalid categorical syllogism.

24.   Master Gerard clearly likes Scholar Marc's third argument very much and says that it
results in an accurate definition of the vegetative soul. Why does Master Gerard believe
that Scholar Marc's conclusion is an accurate definition?

☐   The master holds that it is an accurate definition because it is the
conclusion of a valid argument with true premises.

☐   The master holds that it is an accurate definition because the premises are
true even though the argument is invalid.

☐   The master holds that it is an accurate definition because he is a vegetarian.

25.   At one point in the discussion, Scholar Malphus says, "This just goes to show that
you can take the scholar out of Auvergne, but you cannot keep the Auvergne out of the
scholar!" This comment evokes laughter among the gathered scholars. Why do they
laugh?

☐   They laugh because Scholar Malphus has made a joke about Scholar Georges
who has left behind his native province of Auvergne to attend the university in
Paris, but who cannot bear to leave behind the tasty cheese with which he grew
up.

☐   They laugh because Scholar Georges speaks with his mouth full.

☐   They laugh because everybody knows that composing a categorical syllogism
while eating Auvergne cheese makes the argument invalid.

Exercise 20

Student: _____

Read the following dialogue and answer the questions that follow.

The Wealth of Pelops

One fresh spring day in the year 1310, the sun reflected brightly off the surface of the Adriatic Sea and there was just enough wind to fill the sail. Two university students leaned on the ship's rail lazily watching the dolphins swimming alongside the ship.

Scholar Giordano:	What a pleasure to be away from the town and all the pressures of our studies—out here at sea where the air is so clear!
Scholar Marco:	It was a stroke of good fortune that my father was not ready to put to sea until we arrived. We would have missed the opportunity to travel with him to the Greek Isles.
Scholar Giordano:	Look at those beasts down there, they neither toil nor accumulate wealth, yet they seem quite happy. I wish I had no cares or responsibilities and could be as free as a dolphin skimming through the sea.
Scholar Marco:	Well, if we were free like dolphins we would not be here. Remember, my friend, the purpose of our journey is trade. As a merchant, my father travels to the Isles of Pelops every year at this time to trade for oil. The silver olive trees of the isles produce the best oil to be found on the whole coast. It is the source of our family's wealth and the reason why I am free to attend the university.
Scholar Giordano:	Ah, there's the rub! We humans are free only when we have wealth, whereas that swimming beast down there is free simply being what he is.
Scholar Marco:	Do not be so gloomy, my friend! You cannot defy fate. It is man's fate that his happiness is to be found in wealth.
Scholar Giordano:	But why should it be so? I do not wish it so. Nay, I refuse to believe it!
Scholar Marco:	It is simply a matter of logic. You are a logical fellow, so consider this: man's happiness is that to which his affections are most truly and completely drawn. That is why man's happiness is wealth. It is a simple syllogism.
Scholar Giordano:	Simple enough and valid. I even grant you your first premise. Yet, I wonder whether your second premise is true.
Scholar Marco:	How not?

Scholar Giordano:	Well, the purpose of attaining wealth is to buy something valued more than wealth itself.
Scholar Marco:	Yes, I see that.
Scholar Giordano:	Nothing valued more than wealth itself can be what draws human affections less than wealth.
Scholar Marco:	Very well, I grant you that.
Scholar Giordano:	It follows that the purpose of attaining wealth cannot be what draws the affections less than wealth.
Scholar Marco:	I am not sure I see your point.
Scholar Giordano:	The point, my good friend, is that wealth cannot be what people desire the most.
Scholar Marco:	But why not?
Scholar Giordano:	Because whatever people desire the most is sought for its own sake and wealth is never sought for its own sake.
Scholar Marco:	Are you saying that there is no point in making this journey?
Scholar Giordano:	I am saying that the point of this journey, which is to attain wealth through trade, is something we desire because we desire something else.
Scholar Marco:	But what else?
Scholar Giordano:	Obviously, whatever wealth can buy.
Scholar Marco:	Oh. I will have to think about that.

1. Why are the two university students in the story sailing to the Greek Islands of Pelops?

    _____

    _____

    _____

2. According to Scholar Marco, what is the fate of human beings?

    _____

    _____

3.   When Scholar Giordano rebels at the idea that human happiness is found in the attainment of wealth, his friend Marco says that he must accept this idea. Marco supports his claim with an argument. What is Marco's argument?

Premise 1:   _____

_____

Premise 2:   _____

_____

Conclusion: _____

_____

4.   The logical form of Scholar Marco's argument is

☐   a categorical syllogism, because it has two premises and exactly three distinct terms in the two premises and the conclusion.

☐   a categorical syllogism, because it has two universal affirmative premises.

☐   a categorical syllogism, because it is valid.

5.   Draw a diagram of Scholar Marco's argument.

6.   Scholar Giordano says that Scholar Marco's argument is valid. Based on your diagram analysis, is Giordano correct?

☐   Yes, he is correct as confirmed by my diagram analysis.

☐   No, he is incorrect as confirmed by my diagram analysis.

☐   The correctness of Scholar Giordano's claim cannot be determined by a diagram analysis.

7. While Scholar Giordano admits that Scholar Marco's argument is valid, he challenges one of Marco's premises. Which of Marco's two premises does Giordano believe may be false?

    Premise: _____

    _____

8. Scholar Giordano supports his hesitation to accept Scholar Marco's premise with an argument. What is Giordano's argument?

    Premise 1: _____

    _____

    Premise 2: _____

    _____

    Conclusion: _____

    _____

9. Draw a diagram of Scholar Giordano's argument.

10. Is Scholar Giordano's argument valid?

    ☐   Yes, it is a valid immediate inference by equivalence.

    ☐   Yes, it is a valid immediate inference by implication.

    ☐   Yes, it is a valid categorical syllogism.

    ☐   No, it is an invalid categorical syllogism.

11.   While Scholar Giordano supports his challenge to Scholar Marco's premise with an argument, Marco does not seem to get the point. Giordano responds by attempting to clarify the point with another argument. What is Scholar Giordano's second argument?

Premise 1: _____

_____

Premise 2: _____

_____

Conclusion: _____

_____

12.   Draw a diagram of Scholar Giordano's second argument.

13.   Is Scholar Giordano's second argument valid?

☐   Yes, it is a valid immediate inference by implication.

☐   Yes, it is a valid categorical syllogism.

☐   No, it is an invalid categorical syllogism.

14.   On the basis of Scholar Giordano's arguments, it is clear that he believes

☐   wealth could be sought for its own sake, if the wealthy person never spent any money but just put it in the bank.

☐   wealth cannot be sought for its own sake, because wealth is always a means to attaining some other good and not a good in itself.

☐   wealth cannot be sought for its own sake, because only the wealthy have wealth.

☐   dolphins are the wealthiest animals on the planet.

Exercise 21

Student: _____

Provide a complete analysis of each of the following elliptically expressed categorical arguments.

1. Divine action is not a process with a beginning or an end and that is why it is eternal.

Premise 1: _____

_____

Premise 2: _____

_____

Conclusion: _____

_____

Diagram analysis:

    ☐   This argument is a valid categorical syllogism.

    ☐   This argument is an invalid categorical syllogism.

2.   No divine thing is subject to change, because all changeable things exist in time.

Premise 1:   _____

_____

Premise 2:   _____

_____

Conclusion: _____

_____

Diagram analysis:

☐   This argument is a valid categorical syllogism.

☐   This argument is an invalid categorical syllogism.

§9 Being Complex

An individual categorical syllogism is a relatively simple form of argument: it is composed of only two premises and a conclusion and the premises and conclusion are composed of only three distinct terms. Yet, much of the argument by which we articulate our scientific explanations seems much more complex than this. How can it be rightly said, then, that all of our scientific explanations can be articulated in the form of categorical syllogisms? An important part of the answer to this question is the fact that several individual categorical syllogisms are often used together in complex arguments to establish scientific conclusions. There are two common ways in which this is done.

Soritical Arguments

One common way in which a series of categorical syllogisms can be used together to establish a final conclusion is called a *soritical argument* or *syllogistic chain*. One might attempt to establish a conclusion by an interconnected series or chain of individual categorical syllogisms where the conclusion of one syllogism is used as one of the premises of another syllogism to prove a further conclusion and then that conclusion is used as one of the premises of the next syllogism to prove a further conclusion and so on until one reaches a final conclusion. Consider an argument intended to establish the conclusion *all truly human actions are directed at a known goal*. In order to attain such a conclusion by means of a valid argument, the arguer may have to draw a series of preliminary conclusions as a means to establishing this final conclusion:

[1]   All truly human actions are actions of which the person is the master.
       All actions of which the person is the master are performed knowingly.
       Therefore, all truly human actions are performed knowingly.

       All truly human actions are performed knowingly.
       Any actions performed knowingly are chosen.
       Therefore, all truly human actions are chosen.

       All truly human actions are chosen.
       Any chosen action is directed at a known goal.
       Therefore, all truly human actions are directed at a known goal.

Notice that this complex argument is composed of three individual categorical syllogisms. Like every categorical syllogism, each of these individual arguments is composed of two premises and a conclusion in which there is some distribution of exactly three distinct terms. In order to establish the final conclusion *all truly human actions are directed at a known goal,* the arguer draws two preliminary conclusions *all truly human actions are performed knowingly* and *all truly human actions are chosen* and uses these conclusions as premises in the next stage of the complex argument. Thus, the conclusion of the first individual categorical syllogism in the syllogistic chain establishes the conclusion *all truly human actions are performed knowingly*. This proposition is then used as the first premise of the next individual categorical syllogism in the chain to establish the conclusion *all truly human actions are chosen*. This proposition is, in turn, used as the first premise of the next categorical syllogism in the chain to establish the final conclusion *all truly human actions are directed at a known goal* that the arguer was attempting to prove.

This way of using individual categorical arguments together in a complex argument truly establishes its final conclusion when each individual stage of the argument is a valid categorical syllogism. This can be shown by drawing an argument diagram for each individual argument in the syllogistic chain. In argument [1], the syllogistic chain is composed of three individual categorical arguments and, therefore, can be shown to be valid by means of three argument diagrams.

Lemmastic Arguments

Another common way in which a series of categorical syllogisms can be used together to establish a final conclusion is an argument with lemmas. A *lemma* is an auxiliary or assisting argument. Suppose one knows that one can prove a certain conclusion by means of a valid categorical syllogism with two particular premises, but one is uncertain whether these two premises are true. One then might attempt to draw each of the premises as conclusions from known premises and then, having proven them true, use them in the main categorical syllogism to prove the final conclusion. This kind of complex argument may be called *lemmastic argument*. Consider the following complex argument:

    [2] Main Argument: Two quantities equal to a third are equal to each other.
                         Two quantities equal to each other are convertible.
                         Therefore, two quantities equal to a third are convertible.

        Lemma 1:   Two quantities equal to a third are the same size.
                    Two quantities of the same size are equal to each other.
                    Therefore, two quantities equal to a third are equal to each other.

        Lemma 2:   Two quantities equal to each other are interchangeable.
                    Two interchangeable quantities are convertible.
                    Therefore, two quantities equal to each other are convertible.

In this complex argument, the arguer is attempting to establish the conclusion *two quantities equal to a third are convertible*. He knows that this conclusion validly follows from the two premises *two quantities equal to a third are equal to each other* and *two quantities equal to each other are convertible*, but he is uncertain whether these two premises are true. In order to show that the conclusion of his main argument validly follows from true premises, he constructs two lemmas, each proving one of the premises of his main argument. If he is successful in proving by valid lemmas each of the premises of his main argument, then he can be sure that he is arguing from true premises in his main argument. If his main argument is valid, then he has successfully established his final conclusion.

The analysis of lemmastic arguments makes use of argument diagrams in the usual way. The main argument is shown to be valid by an argument diagram and two argument diagrams showing that each of the lemmas are valid completes the analysis of the logical form of the whole complex argument and confirms the validity of each of its parts.

Exercise 22

Student: _____

Read the following dialogue and answer the questions that follow.

A Rare Bear in Oxford

It was early November in the year of our Lord 1299. The leaves were falling from the trees in a colorful cascade as two university students greeted each other on the High Street in Oxford.

John of Occam:	Alan, my good friend, I have been searching for you everywhere.
Alan of Hale:	Why? Do I owe you money?
John of Occam:	Now, now, do not be cynical, good friend. I do not always seek out my friends as sources of funds.
Alan of Hale:	I am not so sure. I have not seen you for nearly a year and the last time I did, you managed to talk me into that crazy investment scheme concerning that bridge over in . . .
John of Occam:	Forget the past! Today is a new day.
Alan of Hale:	Well, it is a day that finds me with a limp purse. I do not even have a penny to my name. So, if you are looking for someone to pay for all the drinks again like last Christmas, you have come to the wrong person.
John of Occam:	You have me wrong, friend Alan. It is I who will pay for the drinks today. Come with me to the Three Crowns and I will not only buy you a drink, but a good meal as well.
Alan of Hale:	Since when are you so well supplied with funds? Usually, you are the one with the empty purse come begging the price of a drink.
John of Occam:	Quite the contrary today. My father has sent me ten silver shillings as a gift. So, today the drinks are on me!
Alan of Hale:	Is this news supposed to allay my suspicions? The last I heard, your father had promised to completely cut off your funds until you passed your theology exams. Knowing your dismal scholarly record, I cannot believe that the faculty has passed you out yet.
John of Occam:	You insist on looking on the bleak side of things, my friend. Let me calm your suspicions and tell you the story. My father, last year so stern, has turned over a new leaf. He is now the most generous of benefactors. It seems that he invested in a merchant enterprise and the ship recently put into harbor with a load of Arabian spices worth thousands. My

115

father, who thought the ship lost during a storm at sea, was so relieved at the return on his investment that he sent something to everyone in the family, even me. So, buck up and come share a drink with me.

So, the two students headed down the High Street and turned in at the sign of the Three Crowns opposite the Church of the Holy Virgin. They went straight to the back where they sat in a pleasant walled garden as the tavern keeper brought ale and a plate of pickled fish and vegetables.

Alan of Hale: Forgive my suspicions and gloom, friend John. It has been a difficult day. You see, I met with my mathematics examiners this morning and it was not a pretty sight. I was nervous as a chicken. My brain was so addled that I could not think and my tongue was so thick that I could hardly form my Latin words. I shudder to think how well I did on the exam. My examiners gave no hint and told me they would announce the results tomorrow. I fear the worst.

John of Occam: Well, calm yourself, friend. Here you need not speak the proper Latin of the textbooks. The common Latin of the drinking songs will do. As for geometry, I will ask you about neither axioms nor theorems. In fact, I will only demand enough logic of you to follow the amusing story of an encounter I once had in this very tavern.

Alan of Hale: Not another of your far-fetched stories! That is just what I need! The last story you told was so preposterous . . .

John of Occam: But this one is God's truth. I swear! It happened last year on the Feast of St. Andrew. The bishop and his people were having their usual psalm-singing processions in the streets and I, being the pious fellow I am, naturally took refuge in here.

Alan of Hale: Now, that I believe. The devotion of your faith has always run more to food and drink than to the deeds of the saints.

John of Occam: Let us just say that I have my own way of celebrating the feast day of St. Anthony.

Alan of Hale: Hmm. I am sure. So, what happened when you came into the tavern?

John of Occam: Well, there I was sitting at the bar nursing a cup of the tavern keeper's finest red when in comes this bear.

Alan of Hale: Oh, here we go!

John of Occam: Yes, truly. He was one of those big brown furry types. He comes right in and sits down at the bar next to me. He turns to me and, in perfect Latin, wishes me a good afternoon.

Alan of Hale: Sure.

John of Occam: Not wishing to be impolite, I returned the greeting. The tavern keeper was beside himself with surprise and, to be frank, fear. So, when the

116

bear ordered a beer, all the tavern keeper could do was stutter incoherently.

Alan of Hale:	But you, of course, kept your cool head.
John of Occam:	Yes, of course. I turned to the bear and remarked that I did not realize that bears drink beer. The bear not only responded, but did so in the form of a syllogism. He said, "Yes, all bears drink beer and, since all beer drinkers sooner or later come to a tavern, all bears eventually visit a tavern."
Alan of Hale:	How logical.
John of Occam:	Indeed, but that was not all. The bear continued, "But all bears are honest while some tavern keepers are not. This is why there are tavern keepers who are not bears."
Alan of Hale:	Apparently, your bear is as honest as he is talkative.
John of Occam:	Honest, perhaps, but not bright. I took the tavern keeper aside and suggested that, because bears are as stupid as they are honest, he could over-charge the bear by as much as ten times the usual price. Fearful, the tavern keeper hesitated only briefly before his greed got the better of him. He said to the bear, "That will be one gold crown, please." Believe it or not, the bear actually paid the outrageous price.
Alan of Hale:	The bear did not complain?
John of Occam:	Not at all. So, I asked him why bears do not visit taverns more often. He replied, "Bears do not visit taverns often because they dislike paying the high cost of beer."
Alan of Hale:	I suppose that you are now going to tell me that is why I have never seen a bear in here.
John of Occam:	Yes, of course. You have to admit it is logical.
Alan of Hale:	I think that I trust the bear's logic more than yours.

1. This story clearly takes place in medieval Oxford. You, of course, are reading the story in modern English. What language are the characters in the story speaking?

☐ They are speaking modern English, as the printed words show.

☐ They are speaking Latin, the language of medieval universities.

☐ They are speaking some dialect of Bear.

2.   What is the name of the tavern where Scholar John of Occam, according to his own story, had an unusual encounter?

     _____

3.   According to Scholar John's story, the tavern keeper was surprised by and afraid of John's drinking companion on the feast day of St. Andrew. Why was he afraid?

     _____

     _____

4.   When Scholar John remarks to his drinking companion that he did not realize that bears drink beer, his companion responds with an argument. What is the logical form of this argument?

     ☐   Hypothetical Syllogism

     ☐   Categorical Syllogism

     ☐   Ursine Syllogism

5.   Scholar John's furry drinking companion confirms that bears drink beer and then proceeds to draw a conclusion from this fact. What is the conclusion?

     Conclusion: _____

     _____

6.   What is the logical form of this conclusion (the one you wrote at number 5)?

     Quantity: _____

     Quality: _____

7. What reasons does Scholar John's furry drinking companion give in support of his conclusion (the one you wrote at number 5)?

Premise 1: _____

_____

Premise 2: _____

_____

8. Provide a diagram analysis of the argument you outlined in numbers 5 and 7.

9. Is the argument you analyzed in number 8 valid?

☐ Yes. Apparently this bear is not only a beer drinker, but also knows how to construct a valid categorical argument.

☐ No. This bear may be a beer drinker, but he could not reason his way out of hibernation.

☐ The categorical syllogisms of bears, even in stories, cannot be analyzed by the diagram method.

10. As Scholar John, according to his story, continues his conversation with his ursine drinking companion, the bear provides an argument to explain why at least some tavern keepers are not bears. What is the argument?

Premise 1: _____

_____

Premise 2: _____

Conclusion: _____

_____

11. Use the diagram method to analyze the bear's second argument.

12. Is the argument you analyzed in number 11 valid?

☐   Yes, the bear's argument is paws-down valid.

☐   No, the bear's argument is no more valid than a snort through a snout.

☐   The categorical syllogisms of bears, even in stories, cannot be analyzed by the diagram method.

13. When Scholar John conversationally asks his drinking companion why bears do not visit taverns more often, he gets an answer in the form of a categorical syllogism. What is the argument?

Premise 1: _____

_____

Premise 2: _____

_____

Conclusion: _____

_____

14.   Using the diagram method, analyze the logical form of this final argument.

15.   Is the argument you analyzed in number 14 valid?

☐   Yes, it clearly explains why bears do not visit taverns often.

☐   No, it leaves open the possibility that one day bears may visit taverns with some frequency.

☐   The categorical syllogisms of bears, even in stories, cannot be analyzed by the diagram method.

16.   Having completed this exercise, which of the following do you believe is true? (There may be more than one correct answer.)

☐   Medieval bears were far more sophisticated than modern bears.

☐   Oxford students had strange imaginations back in medieval times.

☐   The author of this exercise spends *way* too much time thinking about medieval universities.

☐   The author of this exercise spends *way* too much time drinking beer with bears.

Exercise 23

Read the following dialogue and answer the questions that follow.

The Laughing Dogs of Arabia

There was snow on the ground in Oxford on St. Stephen's Day in the year 1291. Three university students were walking through the cold narrow streets of the old town in search of an inn where they could get a good hot meal.

John of Dorset: There are few people about today.

Robert Bacon: Can you blame them? This must be the coldest winter in Oxford for years. I would not be about myself except that I have not had a decent meal for days. What a way to spend Christmas! No food, no money, no peat to keep the fire going in our rooms. My feet were so cold last night that I could not sleep!

William Hale: Stop complaining, my friend. Has not my father sent me three gold sovereigns as a Christmas gift? And have not I invited you, my closest friends in Oxford, to be my guests at a festive meal? So, buck up! You will feel more cheerful once we find a tavern keeper who will open his inn and provide us with our Christmas feast.

Robert Bacon: But my feet are still so cold that . . .

John of Dorset: Let us talk of something else. We must get our minds off this frigid weather.

William Hale: Say, I know—remember that Moor whom we met at the London docks last summer? Do you remember his story about the laughing dogs that live in the Arabian wastelands?

John of Dorset: Yes, I remember. He was telling us about the Arabian hyena. It is about the size of a wolf and is capable of laughter.

Robert Bacon: You did not believe him, John, did you?

John of Dorset: Why not? Is it so incredible?

Robert Bacon: Then you are as much a fool as I am frozen.

William Hale: Robert has a point, John.

John of Dorset:	But why should a hyena be incapable of laughter? After all, the Moor had traveled to Arabia and heard the animal for himself. He had no reason to lie to us.
William Hale:	It is not a question of lying. I am sure that the Moor heard this animal make sounds that seem like laughing, but that is not true laughter.
John of Dorset:	Why not?
William Hale:	The capability of laughter is what we call "risibility."
John of Dorset:	Look, William, a radish may know no Latin, but I do. Of course I know what "risibility" signifies.
William Hale:	You miss my point, friend John. I am initiating a philosophical inquiry. I want to understand what exactly risibility is and how it can be defined with precision. Once we know that, will we be in a position to investigate the risibility of the hyena.
John of Dorset:	Oh. That is different. Sorry I am a bit touchy—it is the cold.
Robert Bacon:	So, just what is risibility?
John of Dorset:	Well, I would say that it is the ability to find something humorous— something that is said or maybe some situation.
William Hale:	I agree. Now, this ability to find something humorous is precisely what?
John of Dorset:	Hmmm. It is the ability to recognize and delight in an incongruity.
William Hale:	Well said, John. It follows from your definitions that risibility is the recognition and delight in something incongruous.
John of Dorset:	Very well. But where does that leave us?
William Hale:	Clearly, the recognition and delight in the incongruous requires rationality.
John of Dorset:	Most certainly.
William Hale:	Therefore, risibility requires rationality.
John of Dorset:	And nothing that requires rationality is within the capacity of a hyena.
Robert Bacon:	That gives us our conclusion: risibility is not within the capacity of a hyena.
John of Dorset:	So why, then, did the Moor, who seemed like an intelligent fellow, tell us that he heard the hyena laughing?

William Hale: Obviously, he did not mean that the hyena is risible, but that the hyena has a cry that sounds like laughter.

Robert Bacon: If you two would stop your clamor about hyenas and pay attention, you will see that the tavern keeper at the end of the street has just come out to light his lamp. This means that he is ready to receive cold and hungry customers and I intend to be one of them. Let us hurry!

1. In order to keep their minds off of the cold, the three students in the story discuss the account they heard from a traveler about the Arabian hyena. In their discussion, they use a complex argument composed of categorical syllogisms to resolve a puzzling question about the hyena. What is the question?

_____

_____

_____

_____

_____

2. What is the final conclusion of the students' whole complex argument that finally resolves this question?

Conclusion: _____

_____

3. When Scholar John of Dorset says "a radish may know no Latin, but I do" is he saying that he thinks the vegetables talk or does he mean something else? If something else, then just what does he mean?

_____

_____

_____

_____

4.　Before setting out their complex argument, the students agree that "risibility" is the common name for the capability they are investigating. What is the meaning of this term?

　　☐　"Risibility" signifies the ability to feel cold.

　　☐　"Risibility" signifies the ability to reproduce.

　　☐　"Risibility" signifies the ability to laugh.

　　☐　"Risibility" signifies the ability to understand speech.

5.　The students begin their complex argument with a categorical syllogism aimed at proving that risibility is the recognition of and delight in the incongruous. What reasons do they give in support of this conclusion?

Premise 1: _____

_____

Premise 2: _____

_____

6.　The premises of this categorical syllogism share the same logical form. What is the form of the two premises?

Quantity: _____

Quality: _____

7.　Using the diagram method, show the logical form of the argument aimed at proving that risibility is the recognition of and delight in the incongruous.

8. On the basis of your diagram analysis, determine the validity of this first argument of the complex series.

    ☐ It is a valid categorical syllogism.

    ☐ It is an invalid categorical syllogism.

9. What is the second argument in the complex series?

    Premise 1:   _____

    _____

    Premise 2:   _____

    _____

    Conclusion: _____

    _____

10. Using the diagram method, provide an analysis of the logical form of the second categorical syllogism in the complex argument showing that it is valid.

11. What is the final argument in the complex series?

    Premise 1:   _____

    _____

    Premise 2:   _____

    _____

    Conclusion: _____

    _____

12.   Using the diagram method, provide an analysis of the logical form of the final categorical syllogism in the complex argument showing it to be valid.

13.   How do the students know that the categorical syllogism that you just set out and analyzed is the final argument of the complex series?

☐   The students know that this is the final argumentative stage in the complex argument because its conclusion solves the problem that gave rise to the argument in the first place.

☐   The students know that this is the final argumentative stage in the complex argument because it is a categorical syllogism.

☐   The students know that this is the final argumentative stage in the complex argument because it is the third stage and all complex arguments have three stages.

14.   What type of complex argument is the students' argument about the Arabian hyena?

☐   It is a categorical syllogism.

☐   It is a soritical argument.

☐   It is a lemmastic argument.

15.   Essentially, the students' complex argument demonstrates that

☐   the hyena is too busy protecting its territory from other predators to attend to humorous situations.

☐   the hyena may make a sound similar to human laughter, but hyenas are not truly laughing, because the ability to truly laugh requires reason and the hyena is a non-rational animal.

☐   there are no hyenas in Oxford.

☐   Scholar John does not get the joke.

§10 The Simple and the Complex

The discussion of propositions in §§3–5 focused only on the most basic forms of simple propositions and their possible relationships with each other. In addition to these simple forms of propositions, complex propositional forms are also possible. All propositions are uses of language that are capable of having truth value. A *simple proposition* is a proposition that is not composed of any parts that are themselves propositions. If one analyzes a simple proposition and breaks it down into its parts, one finds that these parts are not themselves propositions, but terms, logical quality, and logical quantity. It is possible, however, for propositions to be composed of simpler propositions. A *complex proposition* is a proposition that is composed of parts that are themselves propositions. If one analyzes a complex proposition and breaks it down into its parts, one finds that these parts are capable of having truth value and, therefore, are themselves propositions. Consider the following examples:

[1]   University masters lecture in Latin.

[2]   University masters lecture in both Latin and Greek.

[3]   University masters wear either academic gowns or religious habits when lecturing.

[4]   Whenever a university master is giving a lecture, then the master wears an academic gown.

Each of these examples [1]–[4] is a proposition, because each is capable of being true or being false. The first example [1] is a simple proposition, because it is composed of parts that are not themselves propositions. An analysis of this proposition resolves it into the terms *people who are university masters* and *people who lecture in Latin* as well as universal quantity and affirmative quality. Neither these two terms nor the proposition's quantity or quality are propositions. The other examples [2]–[4] are all complex propositions, because each is composed of simpler propositions. Example [2] is composed of the propositions *university masters lecture in Latin* and *university masters lecture in Greek*. These two simpler propositions are joined together by the logical connecting word "and" to form a complex proposition. Example [3] is composed of the two propositions *university masters wear academic gowns when lecturing* and *university masters wear religious habits when lecturing* joined by the logical connective "or." Example [4] is composed of the two propositions *a university master is giving a lecture* and *a university master wears an academic gown* joined by the logical connective "whenever . . . then."

These examples make it clear that there are different ways to construct a complex proposition out of simpler propositions. These different types of complex propositions are determined by the way in which the simpler propositions are joined together in the complex proposition. There are three basic types of complex propositions. One can join two or more propositions in a direct way that states them together. This kind of complex proposition is called a *conjunction* and usually uses the logical connective "and" and sometimes "both . . . and . . ." as in example [2]. One can also join two or more propositions in a way that states them as alternatives. This kind of complex proposition is called a *disjunction* and uses the logical connective "or" and sometimes "either . . . or . . ." as in example [3]. Yet another way of forming a complex is to join two propositions in a way that states one of them as the condition or qualification of the other. This kind of complex proposition is called a *conditional* and uses the logical connective "if . . . then . . ." or "whenever . . . then . . ." or "given that . . . then . . ." or "on the condition that . . . then . . ." or other words that indicate that one thing is a condition for another. Example [4] is an example of a conditional proposition.

Conjunctive Propositions

Conjunctions are the most direct and straightforward way of composing a complex proposition. Instead of separately stating a series of propositions, one can state them together by linking them with the word "and" or some similar word. Conjunctions must be composed of at least two propositions. Often conjunctions of two simpler propositions use the words "both . . . and . . ." as a logical connective. Conjunctions, however, can be composed of more than two simpler propositions. A conjunction is intended to state that each one of the simpler propositions of which it is composed is true. If each of the propositions linked in a conjunction really is true, then the whole conjunction is true. If at least one of the propositions conjoined in a conjunction is false, then the whole conjunction is false.

Disjunctive Propositions

Disjunctions are complex propositions that state alternatives. If two or more simple propositions represent distinct possibilities, then linking them with the word "or" presents them together as alternatives to each other. Like conjunctions, disjunctions must be composed of at least two simpler propositions, because one cannot have a single alternative—every alternative is alternative to something. The shortest disjunction, then, states two alternatives and often makes use of the words "either . . . or . . ." as a logical connective. For negative alternatives, the words "neither . . . nor . . ." are sometimes used. Disjunctions, however, can be composed of more than two simpler propositions where there are more than two alternatives. If at least one of the alternatives is true, then the whole disjunction is true. If all the alternatives are false, then the whole disjunction is false.

Conditional Propositions

Conditionals are complex propositions that state the conditions under which something is true. If the truth of one proposition is a condition for the truth of another, then this can be stated in a conditional proposition using logical connecting words like "if . . . then . . ." or other words that indicate conditionality. Conditional propositions are always composed of two simpler propositions. One of these propositions states the condition and this part of the conditional proposition is called the *antecedent*. The other proposition states that for which the antecedent is the condition and this part of the conditional proposition is called the *consequent*. Consider, for example, the following conditional proposition:

[5]   If a university master intends to resign his appointment, then he must notify the chancellor.

Notice, first of all, that this proposition [5], like all conditional propositions, is complex, for it is composed of the simpler propositions *a university master intends to resign his appointment* and *a university master must notify the chancellor*. The first of these simpler propositions *a university master intends to resign his appointment* is the antecedent of the conditional [5] because it states a condition under which the consequent *a university master must notify the chancellor* is true.

It is very important to understand that the conditional proposition [5] does not state that its consequent *a university master must notify the chancellor* is in fact true. Nor does it state that its antecedent *a university master intends to resign his appointment* is in fact true. What the conditional [5] states is that there is a condition that, when fulfilled, is enough to make its consequent *a university master must notify the chancellor* true. A conditional proposition is true when its antecedent actually is a sufficient condition for its consequent being true. A conditional proposition is false when its antecedent is not a sufficient condition for its consequent being true. This means that it is possible to have a true conditional proposition that is composed of a false antecedent and false consequent. Consider, for example, this conditional proposition:

[6]   If human physiology were like that of a bird, then human locomotion could be by self-powered flight.

This conditional proposition [6] is true because its antecedent *human physiology is like that of a bird* is a sufficient condition for its consequent *human locomotion can be by self-powered flight* being true. That means that the conditional [6] can be true even though it is counterfactual—that is, even though in reality its antecedent is false and so is its consequent. So, this whole conditional is true: If human beings had bodies like birds—which they in fact do not—then human beings could move about by self-powered flight—which in fact they cannot.

Categorical Propositions

This example [6] of a counterfactual conditional shows why conditional propositions are important. They allow for the possibility of propositions that state, not what is factually true or false, but propositions that state what might be true or false but is not what is actually true or false, or should be true or false even when it is not actually true or false, or what will be true or false, but is not true or false now. Conditional propositions allow discourse that goes beyond actual facts to discourse about possibilities, preferences, imperatives, and the future. This shows that conditional propositions are different in this respect from all the other types of propositions. All the kinds of propositions studied so far are used to state what is actually true or false. Propositions that refer to actual or factual reality like this are called *categorical propositions*. The simple propositions that serve as the premises and conclusions of categorical syllogisms are categorical propositions. (Indeed, this is why arguments of this kind are called "categorical," because they are always composed of categorical propositions.) Complex propositions that are conjunctions and disjunctions are also categorical, for they state what is factually true or false together (conjunctions) or what are factually true or false alternatives (disjunctions). Therefore, categorical propositions directly state what is true or false about the real world whereas conditional propositions truly or falsely state factual or counterfactual conditions.

The way in which arguments can be composed of simple categorical propositions has been described in §§5–9. It is also possible that arguments can be composed of complex propositions. Some important forms of argument are attempts to draw a conclusion from a set of alternatives and these arguments have a disjunction among the premises. Other important forms of argument are attempts to draw a conclusion from the fact that one thing is a condition for another and these have conditional propositions among the premises.

Exercise 24

Student: _____

Consider each of the following propositions and determine whether it is simple or complex. If it is complex, underline any word or words indicating a logical connective.

1.   Master William is an expert on Arabic astronomy.

    ☐ simple proposition   ☐ complex proposition

2.   Both Master William and Master Robert have read Al-Kindi's treatise on cosmology.

    ☐ simple proposition   ☐ complex proposition

3.   Every expert on Arabic astronomy at Oxford is a member of the Faculty of Arts.

    ☐ simple proposition   ☐ complex proposition

4.   There are experts on Arabic astronomy at Oxford.

    ☐ simple proposition   ☐ complex proposition

5.   If Master William is an expert on Arabic astronomy, then he is familiar with the astrolabe.

    ☐ simple proposition   ☐ complex proposition

6.   Either Master William is familiar with the astrolabe or Master Robert is.

    ☐ simple proposition   ☐ complex proposition

7.   Master William has constructed his own astrolabe.

    ☐ simple proposition   ☐ complex proposition

8.   Either Master William or Master Robert is lecturing on Al-Kindi's book this term.

    ☐ simple proposition   ☐ complex proposition

9. Master Robert is lecturing on Al-Kindi's book this term.

   ☐ simple proposition   ☐ complex proposition

10. No masters at Oxford know the exact number of the fixed stars.

    ☐ simple proposition   ☐ complex proposition

11. When Master William constructs his astrolabe, then he will demonstrate its use.

    ☐ simple proposition   ☐ complex proposition

12. Arts masters at Oxford lecture on natural philosophy or on logic.

    ☐ simple proposition   ☐ complex proposition

13. There are masters at Oxford who have lectured on Al-Kindi's books.

    ☐ simple proposition   ☐ complex proposition

14. Both Masters Robert and William have lectured on Al-Kindi's books.

    ☐ simple proposition   ☐ complex proposition

15. Given that Master William is an expert on Arabic astronomy, he should give the lecture.

    ☐ simple proposition   ☐ complex proposition

16. Master William is lecturing this term, provided he returns to Oxford.

    ☐ simple proposition   ☐ complex proposition

Exercise 25

Student: _____

For each of the following complex propositions, write out the simpler propositions composing the complex proposition.

1.   Both Master Robert and Master Siger are experts on the science of perspective.

_____

_____

_____

_____

2.   If Master Robert completes his book, then he will lecture on geometry next term.

_____

_____

_____

_____

3.   Master William is at Oxford and is well.

_____

_____

_____

_____

4.   Arts masters at Oxford lecture either on natural philosophy or logic.

_____

_____

_____

_____

5.   Master Robert is lecturing on the science of perspective, provided he is not called to Rome.

_____

_____

_____

_____

6.   Assuming that perspective is a natural phenomenon, it is a middle science.

_____

_____

_____

_____

Exercise 26

Student: _____

Determine whether each of the following propositions is categorical or conditional.

1. Both Master Robert and Master Siger are experts on the science of perspective.

   ☐ categorical proposition   ☐ conditional proposition

2. Provided Master Robert returns from Rome by September, he will lecture on the science of perspective during Michaelmas term.

   ☐ categorical proposition   ☐ conditional proposition

3. If Master Robert presides over the disputation, Scholar John will serve as his reporter.

   ☐ categorical proposition   ☐ conditional proposition

4. All arts masters at Oxford respect Master Robert.

   ☐ categorical proposition   ☐ conditional proposition

5. Either Master Robert or Master Siger has the optical treatise of Al-Kindi.

   ☐ categorical proposition   ☐ conditional proposition

6. Al-Kindi is the author of this classic work on the science of perspective.

   ☐ categorical proposition   ☐ conditional proposition

7. There are masters at Oxford who knew Master Robert in Rome.

   ☐ categorical proposition   ☐ conditional proposition

8. Whenever Master Robert lectures on perspective, many students attend.

   ☐ categorical proposition   ☐ conditional proposition

9.   Given the calculations of Al-Kindi, Master Robert's conclusions follow.

☐ categorical proposition   ☐ conditional proposition

10.   Master Robert's conclusions follow, on the assumption that Al-Kindi's calculations are correct.

☐ categorical proposition   ☐ conditional proposition

11.   When he sees the calculations of Al-Kindi, Master Robert will be pleased.

☐ categorical proposition   ☐ conditional proposition

12.   Master Robert has confirmed Al-Kindi's calculations.

☐ categorical proposition   ☐ conditional proposition

13.   The calculations of Al-Kindi are useful, provided Master Robert confirms them.

☐ categorical proposition   ☐ conditional proposition

14.   Given the calculations of Al-Kindi, Master Robert's conclusions follow.

☐ categorical proposition   ☐ conditional proposition

15.   If Master Robert's conclusions follow, then Master Siger is in error.

☐ categorical proposition   ☐ conditional proposition

16.   Master Siger is in error.

☐ categorical proposition   ☐ conditional proposition

Exercise 27

Student: _____

Part I

For each of the following complex propositions, determine the type of propositional complexity it is.

1.   Both Master Robert and Master Siger are experts on the science of perspective.

        ☐ conjunction   ☐ disjunction   ☐ conditional

2.   On the condition that Master Robert returns from Rome, he is lecturing this term.

        ☐ conjunction   ☐ disjunction   ☐ conditional

3.   Master Robert is in Rome and Master Siger is lecturing on optics.

        ☐ conjunction   ☐ disjunction   ☐ conditional

4.   Master Robert is expert on the science of perspective and so is Master Siger.

        ☐ conjunction   ☐ disjunction   ☐ conditional

5.   Neither Master Robert nor Master Siger have read Al-Kindi's book.

        ☐ conjunction   ☐ disjunction   ☐ conditional

6.   If the chancellor consents, Master Robert is lecturing on Aristotle's book.

        ☐ conjunction   ☐ disjunction   ☐ conditional

7.   Master Robert is living at Merton, provided they have rooms for him.

        ☐ conjunction   ☐ disjunction   ☐ conditional

Part II

For each of the following conditional propositions, write out its antecedent and consequent.

1.   When university masters lecture in college, they must wear academic gowns.

      Antecedent: _____

_____

      Consequent: _____

_____

2.   All university masters may lecture in college, provided the dean consents.

      Antecedent: _____

_____

      Consequent: _____

_____

3.   If a university master has permission to lecture in college, he may do so any term.

      Antecedent: _____

_____

      Consequent: _____

_____

4.   Given that a university master has permission to lecture in college, he may do so.

      Antecedent: _____

_____

      Consequent: _____

_____

§11 Either/Or and Therefore

As already discussed, propositions that state alternatives are disjunctions. Disjunctions are important in discourse because in real life it is often necessary to determine which of a set of alternative possibilities or choices is true. This simplest possible disjunction is one in which a set of two alternatives is stated. This kind of disjunction is called a *dichotomy*. The following proposition is an example of dichotomy:

[1]   Law masters teach either civil law or canon law.

It is possible, of course, to have a disjunction that states more than two alternatives. The following disjunction is a *trichomomy*:

[2]   The books of Aristotle may be read in Greek or Arabic or Latin.

A disjunction might also be a *tetrachotomy* (four alternatives), *pentachotomy* (five alternatives), *hexachotomy* (six alternatives), *heptachotomy* (seven alternatives), and so on. In argument, conclusions are typically drawn from a limited set of alternatives, usually from a dichotomy.

Disjunctive Syllogism

A simple form of disjunctive argument is one in which the arguer draws a conclusion from a known set of two alternatives and the exclusion of one of the alternatives. For example:

[3]   Master Isadore is lecturing today on either civil or canon law.
He is not lecturing on canon law.
Therefore, he is lecturing on civil law.

This form of argument is called a *disjunctive syllogism* and is a valid form of argument. A dichotomy is true when at least one of the alternatives stated in it is true. In example [3], then, the first premise is true when *Master Isadore is lecturing on civil law* is true or when *Master Isadore is lecturing on canon law* it is true or when they are both true. The second premise excludes the second possibility *Master Isadore is lecturing on canon law* being true by affirming its negative. This necessarily leaves the first possibility, that he is lecturing on civil law, as the one that is true. Notice that a disjunctive syllogism has two premises. One of the premises is a dichotomy (a disjunction of two alternatives) and the other is the negation of one of the alternatives. The conclusion is the affirmation of the other alternative. Disjunctive syllogism is a common form of argument in everyday life. Suppose that we have narrowed down our choices to two (a dichotomy) and then we rule out one of the possible choices. That necessarily leaves us with the other choice. This shows that disjunctive syllogism is a valid form of argument.

141

Constructive Dilemma

Another kind of argument in which a conclusion is drawn from a set of alternatives is one where either alternative in a dichotomy is known to imply the same result and the arguer concludes that the result must be true. For example:

[4]   Master Isadore is examining us in either civil law or canon law.
If he is examining us in civil law, then we must be prepared to cite cases.
If he is examining us in canon law, then we must be prepared to cite cases.
Therefore, we must be prepared to cite cases.

This form of argument is called a *constructive dilemma* and is a valid form of argument. Given that students are to be examined in at least one of the two possible subjects and that each demands that the students be prepared to cite cases, it clearly follows that the students must be prepared to cite cases. Notice that a constructive dilemma has three premises. One premise is a dichotomy (a disjunction stating two alternatives). The other two premises are conditional propositions, each having as its antecedent one of the alternatives and as its consequent the same result. The conclusion is the same proposition as the consequents of the conditional premises affirming the result.

Constructive dilemmas are often stated elliptically with the two conditional premises left unexpressed. The constructive dilemma [4] might be stated like this:

[5]   Master Isadore is examining us in either civil or canon law. Either way we must be prepared to cite cases.

This is a very common way in which this form of argument appears in everyday speech or writing. The arguer expresses the two alternatives in a disjunction and then expresses the conclusion prefaced by the expression "either way . . ." This expression stands in for the two conditional premises. When analyzing this argument to understand its form and see its validity, it is necessary to know what all three premises are and to be prepared to express them fully.

In everyday life, constructive dilemmas draw a conclusion from a dichotomy. Yet, it is possible to argue with a more complex constructive dilemma, such as one that has a disjunctive premise that is a trichotomy:

[6]   Master Alexander has read Aristotle's book in either Greek or Arabic or Latin.
If he read Aristotle's book in Greek, then he knows the four causes.
If he read Aristotle's book in Arabic, then he knows the four causes.
If he read Aristotle's book in Latin, then he knows the four causes.
Therefore, he knows the four causes.

Notice that a constructive dilemma with a trichotomy has four premises—one conditional premise for each alternative in the disjunctive premise. (In a similar way, more complex constructive dilemmas would have additional premises: a dilemma with a tetrachotomy would have five premises, a dilemma with a pentachotomy would have six premises, and so on.) Like a constructive dilemma with a dichotomous premise, a more complex dilemma can be expressed elliptically. The trichotomous dilemma [6] can be elliptically expressed like this:

> [7]   Master Alexander has read Aristotle's book in either Greek or Arabic or Latin. No matter which, he knows the four causes.

Here the phrase "no matter which . . ." stands in for the three conditional premises.

Destructive Dilemma

Another type of dilemma is an argument in which a conclusion is drawn from a set of negative alternatives. Given that an arguer knows that a dichotomy of negative alternatives is true and that a certain situation implies the affirmation of each alternative, then he can validly conclude that the situation does not obtain. Consider this example:

> [8]   Master Isadore is not examining us on the Theodosian Code or on the Justinian Code.
> If he were examining us on Roman Law, then he would examine us on the Theodosian Code.
> If he were examining us on Roman Law, then he would examine us on the Justinian Code.
> Therefore, he cannot be examining us on Roman Law.

This form of argument is called a *destructive dilemma* and is a valid form of argument. Given that students know that they will not be examined on either the Theodosian or Justinian Codes and that being examined in Roman Law necessarily involves being examined in both of these codes, they can conclude with confidence that their exam is not going to be on Roman Law. Notice that a destructive dilemma has three premises. One premise is a dichotomy (a disjunction stating two negative alternatives). The other two premises are conditional propositions, each having as its antecedent something that implies the affirmation of each of the alternatives. The conclusion is the negation of what implied the affirmation of the alternatives.

Like constructive dilemmas, destructive dilemmas are often stated elliptically with the two conditional premises left unexpressed or not fully expressed. The destructive dilemma [8] might be elliptically stated like this:

> [9]   Master Isadore is not examining us on the Theodosian or Justinian Codes. But examination on Roman Law involves examining us on both and, therefore, he is not examining us on Roman Law.

This is a very common way in which this form of argument appears in everyday speech or writing. The arguer expresses the two negative alternatives in a disjunction and then elliptically expresses the two conditional premises followed by the expression of the conclusion. As with any elliptically expressed argument, one must be prepared to fully express all the parts of the argument when analyzing the argument's logical form and testing it for validity.

Again, as with constructive dilemmas, destructive dilemmas may be more complex when they draw a conclusion from a trichotomy or a more complex form of disjunction. Consider this example of destructive dilemma with a trichotomous premise:

[10]   Master Alexander knows neither the principle of matter nor the principle
                of form nor the principle of privation.
        If he read Aristotle's *Physics*, then he knows the principle of matter.
        If he read Aristotle's *Physics*, then he knows the principle of form.
        If he read Aristotle's *Physics*, then he knows the principle of privation.
        Therefore, he has not read Aristotle's *Physics*.

Notice that a destructive dilemma with a trichotomy has four premises—one conditional premise for each alternative in the disjunctive premise. (In a similar way, more complex destructive dilemmas would have additional premises.) This example of a trichotomous destructive dilemma, like all dilemmas, is most commonly stated elliptically in everyday speech or writing. Thus, the destructive dilemma [10], would more commonly appear like this:

[11]   Master Alexander knows neither the principle of matter nor of form nor of
        privation. But if he read Aristotle's *Physics*, then he knows all three
        principles. Clearly, he has not read the *Physics*.

Exercise 28

Student: _____

Indicate the logical form of each of the following valid arguments.

1.   Master Robert will lecture on either Al-Kindi's optics or Aristotle's logic this term.
      I just learned that the lecture will not be on optics and, therefore, he is lecturing on
      Aristotle's logic.

         ☐   disjunctive syllogism

         ☐   constructive dilemma

         ☐   destructive dilemma

2.   Neither my theorem nor that of Master Robert is consistent with observation. But the
      calculations of Al-Kindi imply both. Clearly, the calculations of Al-Kindi are in error.

         ☐   disjunctive syllogism

         ☐   constructive dilemma

         ☐   destructive dilemma

3.   We know that Master Robert cannot be giving the Hilary term lectures on
      perspective because he is in Rome. But it could only be he or Master Siger.
      Therefore, Master Siger is giving the lectures on perspective.

         ☐   disjunctive syllogism

         ☐   constructive dilemma

         ☐   destructive dilemma

4.   Master Robert's conclusion is correct or Master Siger's is. Either way, Al-Kindi's
      calculations are in error. We can be sure Al-Kindi's calculations are incorrect.

         ☐   disjunctive syllogism

         ☐   constructive dilemma

         ☐   destructive dilemma

5. Al-Kindi's calculations must be either correct or incorrect. But Master Siger has disproved them. Therefore, they are incorrect.

    ☐   disjunctive syllogism

    ☐   constructive dilemma

    ☐   destructive dilemma

6. Suppose Master Robert's calculations are in error, then Al-Kindi's theorem is confirmed. Suppose that Master Siger's calculations are also in error, then again Al-Kindi's theorem is confirmed. Well, the calculations of either Master Robert or Master Siger are in error and, consequently, Al-Kindi's theorem is confirmed.

    ☐   disjunctive syllogism

    ☐   constructive dilemma

    ☐   destructive dilemma

7. Master Robert has clearly proven that optical phenomena presuppose the laws of projective geometry. Obviously, they either do presuppose projective geometry or they do not. It is clearly an error to hold that optical phenomena do not presuppose the laws of geometry.

    ☐   disjunctive syllogism

    ☐   constructive dilemma

    ☐   destructive dilemma

8. Master Robert's calculations show that the angle of refraction is either 90 degrees or 45 degrees, but I cannot remember which. Our calculations show it cannot be 90 degrees, so the master's calculations must have shown 45 degrees.

    ☐   disjunctive syllogism

    ☐   constructive dilemma

    ☐   destructive dilemma

Exercise 29

Student: _____

Read the following dialogue and answer the questions that follow.

The Proud Peasant

Stephanus of Raetia had been a professor of rhetoric at the University of Paris for eight years when, in the spring of the year 1302, he announced that he would begin a series of lectures on the topical logic of Aristotle. This was an important subject and he had been looking for the opportunity to lecture on it for a long time. Finally, the time had come, but he was pessimistic about the student turn out. In all his years at the university, he had never come across such an unscholarly bunch of students as those who were studying arts that year. However they spent their time, it was clearly not with their studies. Nonetheless, he remained hopeful that he might get some of the students interested in Aristotle. His heart fell, however, as he surveyed the unusually quiet group of students drag themselves into the aula of the Convent of Saint-Sulpice.

Master Stephanus:	Young scholars, you look rather bleary-eyed this morning. May I rightly assume that you were all out late last night celebrating?
Scholar Raymond:	Do you have to shout so loud, Master? My head . . .
Scholar Alanus:	Of course we were out late last night, Master. After all, it was the king's birthday. A good subject must do his duty.
Master Stephanus:	[smiling] I see. And your only concern was to show your loyalty to the crown.
Scholar John:	To be sure, Master. Well, if a bit of food and drink came our way we, naturally, did not turn it down.
Master Stephanus:	I see that this will not be a day for Aristotle.
Scholar Alanus:	Well, at least we are here. That is more than we can say for our fellow scholar Paul whom we left at . . .
Master Stephanus:	Never mind where you left your companion, I have no need to hear the story. Had all my scholars arrived clear-headed and alert this morning, I would have given you a fine lecture on Aristotle's treatment of the topical syllogism. But, as I say, this is clearly not a day for Aristotle.
Scholar Alanus:	Perhaps instead of the usual dose of Aristotle, Master, you might tell us one of your delightful and instructive stories.
Scholar John:	Yes, Master, please do. You are the best story-teller on the arts faculty.
Scholar Raymond:	We always profit from your moral tales.

Master Stephanus:	[shaking his head with a knowing smile] I wonder if you do.
Scholar Alanus:	We do, indeed, Master. Besides, the learned Aristotle himself said that the moral education of youth is best pursued through instructive stories.
Scholar John:	You well know how much we respect Aristotle.
Scholar Raymond:	And how much we seek moral instruction.
Master Stephanus:	Enough! You scholars remind me of the peasant farmer who sought to outdo all of his neighbors in building an impressive mound of cow manure. He labored mightily for many days, placing layer upon layer, building up terrace upon terrace. His mound grew in height until it was taller than his barn and could be seen from miles away. One day a nobleman was passing through the district and stopped to look at the mound. The proud peasant approached the nobleman and asked "What do you think of my mound, my lord?" The nobleman thought for a moment and then replied "This is either the tallest man-made mound in the kingdom or it is the best constructed mound in the kingdom. Yet, either way, it remains nothing but a pile of manure."
Scholar Alanus:	Is not our flattery and our eagerness for your instruction sweet, Master?
Master Stephanus:	I would say it was as fragrant as the peasant's mound.
Scholar Raymond:	Ooooo! That hurts as much as my head.
Scholar John:	A witty retort, Master. We stand humbled, even if not contrite.
Master Stephanus:	To your beds, young scholars! Today you need sleep more than Aristotle or even moral instruction. We will try again tomorrow.

1.   On the morning that the story takes place, why did Master Stephanus decide not to lecture on Aristotle as he had planned?

_____

_____

_____

_____

2. When his students begin to jokingly insist on their eagerness for moral instruction, Master Stephanus tells them a story of a peasant farmer and his mound. What is the point of his comparison between the peasant's mound and the students' expressed eagerness for moral education?

    _____

    _____

    _____

    _____

3. When the peasant in Master Stephanus' story asks the nobleman his opinion of his mound, the nobleman answers him in the form of an argument. What is the nobleman's argument?

    Premise 1: _____

    _____

    Premise 2: _____

    _____

    Premise 3: _____

    _____

    Conclusion: _____

    _____

4. The premises of the nobleman's argument are all complex propositions. What two types of complex propositions are found in the three premises of this argument?

    _____

    and

    _____

5.   What form of argument is the nobleman's argument?

    ☐   categorical argument

    ☐   disjunctive syllogism

    ☐   constructive dilemma

    ☐   destructive dilemma

6.   Given the overall tone of the dialogue, what do you think Master Stephanus' attitude toward his students is?

    ☐   Master Stephanus believes that his students are brilliant and diligent scholars who spend most of their time reading the classics.

    ☐   Master Stephanus is angry at his students for messing up his plans to lecture on Aristotle's logic by coming to his lecture in a state in which they are not prepared to study anything serious.

    ☐   Master Stephanus is bemused at the state of his students who were up all night celebrating the king's birthday (a good excuse for a party) and he cannot resist teasing his students a bit about the fact that they are not prepared to study Aristotle or any other serious subject.

    ☐   Master Stephanus is envious of his students' carefree attitude and is hinting that he plans to destroy their careers in revenge.

Exercise 30

Student: _____

Read the following dialogue and answer the questions that follow.

The Storks of Lemnos

Master Tommaso di Ravenna, a professor of natural philosophy at the University of Padua, was quite excited one day in October of the year 1298. He was expecting a visit from a good friend of his, a Greek scholar from Constantinople named Nicholos Nicomedes. Nicholos was an expert on the books of the ancient philosopher Aristotle and his visits to Padua were often the occasion for fascinating intellectual discussions. Having met in town, the two friends retired to a charming inn just outside Padua on the Brescia Road.

Master Tommaso:	Nicholos, my good friend, let us order some wine and then get down to talk. I understand that you have brought with you copies of some epistles of the great Aristotle that I have not seen yet. Is this true?
Nicholos:	Yes, it is quite true. They were found in the library of the Comnenos castle in the hill country outside of Nicaea. The young Princess Nikola Comnena gave them to me to study, asking me to determine their authenticity. She told me that they were part of a large collection of Aristotle's writings that were collected by her great-great-grandmother Anna, who was a famous scholar. As you well know, we owe the recovery of many of Aristotle's most important books to Anna Comnena and her staff of scribes. Most of these books are now known to be rightly attributed to Aristotle, but the collection of epistles presents some problems. Some of them seem to have been written long after the time of Aristotle himself by students of his. In any case, Princess Nikola has given me permission to bring these copies to you here in Padua for your opinion.
Master Tommaso:	My eagerness to look at these epistles is second only to my admiration of your patroness Nikola Comnena. Her scholarly devotion is rare in such a young woman. She cannot be more than twenty years old.
Nicholos:	She is nineteen years old and she is indeed a remarkable person. Following in the footsteps of her ancestor Anna, she has already published a very scholarly history of her family going back to the Trebizond dynasty. She is now working on a digest of the medical treatises of Galen that she found in the family library.
Master Tommaso:	Most impressive. But tell me about this ancient epistle that you found in the Comnenos castle library. I understand that it purports to be written by Aristotle's student Harmodios to his former teacher during the time when Harmodios was headman on the island of Lemnos.

151

Nicholos:	Yes, that is correct. I brought it with me. You can read it for yourself, for I have made a Latin translation. Read it aloud and then we can discuss it.
Master Tommaso:	[reading] *To Aristotle of Stagira, trusted advisor to the court of King Philip of Macedonia, from Harmodios, Archon of Lemnos and High Priest of Apollo: Respectful greetings.*

We here on our small island hear many good things from Macedonia about King Philip's good government and the prospering of his house. Please greet the king for me and assure him of our continued good will and respect for the sacred treaties which bind us.

Many years ago, when I was young and had the great privilege to study with you, I was gratified by your support of my interest in the study of animal life. You often reminded me of the importance to ground all of my scientific conclusions in the evidence of my senses and sound inferences from sense experience. I recall with fondness and gratitude the many hours you devoted to guiding my early scientific efforts.

All of this came back to mind during my recent visit to Pharsalia, a small place to which I paid a state visit during their annual Stork Festival in honor of the god Apollo Pharsalos. The good people of this small out-of-the-way place invited me to attend both in my capacity as archon as well as priest of Apollo, for the festival is marked by sacrifices to the god, a procession of the elders dressed in stork feathers, and a great communal feast. I must confess that I went as much for the satisfaction of my curiosity as the fulfillment of my duties, for this is the place where the storks of Thrace spend the winter months, having migrated from their northern home across the sea to our little island. I have often wondered how these birds are able to migrate with such accuracy, for they unfailingly arrive in the same place on our island each year.

It occurred to me that there must be only two possibilities. One is that the storks have some inner sense which guides them to their destination. The other is that the storks are able to recognize landmarks which they see on the way, just as the pilot of a ship sights the landmarks on the shore and safely guides the ship into harbor. I was able to eliminate the second possibility, because the storks fly over many miles of open sea where no landmarks can be sighted. I concluded that these birds must possess some inner sense that guides them. This reasoning, in turn, led me to wonder at the nature of this inner sense. I reasoned further: stork navigation is by an inner sense; navigation by an inner sense is not navigation dependent on visual sightings; therefore, stork navigation is not dependent on visual sightings. So much was clear from my arguments, but this was as far as my reasoning took me. The precise nature of the stork's ability to accurately navigate over many miles of open sea escaped me. Perhaps natural philosophers of the future will be able to discover the solution to this puzzle.

Wishing you health and long life, Master, I ask the blessings of the god on you and your work.

Nicholos: You must admit that, authentic or not, this epistle presents a fascinating picture of the work of Aristotle and his students in natural philosophy.

Master Tommaso: You are right there, my friend. Let us have another cup of wine and then get down to work comparing this epistle with others we know to be authentic.

1. Nicholos Nicomedes is aware that his Italian friend Tommaso di Ravenna knows the reputation of the Greek princess Anna Comnena. For what is she famous?

_____

_____

_____

_____

_____

2. Why does Master Tommaso admire the Greek princess Nikola Comnena?

_____

_____

_____

_____

3. Who is Harmodios of Lemnos and what is his relationship to Aristotle?

_____

_____

_____

_____

4.　　According to his epistle, what was the *official* reason for the visit of Harmodios to the little village of Pharsalia on the north coast of the island of Lemnos?

_____

_____

_____

_____

5.　　According to his epistle, what was the *unofficial* reason for the visit of Harmodios to the little village of Pharsalia on the north coast of the island of Lemnos?

_____

_____

_____

_____

6.　　As part of his study of stork migration, Harmodios draws two conclusions from two separate arguments. What is the first of these arguments?

Premise 1:　　_____

_____

Premise 2:　　_____

_____

Conclusion:　　_____

_____

7.　　What is the logical form of the argument you outlined in number 6?

☐　　　This argument is a categorical syllogism.

☐　　　This argument is a disjunctive syllogism.

☐　　　This argument is a constructive dilemma.

☐　　　This argument is a destructive dilemma.

154

8.   Is the argument you outlined in number 6 valid?

☐ Yes, this is a valid argument.   ☐ No, this is an invalid argument.

9.   What is Harmodios' second argument about stork migration?

Premise 1:   _____

_____

Premise 2:   _____

_____

Conclusion: _____

_____

10.   What is the logical form of the second argument you outlined in number 9?

☐   This argument is a categorical syllogism.

☐   This argument is a disjunctive syllogism.

☐   This argument is a constructive dilemma.

☐   This argument is a destructive dilemma.

11.   Toward the end of his epistle, Harmodios refers to a scientific puzzle that he is attempting to solve by means of his observations and arguments. What is this puzzle?

_____

_____

_____

_____

§12 If/Then and Therefore

Disjunctions are not the only complex propositions from which a conclusion can be drawn. Arguments that draw conclusions from conditional propositions also play an important role in everyday reasoning as well as in scientific investigations. When studying arguments with conditional premises, it is important to keep in mind the distinction between categorical and conditional propositions. Categorical propositions state what is true or false in a direct and unqualified way. Conditional propositions state what is true or false with respect to that which is a condition or qualification for something. Conditional propositions may be counterfactually true when the antecedent is truly a condition for the consequent, but neither the antecedent nor the consequent is true. Categorical propositions are never counterfactually true: they are factually true or factually false.

Modus ponens

A simple form of argument that illustrates the meaning of conditional propositions is one in which a categorical conclusion is drawn from a conditional premise and a categorical premise. In an argument with a conditional premise, the arguer knows that the subject matter of the antecedent is a condition for the subject matter of the consequent. Assume also that the arguer knows that the condition stated in the antecedent is fulfilled. The arguer can then validly conclude that for which the antecedent is a condition—namely, the consequent. Consider this example:

[1]   If Master William is lecturing on Ptolemy's book this term, then all
              students interested in astronomy are attending.
        Master William is lecturing on Ptolemy's book this term.
        Therefore, all students interested in astronomy are attending.

Notice that this argument [1] has two premises. One premise is a conditional proposition. The other premise is the antecedent of the conditional premise. The conclusion is the consequent of the conditional premise. Logic masters in medieval universities called this form of argument *modus ponendo ponens* which means the method of positing what is to be posited. Today this Latin phrase is still used to refer to this way of arguing and most people call it *modus ponens* for short. Modus ponens is a valid form of argument, because if A really is a condition for B and condition A is fulfilled, it follows necessarily that B must be true. This can be easily seen by considering the following situation. Let us say that a certain student, Scholar John, is worried about being allowed to return to the university next term. He knows that if he passes his mathematics exam this term, he will be allowed to return next term. Let us further assume that Scholar John learns that he has in fact passed his mathematics exam this term. He can then safely assume that he will be allowed to return to the university next term. His assumption is based on the validity of the following modus ponens argument:

[2] If Scholar John passes the mathematics exam this term, then he is allowed to return to the university next term.
Scholar John does pass the mathematics exam this term.
Therefore, Scholar John is allowed to return to the university next term.

Modus ponens reveals the nature of conditional propositions. The conditional premise does not say that its antecedent is factually true. In example [2], the conditional premise does not say that Scholar John has in fact passed his mathematics exam this term. It simply says that his passing the exam is a condition for something—namely, that he is allowed to return to the university next term. It is the categorical premise that says that the condition is true. In this case [2], the categorical premise says that Scholar John has actually passed his exam and the condition stated in the antecedent of the conditional premise is fulfilled. It is on these grounds that he can be sure that that for which the antecedent is a condition is true. In this case [2], Scholar John is able to know with certainty that he is allowed to return based on what the premises say.

Any argument that has a true modus ponens form is a valid argument, no matter what its subject matter. There are some arguments, however, that appear to be modus ponens, but actually do not have a true modus ponens form. These arguments may be invalid. Consider, for example, the following argument:

[3] If Scholar Giles is observing the lunar eclipse, then he knows the earth has a curved surface.
Scholar Giles knows the earth has a curved surface.
Therefore, Scholar Giles is observing the lunar eclipse.

This argument [3] appears similar to a modus ponens argument. Like modus ponens, this argument has a conditional premise and a categorical premise and concludes to a categorical conclusion. Yet it is not modus ponens, because the categorical premise is not the antecedent of the conditional premise, but the consequent, and the conclusion is not the consequent of the conditional premise, but the antecedent. In fact, this argument [3] is invalid. Even assuming that the conditional premise is true and that Scholar Giles does in fact know the earth has a curved surface, that does not necessitate that he came to know of the earth's surface from observing a lunar eclipse. He might instead have learned it from some other source: perhaps he observed the curvature of the earth's horizon when at sea or he read about the earth's curved surface in a reliable scientific treatise. It is possible that both premises of this argument [3] are true while the conclusion is false. Thus, this argument [3] is invalid.

Modus tollens

Another simple form of argument that draws a conclusion from a conditional premise is one in which the arguer, knowing that the antecedent is a condition for the consequent and that the consequent does not come true, validly concludes that the condition stated in the antecedent is not fulfilled. Consider this example:

[4]   If Master William is lecturing on Ptolemy's book this term, then there
           must be a copy of that book in Oxford for him to consult.
       But there is no copy of that book in Oxford for him to consult.
       Therefore, Master William is not lecturing on Ptolemy's book this term.

Notice that this argument [4] has two premises. One premise is a conditional proposition. The other premise is the negation of the consequent of the conditional premise. The conclusion is the negation of the antecedent of the conditional premise. Logic masters in medieval universities called this form of argument *modus tollendo tollens* which means the method of negating what is to be negated. Today this Latin phrase is still used to refer to this way of arguing and most people call it *modus tollens* for short. Modus tollens is a valid form of argument, because if A really is a condition for B and B does not happen, it follows necessarily that condition A cannot be fulfilled. This can be easily seen by considering the following situation. Let us say that a certain student, Scholar John, is worried about being allowed to return to the university next term. He knows that if he passes his mathematics exam this term, he will be allowed to return next term. Let us further assume that Scholar John learns that he is not being allowed to return to the university next term. He can then safely assume that he did not pass his mathematics exam this term. His assumption is based on the validity of the following modus tollens argument:

[5]   If Scholar John passes the mathematics exam this term, then he is allowed
           to return to the university next term.
       Scholar John is not allowed to return to the university next term.
       Therefore, Scholar John did not pass his mathematics exam this term.

Like modus ponens, modus tollens depends on the conditional nature of conditional propositions. The conditional premise does not say that its consequent is factually true. In example [5], the conditional premise does not say that Scholar John is in fact being allowed to return to the university next term. It simply says that his being allowed to return to the university depends on a condition being fulfilled—namely, that he passes his mathematics exam this term. The categorical premise says that the consequent is not true—in this case [5] that Scholar John is not being allowed to return. It is on these grounds that he can be sure that the condition stated in the antecedent is not fulfilled—in this case [5] that Scholar John did not pass his mathematics exam.

Any argument that has a true modus tollens form is a valid argument, no matter what its subject matter. There are some arguments, however, that appear to be modus tollens, but actually do not have a true modus tollens form. These arguments may be invalid. Consider, for example, the following argument:

[6]   If Scholar Giles is observing the lunar eclipse, then he knows the earth has
           a curved surface.
       Scholar Giles is not observing the lunar eclipse.
       Therefore, Scholar Giles does not know the earth has a curved surface.

This argument [6] appears similar to a modus tollens argument. Like modus tollens, this argument has a conditional premise and a negated categorical premise and concludes to a negated categorical conclusion. Yet it is not modus tollens, because the categorical premise is not the negation of the consequent of the conditional premise, but the negation of the antecedent, and the conclusion is not the negation of the antecedent of the conditional premise, but the negation of the consequent. In fact, this argument [6] is invalid. Even assuming that the conditional premise is true and that Scholar Giles is not in fact observing the lunar eclipse, that does not necessarily rule out his knowing that the earth has a curved surface. He might have learned it from some other source: perhaps he observed the curvature of the earth's horizon when at sea or he read about the earth's curved surface in a reliable scientific treatise. It is possible that both premises of this argument [6] are true while the conclusion is false. Thus, this argument [6] is invalid.

Hypothetical Syllogism

Yet another simple form of argument that draws a conclusion from conditional premises is one in which the arguer, knowing that one thing is a condition for another and that the other is itself a condition for some third thing, validly concludes that the first is a condition for the third. Consider this example:

[7]   If Master William is lecturing on astronomy this term, then he is making use of Ptolemy's calculations.
      If he is making use of Ptolemy's calculations, then he has a copy of Ptolemy's book.
      Therefore, if Master William is lecturing on astronomy, then he has a copy of Ptolemy's book.

Notice that this argument [7] has two premises. One premise is a conditional proposition that states that its antecedent is a condition for a certain consequent. The other premise is also conditional and states that the consequent of the first premise is a condition for another consequent. The arguer, then, concludes that the antecedent of the first premise is a true condition for the consequent of the second premise. This form of argument is traditionally called *hypothetical syllogism*, because it is composed of conditional propositions. ("Hypothesis" is another word for condition.) Hypothetical syllogism is a valid form of argument, because if A really is a condition for B and B really is itself a condition for C, it follows necessarily that condition A must really be a condition for C. This can be easily seen by considering the following situation. Let us say that a certain student, Scholar John, is worried about completing work for his degree by the end of next term. He knows that, if he passes his mathematics exam this term, he will be allowed to return to the university next term. He also knows that, if he is allowed to return to the university next term, then he will be able to complete work on his degree next term. He can then safely conclude that his passing his mathematics exam this term is a condition for completing work on his degree next term.

Exercise 31

Student: _____

Identify the logical form of each of the following valid arguments.

1.   Master Thomas holds that faith is either an operation of the intellect or an
        appetite.   He says that it is a kind of virtue and not an appetite. Therefore, faith is
        an operation of the intellect.

        ☐ This is a categorical syllogism.   ☐ This is a modus ponens argument.

        ☐ This is a disjunctive syllogism.   ☐ This is a modus tollens argument.

        ☐ This is a constructive dilemma.   ☐ This is a hypothetical syllogism.

2.   If Master Thomas holds that faith is a virtue, then it is a rational operation. He clearly
        states that faith is a virtue and, therefore, it is a rational operation.

        ☐ This is a categorical syllogism.   ☐ This is a modus ponens argument.

        ☐ This is a disjunctive syllogism.   ☐ This is a modus tollens argument.

        ☐ This is a constructive dilemma.   ☐ This is a hypothetical syllogism.

3.   If Master Thomas holds that faith is a virtue, then he holds that it is a matter of
        deliberation. Further, if he considers it is a matter of deliberation, then he holds that
        faith is a rational act. It follows that, on the condition that Master Thomas holds that
        faith is a virtue, he considers it an act of reason.

        ☐ This is a categorical syllogism.   ☐ This is a modus ponens argument.

        ☐ This is a disjunctive syllogism.   ☐ This is a modus tollens argument.

        ☐ This is a constructive dilemma.   ☐ This is a hypothetical syllogism.

4.   Master Thomas is a theologian and all theologians make use of the faculty of reason. So,
        Master Thomas does too.

        ☐ This is a categorical syllogism.   ☐ This is a modus ponens argument.

        ☐ This is a disjunctive syllogism.   ☐ This is a modus tollens argument.

        ☐ This is a constructive dilemma.   ☐ This is a hypothetical syllogism.

5.   Assuming that faith is an appetite, Master Thomas' faith is simply a matter of desire. But his faith is not simply desire and that is why faith cannot be an appetite.

☐ This is a categorical syllogism.   ☐ This is a modus ponens argument.

☐ This is a disjunctive syllogism.   ☐ This is a modus tollens argument.

☐ This is a constructive dilemma.   ☐ This is a hypothetical syllogism.

6.   Master Thomas holds that faith is either an act of reason or emotion. Either way, it is a cognitive act.

☐ This is a categorical syllogism.   ☐ This is a modus ponens argument.

☐ This is a disjunctive syllogism.   ☐ This is a modus tollens argument.

☐ This is a constructive dilemma.   ☐ This is a hypothetical syllogism.

7.   Whenever Master Thomas lectures on faith, he discusses Aristotle's theory of virtue and he is lecturing on faith this term. Therefore, we can expect him to discuss Aristotle's account of virtue.

☐ This is a categorical syllogism.   ☐ This is a modus ponens argument.

☐ This is a disjunctive syllogism.   ☐ This is a modus tollens argument.

☐ This is a constructive dilemma.   ☐ This is a hypothetical syllogism.

Exercise 32

Student: _____

Read the following dialogue and answer the questions that follow.

A Scriptural Paradox

Master Thaddeus had not been a member of the Faculty of Theology of the University of Naples very long before he learned who the wits were among his students. He remembered his own student days in Paris and it was just the same. There were always a few students who took delight in posing absurd and impossible conundrums to young inexperienced masters and then sitting back and, with malicious glee, watching the masters make fools of themselves. He should have realized that it was just a matter of time before he became the victim of such intellectual pranksters himself. So it was in the Lenten term of 1261 when he was lecturing on the Holy Scriptures.

Master Thaddeus: As I was saying yesterday, the Holy Apostle James warns us to avoid pointing out our brother's sins. For no one loves the one who is always harping on the faults of others. And the reason why James insists on this point is his concern for harmony within the community of believers. He says that . . .

Scholar Silas: Excuse the interruption, Master, but must we accept what the Apostle James tells us?

Master Thaddeus: Why, of course. He speaks with the divinely granted authority of an apostle. This is why his admonition is recorded in Holy Scripture which is the word of God.

Scholar Silas: Let me get this right, Master. If Holy Scripture records an admonition—such as the admonition of James you just mentioned, then we must correct our actions accordingly.

Master Thaddeus: Yes, that is correct.

Scholar Silas: And clearly scripture records an admonition: the admonition of the Apostle James against brotherly correction.

Master Thaddeus: Yes.

Scholar Silas: It logically follows that we must correct our actions according to James' admonition against brotherly correction.

Master Thaddeus: But . . .

Scholar Gaimo: You must admit, Master, that Scholar Silas' argument is valid.

163

Master Thaddeus:	Yes, it is valid, but . . .
Scholar Gaimo:	You must further admit, Master, that his argument is supported by other passages in the scriptures such as the proverb of the wise King Solomon that forbids us to reprove the scoffer.
Master Thaddeus:	That proverb applies to the scoffer.
Scholar Gaimo:	Yet, if the scoffer is our brother, then scripture forbids us to reprove our brother. Further, if scripture forbids us to reprove our brother, then we ought not admonish our brother. Therefore, if the scoffer is our brother, then we ought not admonish him. So, the only question is whether the scoffer is our brother.
Scholar Silas:	Does not scripture teach that all men are our brothers?
Master Thaddeus:	Well, yes . . .
Scholar Gaimo:	It follows that the scoffer is our brother. It is a matter of a simple syllogism: all men are our brothers and the scoffer is a man; therefore, the scoffer is our brother. That is valid, is it not?
Master Thaddeus:	It is valid, but . . .
Scholar Silas:	But then we have a problem, do we not, Master?
Master Thaddeus:	How so?
Scholar Silas:	The psalmist enjoins us to admonish the sinner. The psalmist speaks with the authority of Holy Scripture, does he not?
Master Thaddeus:	Of course he does.
Scholar Silas:	And what he says must be true.
Master Thaddeus:	Yes.
Scholar Silas:	If the psalmist says what is true, then we ought to admonish the sinner. You just agreed that the psalmist says what is true. It follows that we ought to admonish the sinner.
Master Thaddeus:	And your point is what?
Scholar Gaimo:	Do you not see, Master? The Holy Scriptures, which always say what is true, are contradictory. The Apostle James and King Solomon say that we ought not to admonish the sinner whereas the psalmist says that we ought to admonish the sinner. So, Master, how are we to act?
Master Thaddeus:	How are you to act? Well, you can begin by praying that I do not lose my patience with you!

1. According to the story, Master Thaddeus is aware that he has a few "intellectual pranksters," as he calls them, among his students. (In modern English we might informally call such students "wise guys.") Two of them, Scholars Silas and Gaimo, argue that the Holy Scriptures are inconsistent. Given the tone of the story, do you think that they truly believe that the scriptures are inconsistent and contain contradictory moral guidelines?

    ☐   Yes, these two scholars are atheists and are arguing that the scriptures are an unreliable source of truth.

    ☐   Yes, these two scholars are believers, but are arguing that there is a serious problem with accepting the scriptures as a reliable source of truth.

    ☐   No, these two scholars know very well that the apparent contradictions of scripture can be reconciled by a careful interpretation and they are just giving Master Thaddeus a difficult time as a kind of practical joke.

2. In his lecture, Master Thaddeus refers to the teaching of the Apostle James on brotherly correction. What is the Apostle's teaching?

    ☐   The Apostle James teaches that we should not correct our brother in order to maintain harmony within the community.

    ☐   The Apostle James teaches that we should always correct our brother in order to maintain the moral purity of the community.

    ☐   The Apostle James teaches that we should sometimes correct our brother in order to maintain personal power within the community.

3. When Scholar Silas asks Master Thaddeus whether the teaching of the Apostle James must be accepted, the master answers in the affirmative. What reason does Master Thaddeus give for his answer?

    _____

    _____

    _____

    _____

    _____

4. In response to the master's explanation of why the teaching of the Apostle James must be accepted, Scholar Silas presents an argument. What is his argument?

Premise 1: _____

_____

Premise 2: _____

_____

Conclusion: _____

_____

5. What is the form of Scholar Silas' argument?

☐ This is a modus ponens argument.

☐ This is a modus tollens argument.

☐ This is a hypothetical syllogism.

6. Scholar Gaimo claims that Scholar Silas' argument is valid. Is he correct and does the master agree?

_____

_____

_____

7. Scholar Gaimo goes on to claim that the teaching against brotherly correction is supported by other passages in the scriptures and he quotes a certain scriptural author. Who is that author?

☐ King Solomon who wrote the book of Proverbs.

☐ King David who wrote the book of Psalms.

☐ Saint John the Theologian who wrote the fourth Gospel.

☐ Pope Leo XIII who wrote the encyclical *Aeterni Patris*.

8. In an effort to show that the supporting scriptural passage makes the same point as made by the Apostle James, Scholar Gaimo gives an argument. What is his argument?

Premise 1: _____

_____

Premise 2: _____

_____

Conclusion: _____

_____

9. What is the form of Scholar Gaimo's argument?

☐ This is a modus ponens argument.

☐ This is a modus tollens argument.

☐ This is a hypothetical syllogism.

10. Is Scholar Gaimo's argument valid?

☐ Yes, it is a valid argument.   ☐ No, it is an invalid argument.

11. Scholar Gaimo goes on to give another argument about whether or not the scoffer is our brother. What is his argument?

Premise 1: _____

_____

Premise 2: _____

_____

Conclusion: _____

_____

12. What is the form of Scholar Gaimo's second argument?

☐ This is a categorical syllogism.

☐ This is a disjunctive syllogism.

☐ This is a hypothetical syllogism.

13. Scholar Gaimo asks the master whether his argument is valid and Master Thaddeus admits that it is. Is it? Provide a diagram analysis of the argument to support your answer.

☐ Yes, it is a valid argument.   ☐ No, it is an invalid argument.

14. Scholar Silas points out that the psalmist authoritatively teaches that we ought to admonish the sinner. He follows this with an argument about what follows from this teaching. What is his argument?

Premise 1: _____

_____

Premise 2: _____

_____

Conclusion: _____

_____

15. What is the form of Scholar Silas' second argument?

☐ This is a modus ponens argument.

☐ This is a modus tollens argument.

☐ This is a hypothetical syllogism.

16. Is Scholar Silas' second argument valid?

☐ Yes, it is a valid argument.   ☐ No, it is an invalid argument.

17. Scholar Silas claims that his argument shows that there is a problem with the authority of scripture. What exactly is the problem?

_____

_____

_____

_____

_____

§13 It Is Absurd and Therefore

All of the various forms of argument studied so far—categorical syllogism, disjunctive arguments (disjunctive syllogism, constructive and destructive dilemma), and conditional arguments (modus ponens, modus tollens, and hypothetical syllogism)—have something in common. They are all direct ways of arguing for a conclusion. They can be considered *direct argument* because, when valid and sound, true premises directly support the truth of the conclusion. Not all arguments, however, are direct. It is also possible to indirectly support a conclusion by showing that the negation of the conclusion is false. In *indirect argument*, a conclusion is established as true because its negation is shown to be impossible. This kind of procedure in argument depends on two fundamental logical laws that apply to all propositions.

Law of Contradiction

As discussed in §5, some propositions are contradictory to others. This happens when two propositions have the same subject matter (share the same subject term and the same predicate term) but differ in quantity and quality such that they are never true together and never false together. In fact, for every proposition there is another possible proposition that must have the opposite truth value—in other words, is its contradictory. In order to see this, consider any proposition—let us call it P—and assign it a truth value. The negation of this proposition must have the opposite truth value. So, given that P is true, not-P must be false. Given that P is false, not-P must be true. This will always be the case, no matter what actual proposition P represents. All propositions are contradictory to their negations. Because this applies to all actual and possible propositions, a logical law can be formulated: the following conjunction is always false:

[1] P and not-P

where P is any proposition. A conjunction is true when all of the propositions conjoined within it are true. Because a proposition will always have the opposite truth value of its negation, the conjunction of a proposition and its negation will always be false.

Essentially, the *Law of Contradiction* says that there is a difference between truth and falsity and that they are entirely incompatible. In the real world, it is impossible that something both be and not be the case at the same time and in the same respect. Consider the following example:

[2]   Scholar John is being examined in geometry and he is not being examined in geometry.

This conjunctive proposition [2] must be false, because it is the attempt to say that a certain proposition is both true and false at the same time and in the same way. This, however, is impossible. If the proposition *Scholar John is being examined in geometry* is true, then its negation *Scholar John is not being examined in geometry* absolutely must be false. If, instead, the proposition *Scholar John is being examined in geometry* is false, then its negation *Scholar John is not being examined in geometry* absolutely must be true. If it were possible that these two propositions could be true at the same time, then nothing makes sense and the world is unintelligible. What would it mean to say *Scholar John is both being examined in geometry and not being examined in geometry right now*? It may seem at first glance that saying such a thing makes sense, but in fact it means nothing. It is impossible that a contradiction be true. In fact, if the Law of Contradiction were not a fundamentally true law governing all discourse, then nothing sensible could be said.

Law of Excluded Middle

All propositions have truth value and there are only two possible truth values: true and false. This means that any given proposition must be either true or false. Another way of saying this is that, for any given proposition, either it or its negation is true. This is because the negation of a proposition always has the opposite truth value as the proposition of which it is the negation, as stated in the Law of Contradiction. Therefore, a logical law that applies to all propositions can be formulated: the following disjunction is always true:

[3]   *P* or not-*P*

where *P* is any proposition. Disjunctions are true when at least one of the propositions disjoined, one of the alternatives, is true. So, this logical law says that any given proposition must be either true or false, either it or its negation must be true. This logical law is called the *Law of Excluded Middle* because it essentially rules out the middle ground between truth and falsity. Consider the following disjunction:

[4]   Master Isadore either is or is not lecturing on Roman Law this term.

According to the Law of Excluded Middle, this disjunction must be a true proposition. It is true when the proposition *Master Isadore is lecturing on Roman Law this term* is true. It is true when the proposition *Master Isadore is not lecturing on Roman Law this term* is true. Both *Master Isadore is lecturing on Roman Law this term* and *Master Isadore is not lecturing on Roman Law this term* cannot be true at the same time, because that would violate the Law of Contradiction. Thus, the Law of Excluded Middle says that it must always be the case that one of these propositions is true while the other is false.

Saying that any proposition must be either true or false is not the same as knowing what the truth value of that proposition is. Consider the following proposition:

[5]   All Oxford masters either do or do not own an academic gown.

According to the Law of Excluded Middle, this disjunctive proposition must be true. That means that one of the two alternatives stated in this disjunction must be true. Yet, that alone does not show which of these is true. One can know that Oxford masters either do or do not own their gowns without knowing whether they actually do so or not.

Reductio ad absurdum

Let us say that an arguer believes that a certain proposition—let us call this proposition *C*—is true, but he cannot think of any true premises that directly support the truth of this proposition *C*. Thus, the arguer cannot formulate a direct argument establishing *C* as a true conclusion. Does this mean that the arguer must be content with believing *C* is true while admitting that he cannot prove that *C* is true? Possibly. Yet, there is another way of using argument to show that *C* must be true that is open to the arguer. Instead of directly proving *C* from a set of premises, the arguer might attempt to indirectly prove *C* is true by showing that its negation not-*C* is false. The Law of Excluded Middle says that, for any proposition, either it or its negation must be true. So, if the arguer can prove that not-*C* is false, then *C* must be true.

This means that there is an indirect form of argument that is capable of establishing a conclusion as true by showing that its negation cannot be true. Yet, how can an arguer show that a proposition cannot possibly be true? How can a proposition be disproved? The Law of Contradiction provides a way of doing this. Let us say that an arguer can show that from a certain proposition not-*C* a contradiction *P* and not-*P* follows by a valid direct argument. This conclusion *P* and not-*P* is, of course, a contradiction. Like all contradictions, it cannot be true because what it states is impossible and absurd. Yet, accepting not-*C* as true committed the arguer to accepting *P* and not-*P* as true because this contradiction followed from not-*C* by a valid argument. *P* and not-*P*, however, cannot be true, because it violates the Law of Contradiction. Therefore, the arguer can reliably conclude that not-*C* cannot be true either. If not-*C* is false, then *C* must be true, by the Law of Excluded Middle. Therefore, *C* has been indirectly proven true, by directly disproving its negation not-*C*.

Logic masters in medieval universities called this sort of indirect argument *reductio ad absurdum* which means the reduction of a proposition to absurdity. By "reduction" they meant showing that something follows from the proposition by a valid argument. By "absurdity" they meant a contradiction, because what contradictions say is always absurd and makes no sense. This Latin phrase is still used today as the name for this type of argument. It is basically an indirect argument strategy: in order to prove a certain conclusion *C*, assume its negation not-*C* as one of the premises and show that a contradiction follows from not-*C*. If this can be done successfully, then one can validly conclude that *C* must be true. Consider the following example:

[6]   A triangle is a plane figure composed of three straight sides that intersect. Such a figure must have three angles where the sides intersect. In order to see that this must be true, assume that a triangle does not have three angles. Now, if this is true, then a triangle does not have intersecting sides. But this is impossible because triangles always do have intersecting sides. Therefore, it cannot be true that triangles lack three angles.

This argument [6] is a reductio ad absurdum argument, because it establishes the conclusion *triangles have three angles* by showing that the negation *triangles do not have three angles* must be false. The way in which this proposition is shown to be false is by showing that the contradiction *triangles do and do not have intersecting sides* follows by a valid argument from the premise *triangles do not have three angles*. To make the logical form of this argument clear, it can be outlined like this:

[7] (1) A triangle does not have three angles.
     (2) If a triangle does not have three angles, then a triangle does not have intersecting sides.
     (3) A triangle has intersecting sides.
     (4) So, a triangle does not have intersecting sides.
     (5) So, a triangle does and does not have intersecting sides.
     (6) Therefore, a triangle does have three angles.

Lines 1–3 of this argument [7] are the premises of the argument. Premises 2 and 3 are accepted because they are known to be true. Premise 1 is the proposition that the arguer is attempting to disprove. At line 4, the arguer draws a preliminary conclusion from premises 1 and 2 by modus ponens. At line 5, the arguer conjoins the preliminary conclusion from line 4 with premise 3 to form a clear and explicit contradiction. So, the arguer has shown that a contradiction follows from the three premises. This means that it is clear that at least one of these premises must be false. Premises 2 and 3 were assumed because they are known to be true. Premise 1 is the proposition the arguer is out to disprove. So, the arguer blames the contradiction on premise 1 and validly concludes to its negation at line 6.

The crucial step in a reductio ad absurdum argument is showing that a real contradiction follows from the premise the arguer is out to disprove. In analyzing such an argument, it is important to make sure that the contradiction is real and not just apparent. The best way to do this is to state the contradiction clearly and explicitly in the form of a conjunction of a proposition and its negation: *P* and not-*P* where *P* is any proposition. Notice that the outline of the argument given at [7] clearly and explicitly states the contradiction at line 5: *a triangle does and does not have intersecting sides*. In ordinary conversation and writing, reductio ad absurdum arguments are often stated elliptically. When analyzing such arguments and investigating their validity, it is necessary to clearly state all the parts of the argument, especially the contradiction.

Generally, reductio ad absurdum arguments are complex arguments. This means that they are arguments that are composed of simpler arguments. This is necessary, because reductio ad absurdum arguments draw a conclusion from the results of another argument that is internal to the reductio ad absurdum argument. In the example outlined at [7], the whole argument supporting the conclusion *a triangle does have three angles* is the reductio ad absurdum argument. Yet, there is another argument within this reductio ad absurdum that is used to derive what is necessary to construct the contradiction. It is the modus ponens argument by which the preliminary conclusion at line 4 is derived from premises 1 and 2 and this preliminary conclusion is used to construct the contradiction at line 5. This is always the case with reductio ad absurdum arguments: they will always contain one or more simpler arguments within them as a mean of deriving from the premises the parts necessary to form a contradiction. These simpler arguments may be of any form, but most often they are modus ponens or modus tollens arguments.

Consider another example of reductio ad absurdum argument:

[8]   Master Robert argues that the order evident in the natural universe shows that God, the creator of the natural universe, must exist. If God did not exist, then the observed natural order must be the result of absolutely random processes. Yet, if this is true, then the natural universe is unintelligible. The natural universe, however, clearly is intelligible as experimental science demonstrates. Therefore, God the creator of the natural universe must exist.

Master Robert's argument [8] is clearly a reductio ad absurdum argument, because he is attempting to show that God exists by disproving the opposite assumption that God does not exist. So, his argument strategy is to assume as one of his premises what he believes to be false—namely, that God does not exist—and then attempt to derive a contradiction from this assumption. Now, he knows that the assumption that God does not exist has certain implications and these provide him with two additional premises. He also knows that experimental science makes sense of the natural universe, so that gives him a fourth premise. From these four premises, Master Robert is able to derive a contradiction by two preliminary argument steps of modus ponens. This gives him what he needs to construct a contradiction on the basis of what follows from the premises. Thus, he is able to conclude to the opposite (the negation) of the assumption that he was out to disprove. The form of Master Robert's argument is made clear by the following outline:

[9]   (1) God does not exist.   Premise (assumption to be disproved)

        (2) If God does not exist,
              natural order results from random processes.   Premise (assumption known to be true)

        (3) If natural order results from random processes,
              natural order is unintelligible.   Premise (assumption known to be true)

        (4) Natural order is intelligible.   Premise (assumption known to be true)

        (5) So, natural order results from random processes.   Conclusion by modus ponens from 1 & 2

        (6) So, natural order is unintelligible.   Conclusion by modus ponens from 3 & 5

        (7) So, natural order is intelligible and unintelligible. Conjunction of 4 & 6 (contradiction)

        (8) Therefore, God exists.   Final conclusion by reductio ad absurdum

Exercise 33

Read the following dialogue and answer the questions that follow.

A Matter of Eternity

In the year of our Lord 1251, a young man named Pierre from the district of Anjou arrived in Paris in the hopes of studying at the university. He had been advised to consult a certain Master Thomas, a professor of theology, about his plans. This is what brought him to the front gate of the Convent of St.-Jacques early one morning. He rang the bell which was promptly answered by the porter who took him to a small room and asked him to wait. His wait was not long.

Master Thomas:	Greetings in the name of the Lord, young sir. I understand that you wish to see me.
Pierre d'Anjou:	Yes, Master. I have a letter of reference from Dom Julian, abbot of the monastery of St.-Denis near Vouillé where I attended the monastery school.
Master Thomas:	Yes, I see that you wish to study for your degree in theology and that you have already received a fine education from the monks in the arts. You have studied grammar and logic as well as arithmetic, geometry, and music. Abbot Julian believes that you are prepared for advanced studies here at the university. Is this why you have come to Paris?
Pierre d'Anjou:	Indeed, it is. I believe that I am ready to take up my studies in theology. I have read the scriptures and the books of the holy fathers as well.
Master Thomas:	What fathers have you read?
Pierre d'Anjou:	I have read the books of the blessed Augustine and the sermons of Bishop Ambrose. I have also read the scripture commentaries of Bishop Basil the Cappadocian.
Master Thomas:	So, you have read among the Greeks as well as the Latins?
Pierre d'Anjou:	Yes, Master.
Master Thomas:	Most impressive. Tell me, is there any particular theological problem that especially interests you?
Pierre d'Anjou:	The holy Basil gives a list of the many names we give to God. This I found most interesting and helpful for understanding sacred doctrine. One particular passage that I read just before I set out on my journey to Paris concerned eternity.

Master Thomas:	Indeed, that is one of the most important names of God.
Pierre d'Anjou:	In his book, Bishop Basil discusses the various kinds of eternity. Clearly, this is important, but I wonder whether it is possible to demonstrate God's eternity.
Master Thomas:	All the holy fathers are agreed that God is the Eternal One. Yet, there is merit in coming to understand this name for God more thoroughly through a demonstration.
Pierre d'Anjou:	This is precisely what I believe.
Master Thomas:	Might it be that you have yourself constructed a demonstration of God's eternity that you wish to tell me about?
Pierre d'Anjou:	My argument begins with the presumption that God is not eternal, a presumption that I make just for the sake of argument.
Master Thomas:	I understand. Proceed.
Pierre d'Anjou:	It must also be accepted that, if God is not eternal, then he is temporal.
Master Thomas:	I agree: lack of eternity in God implies that God exists in time.
Pierre d'Anjou:	I believe, Master, that you will also accept this proposition: if God is temporal, then he does not transcend the temporal world and is part of it.
Master Thomas:	Yes, I accept this as well.
Pierre d'Anjou:	But, of course, we know that God does transcend the temporal world and is not part of it, for he revealed this to Moses on the mountain.
Master Thomas:	Quite correct.
Pierre d'Anjou:	It follows from this last proposition and my second conditional proposition that God is not temporal.
Master Thomas:	Yes, your reasoning is valid.
Pierre d'Anjou:	From this conclusion that God is not temporal and from my first conditional premise it follows that God is eternal.
Master Thomas:	Again, your reasoning is valid.
Pierre d'Anjou:	But we began by assuming that God is not eternal. Thus, our premises have led us into contradiction.
Master Thomas:	Quite right. What, then, do you conclude?
Pierre d'Anjou:	That God must be eternal.

Master Thomas: Very good. Clearly, your demonstration is consistent with the teachings of the holy fathers. It is also clear that true faith is not opposed to right reason.

Pierre d'Anjou: Indeed, Master.

Master Thomas: I hope that you are prepared to remain in Paris and attend the lectures and disputations of the university.

1.   Pierre, a young man from Anjou, has arrived in Paris and consults Master Thomas who is a professor at the university. Why has Pierre come to Paris?

    _____

    _____

    _____

    _____

    _____

2.   Pierre tells Master Thomas that he has read in the book of St. Basil that one of the names of God is the Eternal One. Pierre also reveals that he has constructed an argument demonstrating God's eternity. Has he composed this argument because he doubts St. Basil?

    ☐   Yes, Pierre has theological objections to St. Basil's attempts to give names to God and he intends to demonstrate that this cannot be done.

    ☐   Yes, Pierre believes that St. Basil is a heretic and he is setting out to demonstrate this.

    ☐   No, Pierre is an atheist, but is open to being convinced by argument that God exists and is eternal.

    ☐   No, Pierre believes that St. Basil rightly calls God "the Eternal One" and he is attempting to use argument to gain a better understanding of the meaning of this divine name.

3.   What is the final conclusion of Pierre's whole argument?

    Conclusion: _____

    _____

4. Pierre opens his argument with a presumption that he says he makes "just for the sake of argument." What is this presumption?

Premise 1: _____

_____

5. Why does Pierre begin his argument with this presumption?

☐   Pierre believes that this presumption is true.

☐   Pierre believes that this presumption is false, but he makes it a premise of his argument with the intention of disproving it by a reductio ad absurdum argument.

☐   Pierre believes that this presumption is false, but he makes it a premise of his argument in order to deceive Master Thomas about the contents of St. Basil's book.

6. Pierre then states two conditional premises that the master also accepts as true. What are these two conditional premises?

Premise 2: _____

_____

Premise 3: _____

_____

7. Pierre adds another categorical premise that, again, the master agrees is true. What is this premise?

Premise 4: _____

_____

8. From his final premise (Premise 4) and his second conditional premise (Premise 3), Pierre draws a conclusion. What is this conclusion?

Conclusion: _____

_____

9.   By what form of argument does Pierre draw this conclusion from these two premises?

☐ By a modus ponens argument.

☐ By a modus tollens argument.

☐ By a hypothetical syllogism.

10.   From this preliminary conclusion and from his first conditional premise (Premise 2), Pierre draws yet another preliminary conclusion. What is this conclusion?

Conclusion: _____

_____

11.   By what form of argument does Pierre draw this conclusion from these two premises?

☐ By a modus ponens argument.

☐ By a modus tollens argument.

☐ By a hypothetical syllogism.

12.   Pierre then points out that the premises have led to a contradiction. What precisely is the contradiction?

_____

_____

13.   Is Pierre's complex argument valid?

☐   Yes, Pierre has successfully derived a contradiction from the assumption that God is not eternal thereby disproving it and validly demonstrating that God must be eternal.

☐   No, Pierre's argument contains a contradiction and, because contradictions are always false, he has failed to establish by a valid argument that God is truly eternal.

☐   No, Pierre has failed to derive a true contradiction from his premises and has not demonstrated that God cannot lack eternity.

Exercise 34

Student: _____

Read the following dialogue and answer the questions that follow.

Too Many Numbers

Master Gilbert, a professor of mathematics at the University of Paris, had been asked by a group of students to lecture on the first book of Euclid's *Elements of Geometry*. He was very pleased to accommodate them, for he had recently obtained a new edition of that book while traveling in southern Italy. This new edition contained a much better Latin translation than the old translation of Boethius. The new one had been made from an Arabic version and was much more complete. Yet, when he began his course of lectures during the spring term of 1244, Master Gilbert found that he might as well have used the old incomplete Latin version of Boethius, for his students found the reasoning very difficult and he made slow progress through the book. One day about midterm, one of his students asked him to review the proof of Euclid's famous theorem about prime numbers.

Master Gilbert:	Settle down, scholars, and attend to the theorem that we are about to establish. The ancient mathematician, Euclid, first demonstrated this theorem many centuries ago and our task today is to reconstruct his demonstration. It concerns prime numbers. Let us begin with a definition. What is a prime number?
Scholar Pipen:	A number is prime when it has only one and itself as factors.
Master Gilbert:	Good. So, a prime number, when divided, will only divide evenly when divided by itself or one. Now, let us have an example of a number that is prime.
Scholar Ulrich:	Seven is a prime number.
Master Gilbert:	Good. Are there other prime numbers?
Scholar Michael:	There are many prime numbers.
Master Gilbert:	How many?
Scholar Michael:	I do not know. Very many, I would suppose.
Scholar Ulrich:	Yet, not every number is prime, so that would suggest that there exist only so many prime numbers.
Master Gilbert:	It is quite true that not all numbers are prime, but that does not exclude the possibility of an infinity of prime numbers does it?

183

Scholar Pipen:	Were there an infinity of prime numbers, that would mean that there is no prime number that is the largest.
Master Gilbert:	Quite right. Were there a largest prime number, then there would be a finite number of primes. Consider the series of prime numbers 2, 3, 5, 7, 11, 13, and 17. If 17 were the largest prime number, then this series would represent all the prime numbers there are and this series is, of course, finite.
Scholar Pipen:	Yet, 17 is not the largest prime number, because we can prove that 19 is also prime. It is easy to show that its only factors are 1 and 19.
Master Gilbert:	True enough, Scholar Pipen. How, though, can we know that 19 is not the largest prime number?
Scholar Pipen:	Clearly, by discovering an even larger prime number, say, 23.
Master Gilbert:	What of the question of whether there is an infinity of prime numbers? Can we use this method to discover whether there is a largest prime number?
Scholar Michael:	Clearly not, for no matter how many numbers we attempted to test by this factoring method, we would have many more to test. In fact, we would never finish because there is an infinity of numbers to test.
Scholar Ulrich:	Too many numbers!
Scholar Pipen:	Just thinking about it makes one dizzy!
Master Gilbert:	Perhaps there is a method by which we could determine this question without our heads spinning off.
Scholar Pipen:	How could we, Master? We certainly cannot consider one by one every number there is or could be. What other method is possible?
Master Gilbert:	Instead of taking a direct approach like this, perhaps we can take an indirect approach to the task of proving that there is no largest prime number.
Scholar Pipen:	How would one go about indirectly proving that there is an infinity of prime numbers?
Master Gilbert:	By using the method Euclid himself used. Attend.
Scholar Michael:	You have our full attention, Master.
Master Gilbert:	Let us assume, just for the sake of argument, that there is a largest prime number. Now, this could be any prime number, so let us agree to simply call this number K.

Scholar Pipen:	So, we assume that this number K is the largest prime number beyond which there are no other numbers that are prime.
Master Gilbert:	Correct.
Scholar Ulrich:	Then what, Master?
Master Gilbert:	Let us now define another number by multiplying all the prime numbers less than or equal to K. Let us call this number N.
Scholar Pipen:	If K is 7, for example, then N is product of 2, 3, 5, and 7 or 210.
Master Gilbert:	Now, let us add 1 to N. This new number N with the addition of 1 is a prime number and is greater than K.
Scholar Pipen:	Using my previous example where K is 7, N plus 1 is 211. This is a prime number and is clearly larger than 7.
Master Gilbert:	Yes. Because K represents any prime number, N plus 1 will always be a prime number that is at least one larger than K.
Scholar Michael:	But we began our argument by assuming that K is the largest prime number and this has led us to affirm that there must be a prime number larger than K.
Scholar Ulrich:	That is right. We have been led into contradiction.
Master Gilbert:	What can we conclude from this argument?
Scholar Pipen:	That K clearly is not the largest prime number.
Master Gilbert:	Quite correct. And, because K was any prime number, saying that K is not the largest prime number is equivalent to saying that there is no largest prime number. Thus, Euclid's theorem is proven.
Scholar Pipen:	This indirect form of argument is quite powerful, for it has allowed us to prove something true of an infinity of things, in this case an infinity of numbers.
Scholar Michael:	It is clear that Euclid was a very deep thinker and that we must respect his achievement.

1.   What is Euclid's theorem?

_____

_____

_____

2.   Who first proved Euclid's theorem?

      ☐   The ancient Greek mathematican Euclid, which is obviously why it is called "Euclid's theorem."

      ☐   The ancient Roman scholar Boethius, which is why he wanted to translate Euclid's book into Latin.

      ☐   The medieval mathematican Master Gilbert, which is why he is a professor at the university.

      ☐   The medieval university student Scholar Pipen, because he states the conclusion in the dialogue.

3.   Master Gilbert asks his students whether it is possible to use a method of directly testing each number by division to see if it is prime. Why does Scholar Michael believe that it is not possible?

_____

_____

_____

_____

4.   Master Gilbert suggests that Euclid's theorem can be indirectly proven. What form of argument is Master Gilbert speaking of here?

      ☐   Disjunctive syllogism.

      ☐   Modus ponens argument.

      ☐   Reductio ad absurdum.

5.   What is the form of argument by which Euclid originally proved his prime number theorem?

      ☐   Disjunctive syllogism.

      ☐   Modus ponens argument.

      ☐   Reductio ad absurdum.

6.   Master Gilbert begins the argument by assuming that K is the largest prime number. Yet, it is clear that he does not believe that there is a largest prime number. So, why does he assume that there is?

_____

_____

_____

7.   What are the premises of the argument that proves Euclid's prime number theorem?

Premise 1: _____

_____

Premise 2: _____

_____

Premise 3: _____

_____

8.   At one point in the discussion, Scholar Ulrich says that their argument has led them into contradiction. What precisely is the contradiction?

_____

_____

9.   Is Euclid's argument that there is no largest prime number valid?

☐   Yes, it is a valid disjunctive syllogism because it considers all the alternatives to K being the largest prime number.

☐   Yes, it is a valid reductio ad absurdum because an actual contradiction has been derived from the premises and the argument concludes to the negation of one of the premises.

☐   No, it is an invalid reductio ad absurdum because no actual contradiction has been derived from the premises.

Exercise 35

Student: _____

'Read the following dialogue and answer the questions that follow.

The Cosmic Craftsman

As a professor of theology at the University of Paris, Master Joachim of Brabant was responsible for lecturing on the sacred scriptures. During the year 1288, he lectured on the book of Genesis, but he finished his lectures by the Feast of St. Phillip, three days before the end of term. So, on that day he decided to allow his students to ask him any questions they wished. One of his brighter students, Hermann of Saxony, raised the first question.

Scholar Hermann:	I have heard it said, Master, that the ancient pagan philosophers were able to prove that the universe is divinely made. Is this true?
Master Joachim:	Indeed, it is true.
Scholar Hermann:	How can this be? Did they know the books of Moses?
Master Joachim:	Some have thought that the pagan philosophers must have read the account of God's creation of the universe given by Moses in the book of Genesis. Yet, this is not necessary, because the divine origin of the universe can be known through philosophical demonstration. Thus, it is possible that the pagans knew of the creation of the universe through demonstrative argument.
Scholar Hermann:	Can you explain, Master, how the pagan philosophers could have used argument to demonstrate that the universe is created by God?
Master Joachim:	Yes, I can. Let us consider one such argument given by the great pagan philosopher Plato in his book called *The Timaeus*. Plato's argument begins with the obvious fact that the universe is perceptible.
Scholar Hermann:	So, Plato begins with the reasonable assumption that the universe, which is the totality of all things, can be perceived by perceiving beings such as human beings.
Master Joachim:	Yes, that is correct. Now, Plato adds three other premises. First, he claims that whatever is perceptible comes into being. Then he notes that everything that comes into being does so by the agency of some cause. Finally, he adds that everything that comes into being through some cause is brought into being by an agent that crafts it.
Scholar Hermann:	And from these four premises, Plato draws the conclusion that the universe is brought into being by some agent that crafts it—a sort

189

of cosmic craftsman. I can see that this must be a complex argument of several stages.

Master Joachim: Indeed, it is complex, but I think that upon analysis you will find that Plato's argument is valid.

Scholar Hermann: Yet, this argument only gives us the conclusion that the universe is created by something that crafted it. How can we be sure that Plato intends the same thing by his cosmic craftsman as Moses means by God? In other words, how can we be sure that Plato's cosmic craftsman is a *divine* craftsman and not, say, some natural agent?

Master Joachim: An excellent question! You think like a philosopher, Scholar Hermann.

Scholar Hermann: Thank you, Master. But what of my question? How can we be sure that Plato and Moses are talking about the same being?

Master Joachim: Well, let us assume that the cosmic craftsman who created the whole perceivable universe is not divine.

Scholar Hermann: Very well.

Master Joachim: What then does this imply about the cosmic craftsman?

Scholar Hermann: If the craftsman who created the universe is not divine, then he is created and part of the created universe.

Master Joachim: Quite right. Further, if the craftsman who created the universe is part of the created universe, then he cannot have created the universe for he was created by whatever craftsman did create the universe.

Scholar Hermann: Yes, I see that.

Master Joachim: From our first two premises it follows that the cosmic craftsman is part of the created universe.

Scholar Hermann: And from that conclusion and our third premise it follows that the cosmic craftsman did not create the universe.

Master Joachim: Yes. But remember, we are speaking of the cosmic craftsman, which means the craftsman who created the universe.

Scholar Hermann: So, we have a contradiction.

Master Joachim: Indeed we do. We can now draw the conclusion that the cosmic craftsman who created the whole perceivable universe must be divine.

Scholar Hermann: So, we have another complex argument, but this time one that shows why some have thought that Plato and Moses were talking about the same being: God the Creator.

Master Joachim: It is marvelous how much agreement there is between the sacred author Moses and the pagan philosopher Plato.

Scholar Hermann: Marvelous indeed, Master.

1.   Master Joachim tells his students that some scholars have thought that some ancient Greek philosophers, such as Plato, who held that the universe was created by a divine being must have gotten the idea from reading ancient Jewish books, such as the book of Genesis. (Medieval scholars such as Master Joachim believed that Moses wrote the book of Genesis.) Master Joachim, however, points out that this is not the only possibility. What other way might the pagan Greek philosophers have come to the idea that God created the universe?

_____

_____

_____

_____

2.   What is the name of Plato's book in which he gives his cosmic craftsman argument?

_____

3.   Master Joachim summarizes Plato's argument by stating four premises. Following the reasoning, Scholar Hermann realizes that Plato's argument is a complex argument composed of several simpler arguments. In fact, it is composed of three simpler arguments. What form of complex argument is Plato's cosmic craftsman argument?

☐   It is a complex chain of categorical syllogisms (a soritical argument).

☐   It is a complex of categorical syllogisms that includes lemmas.

☐   It is a complex constructive dilemma.

☐   It is a complex reductio ad absurdum argument.

4. What is the first stage of Plato's cosmic craftsman argument?

Premise 1: _____

_____

Premise 2: _____

_____

Conclusion: _____

_____

5. What is the second stage of Plato's cosmic craftsman argument?

Premise 1: _____

_____

Premise 2: _____

_____

Conclusion: _____

_____

6. What is the third stage of Plato's cosmic craftsman argument?

Premise 1: _____

_____

Premise 2: _____

_____

Conclusion: _____

_____

7.　Master Joachim claims that an analysis would show Plato's argument to be valid. Explain how one could show that this complex argument is valid.

_____

_____

_____

_____

_____

8.　Scholar Hermann agrees that Plato's argument is valid, but he does not think that this argument alone solves the problem of whether Plato and Moses are talking about the same thing. What else has to be proven to show that Plato and Moses are talking about the same being?

_____

_____

_____

_____

_____

9.　Master Joachim proceeds to give an argument showing that Plato and Moses are indeed talking about the same being. What form of argument does Master Joachim use?

☐　　Categorical syllogism.

☐　　Hypothetical syllogism.

☐　　Reductio ad absurdum.

10.　What exactly is Master Joachim attempting to prove in his argument?

Conclusion:　_____

_____

11.   What are the premises of Master Joachim's argument?

        Premise 1:   _____

        _____

        Premise 2:   _____

        _____

        Premise 3:   _____

        _____

        Premise 4:   _____

        _____

12.   Master Joachim draws a conclusion from his first two premises. What is this
        conclusion?

        Conclusion: _____

        _____

13.   By what form of argument does Master Joachim draw this conclusion from his first two
        premises?

        ☐   Modus ponens.

        ☐   Modus tollens.

        ☐   Reductio ad absurdum.

14.   Master Joachim goes on to draw another conclusion; this one from his third
        premise and the conclusion drawn from his first two premises. What is this
        conclusion?

        Conclusion: _____

        _____

15. By what form of argument does Master Joachim draw this conclusion from his third premise and his first preliminary conclusion?

☐　　Modus ponens.

☐　　Modus tollens.

☐　　Reductio ad absurdum.

16. Scholar Hermann points out that the reasoning in Master Joachim's complex argument results in a contradiction. What precisely is the contradiction?

_____

_____

17. Is Master Joachim's complex argument valid?

☐　　Yes, it is a valid reductio ad absurdum proving that Plato's cosmic craftsman who created the universe is divine.

☐　　No, it is an invalid reductio ad absurdum because no actual contradiction has been derived from the premises.

§14 Therefore It Is Probable

A valid argument is one in which, when all the premises are true, the conclusion absolutely must be true. Valid arguments, then, are necessary arguments. One might think of them as proofs in the strict sense, because such arguments are attempts to show that, given a certain set of premises, a certain conclusion is necessarily true. An arguer may, of course, attempt to strictly prove a certain conclusion is necessarily true on the basis of certain premises, but fail. In such a case, the arguer's argument would be invalid. All of the various forms of argument studied so far are like this: they are all attempts to show that a conclusion follows from its premises with absolute necessity. If the form of argument is valid, then this attempt is successful. If the form is invalid, then this attempt is unsuccessful. Yet, not all arguments are attempts to show that a conclusion is absolutely necessary. There are times when an arguer is only trying to show that his conclusion is more likely true than false. Such less-than-necessary arguments may be useful and that means that not every form of argument is the sort of argument that is either valid or invalid. In fact, every argument falls into one of two general categories: those that aim at proving the conclusion is necessarily true and those that aim at showing that the conclusion is probably true.

Deductive Argument

Every form of argument studied so far—categorical syllogism, disjunctive syllogism, constructive and destructive dilemma, modus ponens, modus tollens, hypothetical syllogism, and reductio ad absurdum—are all types of argument that aim to prove the conclusion is necessarily true. This general type of argument is called *deduction*. A deductive argument is one in which the arguer is attempting to show that the premises necessitate the conclusion such that, when all the premises are true, then the conclusion absolutely must be true. A successful deduction is a valid argument and an unsuccessful deduction is an invalid argument.

Deductive argument can be considered the strongest kind of argument. When it is valid, it is a demonstration that one cannot accept the premises as true without also admitting that the conclusion is true. Were one to say of a valid deduction: "I agree that all the premises are true, but I deny the truth of the conclusion" then one is simply being illogical. One has either failed to understand the argument's validity or one is simply acting irrationally. That means that evaluation of deductive arguments is strictly dichotomous: they are either valid or invalid; they either prove the conclusion or fail to prove the conclusion. There is no other possibility.

The study of the various forms of deduction indicates that validity depends entirely on the form of the argument. Given that an argument has, say, a modus ponens form, it is valid, no matter what the subject of the argument is. Validity and invalidity are determined by logical form and not by subject matter. The study of categorical syllogisms in §§6–9 showed that not all forms of this type of argument are valid, only some forms. The other types of argument studied in §§10–15 are all valid forms when they truly fit the pattern designated by the name of the argument. So, there are many types of deduction, but only the valid forms show that the conclusion is necessary.

Inductive Argument

There are important conclusions that cannot be strictly proven by deductive argument. Some conclusions cannot be demonstrated as necessarily true. The best that can be done is to show that there are some good reasons to believe that these conclusions are probably true. Yet, this sort of argument can be quite useful in real life. If one has gathered evidence that points to a certain conclusion, but does not absolutely necessitate that conclusion, it still might be useful to present that evidence in a way that shows how it makes the conclusion probable. This way of arguing is called *induction*. An inductive argument is one in which the arguer aims to show that a conclusion follows from a set of premises with a certain degree of probability.

Inductive arguments are never valid, because the conclusion is never absolutely necessitated by the premises. That means that the evaluation of induction is very different from the evaluation of deduction. Deductive arguments either demonstrate their conclusions with necessity and are valid or fail to demonstrate their conclusions are necessary and are invalid. Inductive arguments show the degree of probability with which the conclusion follows from the premises. If the degree of probability of the conclusion being true is high, then the inductive argument is a *strong induction*. If the degree of probability of the conclusion being true is low, then the inductive argument is a *weak induction*. The stronger the induction, then, the more successful it is. Notice that the evaluation of induction is not strictly dichotomous as is the evaluation of deduction. Deductions are either valid or invalid. Inductions can be more or less strong: an arguer might present a very strong induction showing that the conclusion is very probably true or a somewhat less strong induction showing that the conclusion might be true or a weak induction showing that the conclusion can be true but probably is not. Unlike deductions, then, the evaluation of inductive arguments is a matter of degree.

This difference between deductions and inductions in their modes of evaluation indicates another difference between these two general types of argument. In deduction, the success of the argument depends entirely on its logical form, because validity is a matter of the form of the argument and not its subject matter. In induction, however, logical form is not the only determining factor for the success of the argument. The degree of probability of an inductive conclusion might differ among inductions of the same basic form depending on the nature of the subject matter. It might take more inductive evidence in the premises to show that a certain inductive conclusion is probable given its subject matter than it does for a different inductive conclusion of a different subject matter.

A common feature of inductive arguments is that they proceed from the particular in the premises to the general in the conclusion. Typically, inductions are composed of premises that are universal particularizations and conclude to a universal generalization. For example, one might inductively argue from the evidence of a number of particular cases that are alike to the probable truth of a general conclusion that all such cases are alike. While this structure is common to inductions, there are different ways in which this common structure is manifest in different forms of inductive argument.

Induction by Simple Enumeration

The most basic form of inductive argument is one in which the premises enumerate a series of individual cases as evidence in support of a general conclusion about the species of the subjects individuated in the premises. For this reason, an induction of this sort is called *induction by simple enumeration*. Such arguments often have many premises, because each premise is a statement about what is true of a particular case and many such cases may need to be cited to support a general conclusion. Consider, for example, the following inductive argument:

[1] After observing many cases of the hunting behavior of the peregrine falcon, Master Albert concluded that these birds confine their predatory attentions to water fowl the size of a wild duck or smaller. When he was traveling through the wetlands of Frisia, he observed at least a hundred cases of falcon predation and all were of small ducks. He also recorded over two hundred of his observations of these birds hunting water fowl in the lakes of Dacia and every case was of a wild duck or smaller bird. Master Albert has also recorded in his book the observations of fishermen and falconers from Pomerania and they confirmed his findings by their many hundreds of observations. On the basis of this extensive evidence, Master Albert concluded that the peregrine falcon never preys on water fowl larger than the common wild duck.

Notice that the argument described in example [1] is inductive. Master Albert draws a general conclusion from many hundreds of observed individual cases that all turned out the same way. His conclusion is not absolutely necessary, because there is nothing about the cases he and others have observed that show that peregrine falcons will absolutely never prey on water fowl larger than a wild duck. However, given that neither he nor others have ever observed in their extensive experience falcons preying on larger birds, it seems reasonably probable that this is always true of falcons. So, his argument is inductive and not deductive. Further, Master Albert's argument is an induction by simple enumeration as indicated by the following outline of his argument:

[2] 1st observation in Frisia: A hunting peregrine falcon preyed on nothing larger than a wild duck.

2nd observation in Frisia: A hunting peregrine falcon preyed on nothing larger than a wild duck.

3rd observation in Frisia: A hunting peregrine falcon preyed on nothing larger than a wild duck.

.
.
.

100th observation in Frisia: A hunting peregrine falcon preyed on nothing larger than a wild duck.

1st observation in Dacia: A hunting peregrine falcon preyed on nothing larger than a wild duck.

2nd observation in Dacia:	A hunting peregrine falcon preyed on nothing larger than a wild duck.
3rd observation in Dacia:	A hunting peregrine falcon preyed on nothing larger than a wild duck.

$$2^{nd} \text{ observation in Dacia:}$$

2nd observation in Dacia: A hunting peregrine falcon preyed on nothing larger than a wild duck.

3rd observation in Dacia: A hunting peregrine falcon preyed on nothing larger than a wild duck.

.
.

.

200th observation in Dacia: A hunting peregrine falcon preyed on nothing larger than a wild duck.

1st report from Pomerania: A hunting peregrine falcon preyed on nothing larger than a wild duck.

2nd report from Pomerania: A hunting peregrine falcon preyed on nothing larger than a wild duck.

3rd report from Pomerania: A hunting peregrine falcon preyed on nothing larger than a wild duck.

.
.

.

Therefore, all hunting peregrine falcons prey on nothing larger than a wild duck.

Notice that there are many premises in this argument—hundreds, in fact. Each premise is about a particular case of a certain kind. By enumerating hundreds of these cases and noting that each case is alike, Master Albert draws the general conclusion that all such cases are alike. The conclusion of the argument is a universal generalization. What makes Albert's argument a strong induction is that the number of particular cases cited in the premises is very large. He did not simply base his general conclusion on a few observed cases, but many such cases. Generally speaking, the more particular cases used in the premises, the stronger the induction by simple enumeration.

Induction by Method of Agreement

While induction by simple enumeration is the most basic form of induction, variations are possible. One variation is when the arguer cites a number of cases in the premises that are all different in various ways. Yet, these cases all have something in common. The arguer can inductively conclude that all such cases will have this common feature. This is called the *method of agreement*. Consider the following example:

[3]   Master Albert was discussing infectious diseases of horses with the emperor's stable master. He asked the stable master the circumstances under which diseases spread through the stables. The stable master told him that there were a variety of situations in which he and his staff observed a healthy horse getting ill. There were a large number of cases where an ill horse urinated near its stable-mate which then became ill. There were also some cases where an ill horse would bite a healthy horse

which then became ill. There were quite a few cases of healthy horses which came into contact with the blood of an ill horse becoming ill too. Finally, there were several observed cases of ill horses leaving a corrupted discharge on a post or rail or similar structure that then came into contact with a healthy horse which became ill. Master Albert took notes on every one of these cases and studied them carefully. While no two cases were alike, he did find a common element present in each and every case. No matter how the cases differed, Master Albert noted that in each case there was transfer of some kind of bodily fluid from an infected horse to a healthy horse: urine, blood, saliva, drainage from wounds, and so on. He then drew the conclusion that every case of infection resulted from contact with bodily fluids of an ill horse.

Notice that Master Albert's argument [3] has in its premises cases that differ from each other in various ways. By looking for the common element, the way the cases agree despite their differences, he is able to conclude to something that is true of all the cases. Consider the outline of Master Albert's argument:

[4]   Case 1:   A healthy horse was playfully bitten by an ill horse, thereby transferring a bodily fluid, and the previously healthy horse became ill.

           Case 2:   A healthy horse was spit upon by an ill horse, thereby transferring a bodily fluid, and the previously healthy horse became ill.

           Case 3:   A healthy horse came into contact with blood from an ill horse, thereby transferring a bodily fluid, and a previously healthy horse became ill.

           Case 4:   A healthy horse rubbed up against post upon which an ill horse left some discharge from a scratch on his flank, thereby transferring a bodily fluid, and a previously healthy horse became ill.

           Case 5:   A healthy horse was bitten in anger by ill horse, thereby transferring a bodily fluid, and a previously healthy horse became ill.

           Case 6:   A healthy horse lay down in hay in which ill horse had urinated, thereby transferring a bodily fluid, and a previously healthy horse became ill.

           .
           .
           .

Therefore, every healthy horse that became ill had transferred to it a bodily fluid from an ill horse.

Another variation on induction by simple enumeration is an argument in which the arguer seeks a crucial difference among cases that are otherwise alike in various ways. This type of induction is called the *method of difference*. Often this kind of induction is used in connection with an experiment to draw a general conclusion from individual cases of experimental evidence. Consider this example:

[5]   Master Robert suspected that the rate of vibration of a brass gong determined the pitch of the gong's sound. In order to test this, he hung a gong so that it freely swung from two points of suspension. Sounding the gong with a wooden mallet, he took note of the pitch of the sound and the rate of vibration. He did it again and got the same result. He then changed the way in which the brass gong was suspended such that it swung with less freedom. Sounding the gong with a wooden mallet, he again noted the pitch of the sound and the rate of vibration. He then drew the conclusion that the pitch of a resonating brass gong is always determined by the rate of the gong's vibration.

In order to determine the probability that his suspected relation between vibration and pitch is correct, Master Robert performs a simple experiment and draws an inductive conclusion from the results. Noting the collation of a difference of pitch and a difference of rate of vibration and comparing that to the lack of such difference in other cases, he draws his conclusion. This argument is inductive, for his conclusion is only probable. Yet, it is a useful argument for it shows that there is a probable relationship between one change and another. Master Robert's argument can be outlined like this:

[6]   Control case: A gong allowed to vibrate at a high rate produces a
                         certain pitch of sound.
        Test case: A gong restricted in its rate of vibration produces a
                         different pitch of sound.
        Therefore, rate of vibration always determines pitch of sound in a
        resonating body (gong).

Exercise 36

Student: _____

Consider the following arguments and, for each, determine whether it is deductive or inductive and identify the specific form of argument it is.

1.   If the perennial herb *Mentastri montani* is crushed and mixed with water and pulverized bone, it can be administered orally. If it is administered orally, then it relieves headache. Therefore, on the condition that the herb *Mentastri montani* is crushed and mixed with water and pulverized bone, it relieves headache.

☐ Deductive argument.   ☐ Inductive argument.

Form of deduction or induction: _____

2.   The medicinal properties of the perennial herb *Mentastri montani* have been confirmed by testing. The herb was orally administered to twelve patients complaining of indigestion. Four patients took the herb after eating and six patients took the herb while fasting. Two patients took the herb mixed in warm mulled wine. Despite the differences in these cases, the common effect was the relief of indigestion.

☐ Deductive argument.   ☐ Inductive argument.

Form of deduction or induction: _____

3.   The perennial herb *Mentastri montani* has analgesic effects only when boiled. Twenty-two patients suffering from headache were given equal doses of the herb. Half consumed the herb raw and half consumed the herb as a tea or a boiled mash. Only those who had consumed the herb after it had been cooked in some manner reported relief from headache. This confirmed the observation that the herb *Mentastri montani* must be boiled before its analgesic properties are effective.

☐ Deductive argument.   ☐ Inductive argument.

Form of deduction or induction: _____

4.   The perennial herb *Mentastri montani* is a known analgesic. Known analgesics are commonly prescribed for headache. That is why the perennial herb *Mentastri montani* is commonly prescribed for headache.

☐ Deductive argument.   ☐ Inductive argument.

Form of deduction or induction: _____

5.   The perennial herb *Mentastri montani* is either an analgesic or soporific and tests show that it has no soporific effects. Thus, it is an analgesic.

☐ Deductive argument.   ☐ Inductive argument.

Form of deduction or induction: _____

6.   The perennial herb *Mentastri montani* was administered to fifty-six patients. In each and every case there was some analgesic effect, such as relief of headache, joint pain, or some other pain. The conclusion can be drawn that administration of the herb *Mentastri montani* always has an analgesic effect.

☐ Deductive argument.   ☐ Inductive argument.

Form of deduction or induction: _____

7.   It has been reported that peasants who live in the alpine regions chew the raw leaves of the perennial herb *Mentastri montani* for relief of pain. This herb is also known to relieve pain when cooked and served as a mash or mixed in hot water. The analgesic effects of this herb have also been observed in cases where it was consumed as a tea made by steeping the leaves of the plant in boiling water for ten minutes or more. Finally, administration of the essence of this herb mixed with hot water or some other hot liquid was also observed to relieve pain. Thus, this perennial herb always exhibits analgesic effects when consumed in some manner.

☐ Deductive argument.   ☐ Inductive argument.

Form of deduction or induction: _____

Exercise 37

Student: _____

Read the following dialogue and answer the questions that follow.

The Master's Headache

Roger of Hereford was a professor of medicine at the University of Oxford. During Hilary term in the year 1244, he lectured on the classic *Canon of Medicine* of the Baghdad physician Avicenna. When his series of lectures was finished, his students had many questions.

Master Roger:	Scholar Walter, I believe that you have a question about one of the substances discussed by the learned Avicenna.
Scholar Walter:	Yes, Master, I do. It concerns the substance Avicenna calls *kaffee*.
Master Roger:	Avicenna does indeed mention *kaffee* as a sovereign remedy for headache.
Scholar Walter:	Yes, that is the substance I mean. Can you tell me, Master, what sort of substance this *kaffee* is? From where does it come? How must it be prepared for administration to the suffering patient? Why is it effective? Will it be as effective a remedy for other pains beyond headache? How does one recognize this . . .
Master Roger:	Whoa, young Walter! You have more questions than there are ancient authorities who discuss *kaffee*! I cannot address them all today, but maybe we can make some progress in learning of this most useful medicinal substance by discussing it in a more systematic manner.
Scholar Egbert:	[laughing] This is just like our Walter, Master. He has so many questions that they all try to come out of his mouth at once and get caught and confused in his throat!
Scholar William:	[laughing] In all of Oxford, there is no one as eager to learn as Walter!
Scholar Adam:	[laughing so hard he can hardly speak] Or as confused!
Master Roger:	Now scholars! Calm yourselves. Let us not laugh at Walter. After all, he does have some good questions. Besides, this *kaffee* is an interesting and somewhat mysterious substance.
Scholar Walter:	[embarrassed] I am sorry, Master. I just want to know more about *kaffee*.
Scholar William:	Yes, Master, dispel some of the mystery for us!

Master Roger:	Well, let us begin with a brief description of this substance and then proceed to some of its medicinal applications. According to the authorities I have consulted, *kaffee* is an Arabic word that refers to the fruit of a plant that is said to grow in the regions around Ethiopia and may have been cultivated for centuries by the Christian monks there. The fruit looks like a cherry when harvested, but takes a dark bean-like form when roasted in fire. What the plant itself looks like, I cannot tell you, as I have never seen it.
Scholar Egbert:	How is the *kaffee* bean prepared for medicinal use?
Master Roger:	It seems that it is boiled in water until its essence is released and then the *kaffee*-water is drunk. Avicenna, the most learned physician among the Arabs, recommends it as a cure for headache.
Scholar Walter:	Is it known how effective it is for the relief of headache?
Master Roger:	That is a good question. I have consulted some Arabic sources and I have found that one physician at Baghdad has tested the medicinal effect of the consumption of *kaffee*-water. He records that he administered it to one hundred twenty patients who were suffering from headache. In each and every case, some relief was reported by the patient. The physician concluded that consumption of *kaffee* will always bring at least some relief to the sufferer.
Scholar Egbert:	That is useful information. Is *kaffee* a remedy for any other illness?
Master Roger:	Avicenna only mentions headache, but other medical books report the use of *kaffee* as a remedy for other types of pain, such as pain in the joints, menstrual pain, and muscular pain.
Scholar Walter:	Can you tell us more about this, Master?
Master Roger:	When I visited the Arabic medical school at Salerno, I heard of a learned scholar who conducted a careful investigation of the analgesic effects of *kaffee*. He gathered evidence from many cases of *kaffee* administration to pain sufferers. No two cases were exactly alike, for he was studying many different types of pain in various parts of the body. Some patients were suffering from pain in the ankle joints and some in elbow and wrist joints. Other patients were afflicted by pain in the muscles of the back. A large number of the patients observed were suffering from headache, some having pain in the back of the head and some having pain around the periphery of the head. A number of the cases were women suffering from menstrual pain. Other patients had pain in wounds and contusions. No matter what type of pain was being suffered, administration of *kaffee* brought some relief and the scholar concluded that all types of pain are relieved by *kaffee*.
Scholar Walter:	This seems quite strong evidence that *kaffee* is a general analgesic.

Scholar Adam: Now, were we to come into possession of some of this *kaffee*, we would have a powerful general analgesic for use in treating all kinds of pain. Perhaps, Master, some of your Arabic friends at the school of medicine in Salerno might favor us with a supply.

Master Roger: That is just what I was thinking. In fact, I have a headache right now caused, no doubt, by you scholars and your many questions. I am sure that a nice hot cup of *kaffee* would do me some good!

1. The Baghdad physician Avicenna lived in the eleventh century. What is the modern English word for the substance to which he refers by the medieval Arabic word *kaffee*?

   _____

2. It is clear from the story that medieval Arabic physicians used *kaffee* medicinally. What type of medicine is *kaffee*?

   ☐   It is an anesthetic, because it relieves pain through loss of consciousness.

   ☐   It is an analgesic, because it relieves pain without loss of consciousness.

   ☐   It is a soporific, because it relieves pain by inducing sleep.

3. For what condition does Avicenna recommend *kaffee*?

   _____

4. At one point in the discussion, Scholar Walter asks how it is known that *kaffee* is an effective remedy for headache. Master Roger answers by giving an argument he read in some Arabic sources. What is the conclusion of this argument?

   Conclusion: _____

   _____

5. What type of proposition is this conclusion?

   ☐   It is a universal generalization.

   ☐   It is a universal particularization.

   ☐   It is an existential proposition.

6. What type of argument is Master Roger using to answer Scholar Walter's question?

☐ It is some form of deduction.

☐ It is an induction by simple enumeration.

☐ It is an induction by method of agreement.

☐ It is an induction by method of difference.

7. In the argument Master Roger is using to answer Scholar Walter's question, how many premises are there?

☐ There is only one premise.

☐ There are exactly two premises.

☐ There are one hundred twenty premises.

☐ There are no premises.

8. In the course of the discussion, the question arises whether *kaffee* is effective as a remedy for pain other than headache. When asked for more information on this, Master Roger gives an argument he heard about when visiting the Arabic medical school at Salerno. What is the conclusion of this argument?

Conclusion: _____

_____

9. What type of proposition is this conclusion?

☐ It is a universal generalization.

☐ It is a universal particularization.

☐ It is an existential proposition.

208

10. What type of argument is the argument given by the scholar at the Arabic medical school at Salerno?

☐   It is some form of deduction.

☐   It is an induction by simple enumeration.

☐   It is an induction by method of agreement.

☐   It is an induction by method of difference.

11. Scholar Walter calls *kaffee* a general analgesic. What does he mean by this?

_____

_____

_____

_____

Exercise 38

Student: _____

Read the following dialogue and answer the questions that follow.

The Stationer's Dilemma

Jacques Domier had been a stationer at Paris since he first arrived in the city in 1302. That was twenty years ago. In that time he had published the books of many university masters. Thus, he was not surprised when Andreas Scotus, a master of theology, came to see him one day with a request. Master Andreas wanted Jacques to publish his lectures of the past two years. The book was to be titled *Lectiones Parisiensiae* and Master Andreas hoped that enough copies could be produced so that each of his many students could purchase a personal copy. Jacques was happy to accept this job, because he had twelve scribes who were not working right now. Yet, Jacques was uncertain about the number of copies he should produce. Paper was expensive and Master Andreas could only promise that sixty of his students would purchase copies. Should Jacques limit his production to sixty or should he aim to produce more in the hopes of selling additional copies to others? Pondering this question, he decided to consult his chief scribe Pierre.

Stationer Jacques:	Have you heard the news, Pierre, that Master Andreas has asked us to publish his Paris lectures?
Scribe Pierre:	Yes, everybody in the workshop is talking about it. Will you take the job?
Stationer Jacques:	I told him I would, although it will be a costly one for us, unless we sell at least one hundred copies.
Scribe Pierre:	Yes, you are quite right; it must be at least one hundred copies. Is it possible that a collection of lectures like that can sell so many?
Stationer Jacques:	Well, Master Andreas himself can only guarantee that sixty of his students will purchase the volume and I expect that number is rather optimistic. You know how students are when they get some money from home—only a portion of it is devoted to books. The truth of the matter is that stationers do not see nearly as much student money as do tavern keepers.
Scribe Pierre:	I see the problem. We limit our production to sixty or we take a chance and produce one hundred copies. Either way, we are likely to lose money on the job.
Stationer Jacques:	That is precisely my dilemma.
Scribe Pierre:	We must be sure that we can sell at least one hundred and we cannot even be certain right now that we can sell sixty. Perhaps, if we compare

211

	the possible sales of this book with other similar books we have published over the past two years, we may be able to make a decision.
Stationer Jacques:	A very good idea, Pierre. Now, let me see . . . there was that book of questions on Aristotle's physics that we published last year for Master Burley: that sold nearly one hundred and fifty copies in the first nine months. Quite good for a work like that. The master was very pleased and we made some money too. But do you remember how that total number of books sold compares to the number of those purchased by Master Burley's own students?
Scribe Pierre:	[leaving the room] Wait just a moment, I think I have those records.
Stationer Jacques:	[calling out after him] Bring my ledger too.
Scribe Pierre:	[returning with a stack of ledgers] It is in here somewhere, let me see . . . yes, here it is! This is a list of people who ordered books containing university lectures last year and the previous year. You will see that I recorded which of these purchases were by students and which were by masters and others. Here, look at this: last year we published six academic books: the *Quaestiones super librum physicorum* for Master Burley that you just mentioned, the *De praedicamenta* of Master Adam, the *Quaestiones super librum logicorum* of Master Gilbert, and three of his commentaries on Aristotle's books: the *Topica*, the *Physica,* and the *Rhetorica.* Each of these sold at least forty-five copies beyond those sold to students.
Stationer Jacques:	Yes, I see. What about the previous year?
Scribe Pierre:	In the previous year, we published nine books. Five of these were the scripture commentaries of Master Thomas on the psalms, on the Gospels, on the book of Daniel, on the book of Genesis, and on the proverbs of Solomon. These, as usual, sold very well and each sold at least fifty copies beyond those sold to students. In addition, we published a new edition of Master Albert's *Metaphysica* that sold forty-one copies beyond those sold to students. Also, we published his *Quaestiones super librum ethicorum* and his *Commentarium super librum patrum.* Finally, we published the *Lectiones Oxoniensis* of Master Robert of Oxford. Each of these last three titles sold forty copies beyond those sold to students.
Stationer Jacques:	So, we have published fifteen university lectures over the last two years.
Scribe Pierre:	Yes, and in every case we were able to sell at least forty copies beyond those sold to students.
Stationer Jacques:	This indicates to me that it is probable that any book of university lectures sold to students will sell at least forty more copies.
Scribe Pierre:	Master Andreas has promised that sixty students will purchase his lectures. Past sales indicate that we will sell at least forty more copies. That brings us to the one hundred books we need to sell to make a profit.

It seems reasonable to produce one hundred copies of Master Andreas' book.

Stationer Jacques: Yes. Consider this, Pierre: Suppose Master Andreas guarantees student sales of sixty books, by purchasing himself the difference between actual sales to his students and the promised sixty. If he makes this guarantee, then we can make a profit on his book. I know he will make this guarantee—he wants his book published, after all. Therefore, we can make a profit on this job.

Scribe Pierre: You are a shrewd man, Jacques.

1.   Why is Stationer Jacques eager to publish Master Andreas' book?

_____

_____

_____

_____

2.   Stationer Jacques' dilemma is, in fact, a valid constructive dilemma. What is his dilemma?

Premise 1:   _____

_____

Premise 2:   _____

_____

Premise 3:   _____

_____

Conclusion: _____

_____

3.   What suggestion does Scribe Pierre make as a method of making a decision in the face of Stationer Jacques' dilemma?

_____

_____

_____

_____

4.   On the basis of evidence found in the ledgers of the stationery business, Scribe Pierre constructs an argument aimed at producing the information Stationer Jacques needs to make a decision about publishing Master Andreas' book. After Scribe Pierre states the premises, Stationer Jacques states the conclusion. What is the conclusion of the argument?

Conclusion: _____

_____

5.   What type of proposition is this conclusion?

☐   It is a universal generalization.

☐   It is a universal particularization.

☐   It is an existential proposition.

6.   The argument based on evidence contained in the ledgers of the stationery business is of what form?

☐   It is some form of deduction.

☐   It is an induction by simple enumeration.

☐   It is an induction by method of agreement.

☐   It is an induction by method of difference.

214

7. How many premises are there in the argument based on evidence drawn from the ledgers of the stationery business?

☐   There is only one premise.

☐   There are exactly two premises.

☐   There are fifteen premises.

8. Having determined that it is possible for him to sell some copies of Master Andreas' book beyond those sold to Master Andreas' students, Stationer Jacques presents an argument to show how he will guarantee a profit from the sales. What are the premises of his argument?

Premise 1: _____

_____

Premise 2: _____

_____

9. What is the conclusion of Stationer Jacques' argument?

Conclusion: _____

_____

10. What is the form of Stationer Jacques' argument?

☐   It a modus ponens argument.

☐   It is a modus tollens argument.

☐   It is some form of induction.

11. Is Stationer Jacques' argument valid?

☐   Yes, it is valid and he has come up with a viable way of making a profit from publishing Master Andreas' book.

☐   No, it is invalid and he is going to lose his shirt on the publication of Master Andreas' book.

§15 To Err Is Human

The discussion of the various forms of argument in §§6–14 is focused on successful argument. Successful deductions are valid arguments and successful inductions are strong inductions. Thus, the emphasis has so far been on distinguishing valid from invalid forms and on the conditions for strong inductions. Another way to approach the study of argument, however, is to focus on logical error—the various mistakes that are often made when constructing arguments. Such errors in reasoning are called *fallacies* and one who makes a logical error in argument is said to *commit a fallacy*. There are many different ways of making a mistake, perhaps an infinite number of ways. Yet, most people are creatures of habit and when they make a mistake they tend to make the same mistake over and over. While it may be impossible to catalogue all the possible fallacies that might be committed, it is possible to list and study the more common fallacies. Even a complete list of known common fallacies, however, would be very long and it would take a long time to study all these possible logical errors. Nonetheless, one can obtain a good idea of what fallacies are like and what some of the more commonly committed errors are by investigating a selection of fallacies of different types.

Formal Fallacies

In studying the various forms of deductive argument, some common fallacies have already been considered. For example, argument diagrams were used to display the logical form of categorical syllogisms and to test them for validity. Diagraming arguments reveals the invalid forms of categorical syllogism as well as the valid forms. Now, suppose that one reads in a book a categorical syllogism that was in fact invalid, but it seemed to the reader to be valid. The reader would be guilty of a fallacy, because he mistook an invalid form of argument to be a valid one. Consider the following example:

[1]   Some arts masters lecture on Aristotle's books.
       Some arts masters lecture on Boethius' books.
       Therefore, some arts masters do not lecture on Aristotle's books.

This is clearly a categorical syllogism, because it has two premises and in the two premises and the conclusion there are exactly three distinct terms. It may also seem to the reader to be a valid argument: given that it is true that some masters lecture on Aristotle and some on Boethius, it seems that it must be the case that some do not lecture on Aristotle—namely, those who lecture on Boethius. Yet, a diagram of this argument will reveal it to be invalid: it may be true that some lecture on Aristotle and some on Boethius, but that does not necessitate that some do not lecture on Aristotle, because those who lecture on Boethius may also lecture on Aristotle.

Whenever one mistakenly considers a deductive argument that is actually invalid to be valid, one commits a fallacy. This type of fallacy is called a *formal fallacy*. A formal fallacy is an error that concerns the form of the argument. Specifically, it is the error of mistaking an invalid form of deduction for a valid form of deduction.

Other examples of formal fallacies that have already been studied are those described in §12. Modus ponens and modus tollens are valid forms of deductive argument. There are invalid arguments, however, that are so similar in form to modus ponens and modus tollens that they are often mistaken for these valid forms. Consider this example:

[2]   If Master Isadore is lecturing on Roman Law this term, then he is lecturing on civil procedure.
Master Isadore is lecturing on civil procedure.
Therefore, Master Isadore is lecturing on Roman Law this term.

This appears to be similar to modus ponens which is a valid form of argument. Yet, it is not modus ponens and is, in fact, invalid. Given that Master Isadore is lecturing on civil procedure this term, it does not follow that he must be lecturing on Roman Law, even if when he does lecture on Roman Law he covers civil procedure. He might instead be covering civil procedure in the course of lecturing on Common Law, not Roman Law. Were one to think that this argument [2] is modus ponens or some other form of valid argument, one would commit the formal fallacy of *affirming the consequent*.
Consider another example:

[3]   If Master Isadore is lecturing on Roman Law this term, then he is lecturing on civil procedure.
Master Isadore is not lecturing on Roman Law this term.
Therefore, Master Isadore is not lecturing on civil procedure.

This appears to be similar to modus tollens which is a valid form of argument. Yet, it is not modus tollens and, in fact, invalid. Given that Master Isadore is not lecturing on Roman Law this term, it does not follow that he must not be lecturing on civil procedure, even if when he does lecture on Roman Law he covers civil procedure. He might instead be covering civil procedure in the course of lecturing on Common Law, not Roman Law. Were one to think that this argument [3] is modus tollens or some other form of valid argument, one would commit the formal fallacy of *denying the antecedent*.

Informal Fallacies

Formal fallacies are logical errors concerning the logical form of deductive arguments where one mistakenly believes that the argument is valid when it is actually invalid. The remedy for formal fallacies is to learn the valid forms of deduction. For categorical syllogisms, this can be done using argument diagrams. For other forms of deduction, this can be done by learning the common valid forms and clearly distinguishing these from other similar forms that may be invalid.
While formal fallacies are common, there are many other types of logical errors. Most types of fallacies are not simply mistaking invalid forms of deduction for valid ones. Sometimes one can commit a fallacy by misunderstanding the meaning of the terms and propositions of which the argument is composed. If one, for example, is

unclear about the meaning of a term in a categorical syllogism so that one makes a mistake about where that term is and is not repeated in the argument, one may be guilty of a *fallacy of ambiguity*. Ambiguity like this can make what is actually an invalid argument seem valid. Sometimes one can commit a fallacy by presenting a valid argument that is only trivial in content and does not really advance knowledge about the subject matter of the argument. In such a case one does not commit a formal fallacy, but one has still committed a kind of fallacy, for the argument does not achieve its purpose. Sometimes one can commit a fallacy by misunderstanding the scope of a universal generalization or a dichotomy and thereby produce an invalid or otherwise fallacious deductive or inductive argument. Sometimes one simply uses personal attack of an opponent in argument instead of valid or sound argument and then pretends that one has defeated one's opponent by argument when one really has not.

All of these different types of logical errors are called *informal fallacies*. They are so called because they are errors that are not simply formal fallacies that directly mistake invalid for valid forms. Rather, they are logical errors that concern the meaning of the parts of the argument or the relation of premises and conclusions, or the use of arguments. There are very many types of informal fallacies. Some of the more common types are considered in the sections that follow.

220

Exercise 39

Student: _____

For each of the following deductive arguments, indicate whether it is valid or invalid and identify the form of the argument.

1. Assuming that Master Thomas gives the St. Hilary Day lecture on the nature of the soul, we will hear criticism of Master Peckham's views. I have just heard that Master Thomas is indeed giving the St. Hilary Day lecture on the soul. We can expect to hear criticism of Master Peckham.

    ☐ This argument is valid. ☐ This argument is invalid.

    Form of argument: _____

2. If Master Thomas agrees with Master Peckham's account of the soul, then he believes that the soul is the form of the body. He does, of course, believe that the soul is the form of the body. Therefore, he must agree with Master Peckham.

    ☐ This argument is valid. ☐ This argument is invalid.

    Form of argument: _____

3. Given that Master Thomas studied with Master Albert, he is familiar with Aristotle's experiments and, if Master Thomas knows of Aristotle's experiments, then he knows of the chicken-egg experiment. Therefore, he knows of the chicken-egg experiment, given that he studied with Master Albert.

    ☐ This argument is valid. ☐ This argument is invalid.

    Form of argument: _____

4. If Aristotle is right, then St. Augustine is in error. As I believe that Aristotle is right, I must accept that St. Augustine is in error.

    ☐ This argument is valid. ☐ This argument is invalid.

    Form of argument: _____

221

5.   If all university masters agree with the chancellor about the appointment of Master Siger, then Master Siger is coming to Paris in the spring. But Master Siger is not coming to Paris. Thus, it cannot be that all the masters agree with the chancellor.

☐ This argument is valid.   ☐ This argument is invalid.

Form of argument: _____

6.   If all university masters agree with the chancellor about the appointment of Master Siger, then Master Siger is coming to Paris in the spring. But not all the masters agree with the chancellor. Therefore, Master Siger is not coming to Paris.

☐ This argument is valid.   ☐ This argument is invalid.

Form of argument: _____

7.   Assuming that Master Thomas is appointed regent master of theology, then Jordan of Saxony is leaving Paris. Master Thomas has been appointed regent master of theology and Jordan the Saxon is soon leaving Paris.

☐ This argument is valid.   ☐ This argument is invalid.

Form of argument: _____

8.   Assuming that Master Thomas is appointed regent master of theology, then Jordan of Saxony is leaving Paris. Jordan the Saxon is soon leaving Paris. Thus, Master Thomas has been appointed regent master of theology.

☐ This argument is valid.   ☐ This argument is invalid.

Form of argument: _____

9.   Master Alexander is preaching the university sermon, provided that Master Gilbert is called to Rome to advise the pope. Yet, Master Gilbert has not been called to Rome. Therefore, Master Alexander is not preaching the university sermon.

☐ This argument is valid.   ☐ This argument is invalid.

Form of argument: _____

§16 The Same, the Different, and the Like

The function of an argument is to establish the truth of its conclusion by providing reasons in support of the conclusion in its premises. In deductive arguments, this function is successfully performed by valid arguments. In inductive arguments, this function is successfully performed by strong inductions. Yet, one cannot determine the logical form and, therefore the success of an argument, unless the arguer has stated the parts of his argument in a clear and unambiguous way. This means that understanding and evaluating arguments depends on a clear determination of when two terms have the same meaning and when they differ in meaning.

Univocal Terms

The study of propositions in §3 shows that there is more than one way to express a term. Sometimes the differences between different expressions of the same term are not great and do not make it difficult to see that the same term is being expressed. Consider the following different expressions of the same term:

> [1]   Being a person who speaks Latin

> [2]   People who speak Latin

> [3]   Latin speakers

These term expressions [1]–[3] are similar enough that there is no difficulty in understanding that the same subject or predicate term is being referred to by each. Yet there are terms for which it might sometimes be difficult to determine that they have the same meaning. Consider these examples:

> [4]   Masters who teach the four basic mathematical arts

> [5]   Masters who teach the quadrivium

It may not be clear to some readers that these terms [4] and [5] refer to the same masters unless they know that "quadrivium" is another word for "the four basic mathematical arts." So, these two terms [4] and [5] mean the same, but it may take some effort or even some research to determine this.

Term expressions that have only one meaning in a given context are called *univocal terms*. In argument, it may be quite important to know when two term expressions are univocal. The logical form of a categorical syllogism, for example, depends on the pattern of term distribution. Determining the specific distribution of terms depends on knowing when term expressions are being used univocally and when they are not. When they are, then the same term is being repeated.

Equivocal Terms

A difference between terms is usually marked by the use of a different term expression. This, however, is not necessary. There are some words and phrases that have more than one meaning. Such words and phrases can be used to indicate different terms. Consider the following propositions:

[6]   Master Bernardo explained that any criminal action is illegal.

[7]   Master Bernardo explained that prosecution for theft is a criminal action.

The same term expression *criminal action* is used in both propositions [6] and [7], yet the meaning is very different in each use. In the first proposition [6], the term expression stands for the term *action that violates the criminal law*. In the second proposition [7], the same term expression stands for the quite different term *action before the court involving the criminal law*. In these two examples [6] and [7], the same phrase is used to indicate two very different terms. This is possible because the phrase *criminal action* can have more than one meaning.

Term expressions that have more than one meaning in a given context are called *equivocal terms*. Just as with univocal terms, it is important in argument to determine when terms are being used equivocally. Were one to come across the two uses of the term expression *criminal action* in a categorical syllogism, for example, it would be important to determine whether or not that the term expression is being used in two different ways and, therefore, two different terms are being indicated.

Analogical Terms

Usually we mark univocal terms by using the same term expression for each case where we intend the same meaning; although, as we have already seen, univocal terms using different term expressions are possible as well. Equivocal terms are usually marked by using different term expressions. Yet again, as we have already seen, equivocal terms using the same term expressions are possible as well. There are, however, times when we use the same term expression to mark different meanings that are not exactly equivocal. They may not even be exactly univocal either. Consider the following examples:

[8]   Master Albert's examination determined that the horse is healthy.

[9]   Master Albert's examination determined that the horse's coat is healthy.

[10]   Master Albert's examination determined that the horse's diet is healthy.

In each of these examples [8]–[10], the predicate term *healthy* is used. This term expression is not used univocally in each case, because saying that a horse is healthy is not quite the same as saying that its coat or diet is healthy. So, the meaning of the term expression *healthy* is different in each case. Yet, it is not exactly equivocal, because saying that a horse's coat or diet is healthy does have something to do with the horse being in good health. Terms that have different meanings but are not entirely equivocal are called *analogical terms*. An analogy is a comparison between two terms and two terms are analogous when they do not have the same meaning, but meanings that are related in some important way. In the examples [8]–[10], the meaning of the term *healthy* is different in each case, but related. The difference in meaning is why they are not univocal and the relatedness in meaning is why they are not equivocal. Notice that the use of the term in the first example [8] is the basic meaning. The horse is healthy in the sense that it is in good health. This is different from saying that the horse's coat is healthy as in the second example [9], but a healthy coat is a sign of being in good health. Again, saying that the horse is healthy is different from saying that the horse's diet is healthy as in the third example [10], but a healthy diet is productive or maintaining of good health. In these examples, then, the term expression *healthy* is being used analogically to indicate related but not identical predications.

Fallacy of Equivocation

In order for an argument to provide good reasons for the truth of its conclusion, it is crucially important that the terms and propositions composing the argument be clear and unambiguous. Were the arguer to fail to keep his terms clearly stable in meaning, it is possible that an ambiguity be introduced into the argument that would make it invalid or otherwise unsuccessful. The failure to keep the meaning of the terms in an argument constant is called the *fallacy of equivocation*. If an arguer attempts to draw a conclusion that depends on the univocity of two terms that are really equivocal, then the arguer *equivocates* on that term. This can cause an apparently valid argument to be actually invalid. Consider the following categorical syllogism:

[11] Observations are made with the eyes.
Master Odo's opinion of Aristotle's account of virtue is an observation.
Therefore, Master Odo's opinion of Aristotle's account of virtue is made with the eyes.

The conclusion of this argument is paradoxical, because it is known to be false but it seems to be proven by a valid argument from true premises. The first premise is true, because the eyes are the bodily sense organ by which things are observed. The second premise is true, because a person's expressed opinion about something is called his observation on that something. So, both premises are true. Further, a diagram analysis would seem to show this argument to be a valid categorical syllogism using the three terms *actions that are observations, being Master Odo's opinion of Aristotle's account of virtue*, and *actions performed by the eyes*. Yet, the conclusion is known to be false. How can this be? The answer to this question is that this is not a valid categorical syllogism as it appears to be due to the fallacy of equivocation. One who believes that this is a valid argument equivocates on the term *observation* by failing to understand that the word has one meaning in the first premise and a completely different meaning in the second premise. So, this argument is not composed of three terms, but four and no valid categorical syllogism is composed of more than three terms.

Consider the following argument:

[12]   If one accepts the reality of miracles, then one must logically accept as true the accounts of miracles in the Bible.
The atheist is one who accepts the reality of miracles, such as the miracles of modern medicine.
Therefore, the atheist is one who must logically accept as true the accounts of miracles in the Bible.

The conclusion of this argument [12] is a paradox, for it states that anyone, including an atheist, must admit the truth of biblical miracles. This is, of course, paradoxical because atheists are people who deny the existence of God and biblical miracles are divine actions. Yet, the argument seems to be a modus ponens argument which is a valid form of argument. The argument also seems to be sound, for both premises seem to be true. Yet, the conclusion is known to be false. How can this be? Again, the fallacy of equivocation has been committed. The arguer has equivocated on the term *miracles*. In the first premise the term refers to divine actions outside the order of nature. In the second premise the term refers to wonderful things that can be done by human beings according to the order of nature. So, the term expression *miracles* is being used to indicate two distinct terms. Thus, the second premise is not actually the antecedent of the first conditional premise, as it seems to be. This means that the argument does not actually have a modus ponens form and is, in fact, invalid.

Fallacy of False Analogy

There are situations in which one comes to learn something important about a previously unknown subject by comparing it to an already well-known subject and noting the similarities. The similarities will be expressed by analogous terms that are neither univocal nor equivocal. They do not refer to exactly the same thing in each subject, but they do not refer to something entirely different either, which is why a comparison is possible. If such a comparison is carefully made in the premises of an argument, then a conclusion about the lesser-known subject can be reliably drawn on the basis of what is known to be true of the better-known subject. Consider the following argument:

[13]   A spherical toy ball casts a curved shadow onto a blank wall in all orientations.
The earth casts a curved shadow onto the face of the moon in all orientations.
Therefore, the earth is spherical.

In this argument [13], a comparison is made between a well-known subject, the toy ball, and a lesser-known subject, the earth, about which the arguer is trying to know better. On the basis of some known similarity of the shadow cast by the ball and the earth in

226

analogous circumstances, what is known to be true of the shape of the ball is attributed to the earth. This way of arguing is called *argument by analogy* because a conclusion is drawn about something on the basis of its analogy to another thing. The two cases are not exactly alike, but they are similar enough and similar in the right ways to reasonably support the conclusion. When the analogous predicate shared by the two subjects being compared in an argument by analogy is sufficiently similar, then the comparison is a *true analogy*. Argument [13] is a true analogy.

It is possible, however, that an arguer may attempt an argument by analogy on the basis of a shared predicate that is not truly analogous, because it is not similar enough or not similar in the relevant way. In such a case, the comparison may be a *false analogy* and the arguer may be guilty of the *fallacy of false analogy*. Consider the following argument:

[14]   Government taxes are a legal appropriation of a person's property.
        Theft is an appropriation of a person's property.
        Therefore, theft is legal.

This argument [14] clearly has a paradoxical conclusion, for theft is not legal. Yet, there does seem to be something analogous about the shared predicate in the two premises. The argument, however, is a false analogy because the two cases of property appropriation are different in a way that is relevant to the comparison being made: one is legal and the other is not. One who draws a conclusion on the basis of such a poor comparison commits the fallacy of false analogy.

228

Exercise 40

Student: _____

For each of the following fallacious arguments, write out the conclusion, identify the type of fallacy, and explain where in the argument the fallacy occurs.

1.   The chancellor announced that Master Matthew died today because his heart has become enlarged. This was expected, because the generous Master Matthew was a big-hearted man.

Conclusion: _____

_____

Name of fallacy: _____

Explanation of fallacy: _____

_____

_____

2.   Master Giles told the story of a woman who was distraught because her son left home on his twelfth birthday. She was sure that he would never return home alive, because her son is like the eaglet that falls from the nest before it is fully grown and dies.

Conclusion: _____

_____

Name of fallacy: _____

Explanation of fallacy: _____

_____

_____

3. In his lecture, Master Albert quoted Aristotle's *History of Animals* concerning bees that produce honey in combs within the hive. In his lecture, Master Siger quoted Aristotle's *History of Athens* concerning Solon the lawgiver who kept a comb near his bed to use on his beard. It is clear that Aristotle believed that Solon used honey on his beard.

    Conclusion: _____

    _____

    Name of fallacy: _____

    Explanation of fallacy: _____

    _____

    _____

4. Master Siger accused Scholar John of a fallacy when he attempted to argue that a geometrical ellipse must have three angles because it is a closed figure as is the triangle which has three angles.

    Conclusion: _____

    _____

    Name of fallacy: _____

    Explanation of fallacy: _____

    _____

    _____

Exercise 41

Student: _____

Read the following dialogue and answer the questions that follow.

A Matter of Great Gravity

Master Albert of Lauingen, a professor of theology at the University of Paris, had a reputation for great learning. He was especially noted for his knowledge of the works of Aristotle, among the most important authorities in the sciences. One morning in the year 1247, a student by the name of Felix, a young man from Raetia, came to see Master Albert with some questions about Aristotle's physics. The master was not looking forward to this visit, for Felix was among the least logical of his students. Nonetheless, when Felix arrived the master politely invited him to enter his study.

Scholar Felix: Master, I have been reading the reports of Scholar Thomas on your lectures on Aristotle's physics. I have found them most helpful in clarifying some of the difficult and confusing things that Aristotle says about motion and change.

Master Albert: Very good. Scholar Thomas is among the best of my students and he understands Aristotle very well. You can be sure that his reports on my lectures are not only accurate, but add insightful comments that will aid your understanding.

Scholar Felix: Yet, I have some questions about some confusing teachings of Aristotle.

Master Albert: Perhaps we can consider your questions one by one.

Scholar Felix: Well, one question that I have concerns the universal law of gravity.

Master Albert: Yes, a fundamental law of physics.

Scholar Felix: You say in your lectures that Aristotle held that the law of gravity could be expressed in a precise mathematical formula and this is why we call it a law.

Master Albert: You are right. It is not the only reason we call it a law, but generally speaking what you say is correct.

Scholar Felix: If the law of gravity is part of mathematics, then it can be expressed in a precise mathematical formula. You have just agreed that this law can be expressed mathematically in a precise formula. It follows that the law of gravity is part of mathematics.

Master Albert: Think carefully, young scholar, and you will find an error in your reasoning.

Scholar Felix: I find no error in my argument, Master. I have proved Aristotle incorrect: the law of gravity is part of mathematics, not part of physics as Aristotle claims.

Master Albert: Be careful not to dismiss the ancient authorities too quickly, especially when your own argument is fallacious.

Scholar Felix: But I have other arguments that cast doubt on Aristotle claims about the law of gravity.

Master Albert: Let us then subject these arguments to the test of reason.

Scholar Felix: Aristotle also says that the law of gravity is a universal law to which all things are subject.

Master Albert: This is true.

Scholar Felix: And Aristotle says in his book on the constitutions of city-states that any law can be repealed by legislative authority.

Master Albert: Aristotle does say this, but what does this have to do with the law of gravity?

Scholar Felix: Well, the law of gravity is, as we just said, a law. Therefore, the law of gravity can be repealed by legislative authority.

Master Albert: Young man, you have committed another fallacy. Before we continue our discussion of physics, we must review some basic logic. Aristotle points out that logic is the art of proper discourse on any subject. So, before we can have an intelligible discussion on the laws of physics, we must make you a more critical thinker.

Scholar Felix: But Master, I am a good critical thinker!

Master Albert: Calm yourself, young scholar. Do you remember the lectures I gave last year on Aristotle's book on syllogisms?

Scholar Felix: Yes, Master.

Master Albert: You will recall, then, that in my introductory lecture I discussed the nature of contradictions. What did I say about the logical form of a contradiction?

Scholar Felix: You said that a contradiction is the conjunction of a proposition and its negation.

Master Albert: Good, for that is correct. Now, keep this in mind as you consider the following argument.

Scholar Felix: Very well, Master.

Master Albert: You claim that you, Scholar Felix, are a good critical thinker. Let us agree, for the moment, that you are correct.

Scholar Felix: I am correct.

Master Albert: Consider this proposition: if Scholar Felix is a good critical thinker, then Scholar Felix does not commit fallacies. Do you agree that this is true?

Scholar Felix: Of course it is true. No one who commits fallacies is a good critical thinker, but I have not . . .

Master Albert: Attend to the argument, young man. We can add to these two propositions another that we know to be true: Scholar Felix does commit fallacies. We know that this is true on the basis of the two fallacies you committed in your arguments about the law of gravity.

Scholar Felix: So what is the point, Master?

Master Albert: The point, young scholar, is that these propositions led us into contradiction.

Scholar Felix: Oh! I see that they do. Does this mean, Master, that I am wrong to claim that I am a good critical thinker?

Master Albert: I think that you can answer this question for yourself. More important than this, however, is that you can become a good critical thinker. Come to see me tomorrow and we will begin to review the basic laws of logic. The road to skill in thinking critically and logically is paved with hours of practice.

Scholar Felix: Yes, Master. Thank you.

1.   According to the story, why has Scholar Felix come to see Master Albert?

_____

_____

_____

_____

2.   What fundamental law of nature is discussed by Master Albert and Scholar Felix?

☐   The Second Law of Thermodynamics

☐   The Law of Contradiction

☐   The Law of Gravity

☐   The Law of Excluded Middle

3. According to Scholar Felix, Aristotle holds that the reason why the law of gravity is a law is that it can be expressed by a mathematical formula. Master Albert agrees, but notes that this is not the only reason why Aristotle holds that the law of gravity is a law. What is the point that Master Albert is making here?

   ☐ Master Albert's point is that, while it is true that mathematical formulae have a precision and universality of their own, physical laws possess their law-like nature in virtue of the fact that they are empirically true of everything in the physical universe. This empirical fact about physical things is not simply a matter of mathematics.

   ☐ Master Albert's point is that, while contradiction invalidates mathematical formulae, it is an empirical fact that contradiction can exist in the physical universe.

   ☐ Master Albert's point is that, while the law of gravity can be expressed mathematically, it is too important a matter to be left to mathematicians alone. Physicists retain the natural right to legislate concerning the laws of the physical universe.

4. Scholar Felix presents an argument concerning the law of gravity and the science to which it belongs. What is his argument?

   Premise 1: _____

   _____

   Premise 2: _____

   _____

   Conclusion: _____

   _____

5. One of the premises of Scholar Felix's argument concerning the science to which the law of gravity belongs is a complex proposition. What form of complex proposition is this premise?

   ☐ It is a conjunctive proposition.

   ☐ It is a disjunctive proposition.

   ☐ It is a conditional proposition.

   ☐ It is a categorical proposition.

6.   Master Albert points out that Scholar Felix's argument is fallacious. Is the master correct?

☐   Yes, the argument equivocates on the term "mathematical formula."

☐   Yes, the argument affirms the consequent.

☐   Yes, the argument contains a false analogy between physical objects and mathematical objects.

☐   No, the argument is a valid modus ponens argument.

☐   No, the argument is a valid categorical syllogism.

7.   Scholar Felix presents a second argument in an attempt to cast doubt on Aristotle's claims about the law of gravity. What is this second argument?

Premise 1:   _____

_____

Premise 2:   _____

_____

Conclusion: _____

_____

8.   What is the apparent form of Scholar Felix's second argument against Aristotle?

☐   Scholar Felix is attempting to refute Aristotle with a categorical syllogism.

☐   Scholar Felix is attempting to refute Aristotle with a disjunctive syllogism.

☐   Scholar Felix is attempting to refute Aristotle with a hypothetical syllogism.

☐   Scholar Felix is attempting to refute Aristotle with a reductio ad absurdum.

9.   Again, Master Albert finds Scholar Felix's reasoning fallacious. What is the name of the fallacy the master believes that Scholar Felix has committed in his second argument against Aristotle?

Fallacy name: _____

10.   Precisely where in Scholar Felix's second argument does Master Albert believe the
        fallacy to have been committed?

        _____

        _____

        _____

11.   If Master Albert is attempting to show that Scholar Felix's claim about his critical
        thinking skills is mistaken, then why does he assume that this claim is true?

        _____

        _____

        _____

12.   What is the argument that Master Albert offers in refutation of Scholar Felix's claim
        about his critical thinking skills?

        Premise 1:   _____

        _____

        Premise 2:   _____

        _____

        Premise 3:   _____

        _____

        Conclusion: _____

        _____

13.   At one point in his argument, Master Albert points out that the premises have led
        to a contradiction. What precisely is the contradiction?

        _____

        _____

        _____

§17 In Common and In Particular

In §3, a distinction was made between two types of universal proposition. Some universal propositions have a subject term that refers to a group of people or things or a species. These are called *universal generalizations*. Other universal propositions have a subject term that refers to a particular individual person or a specific individual object. These are called *universal particularizations*. Both types of universal proposition can be used in any form of argument. Universal generalizations, however, have a crucial function in inductions and a special application in certain uses of deduction.

Inductive Generalizations

In §14, inductive argument was described as a form of probabilistic argument that aims at establishing a universal generalization as its conclusion. In one way or another, inductions proceed from particular cases of evidence in the premises to the probable truth of a general conclusion. Thus, induction can be described as a kind of argument that proceeds from the particular to the general. Consider a typical induction by simple enumeration:

[1]   In the first nesting season that observations were made of the Egyptian goose, many hundred cases of nesting behavior were observed. In the first observed case, the female searched for a body of water over which she could build her nest and did not build a nest until she found a sufficiently large body of water under overhanging branches or shrubbery. This was also the case with the second observed case of nesting behavior. So it also was with the third, the fourth, the fifth, and all the hundreds of cases observed during that season.

The second nesting season that observations were made was a drought year and little standing water was to be found throughout the range of the Egyptian goose. Nonetheless, the hundred or so observations made during that season confirmed the pattern evident from the many cases observed during the first season: the female never built a nest over dry land, but would only build a nest over water, even if she had to search for miles to find sufficient water.

The third season of observation was during a wet year and, again, hundreds of cases of nesting behavior were observed. As in the previous seasons, in every case the female only built a nest over water and never over dry land.

From this substantial body of observed evidence, made up of many hundreds of individual cases of nesting behavior, the following conclusion was drawn: The female Egyptian goose will always build her nest over water and never over dry land.

Notice that this argument [1] has many hundreds of premises—each premise being a particular observed case of Egyptian goose nesting behavior. So, each premise is a universal particular proposition. From these many particular premises a general conclusion is drawn: the universal generalization that *every female Egyptian goose will always build her nest over water*. Inductive arguments always aim to establish the probability of the truth of an inductive generalization in the conclusion on the basis of inductive particularizations in the premises. This is evident in the most basic form of induction, arguments by simple enumeration, such as example [1]. It is also the case with inductions by method of agreement and method of difference.

Law-Like Generalizations

Another important use of universal generalizations in argument is where an arguer attempts to apply a general rule or law to a particular case and draw some conclusion. Consider the following example:

> [2]   Any organism that prepares its own food by photosynthesis contains the complex chemical substance chlorophyll.
> The pumpkin vine in my garden is an organism that photosynthesizes.
> Therefore, the pumpkin vine in my garden contains chlorophyll.

Notice that in the categorical syllogism [2], the first premise is a universal generalization that states a general law—in this case a law of biology. The second premise is a universal particularization that refers to a particular subject and predicates of it the subject of the general law stated in the first premise. On the basis of this general law and its application to the particular case, then, a conclusion about the particular case is drawn. This is a common use of universal generalizations in deductive arguments. One of the premises states a general law or rule and the other premise applies it to a particular case allowing some conclusion about the particular case to be drawn. If the deduction is valid and the particular case is the sort of case to which the general law applies, then the rule-application results in reliable knowledge.

Rules or laws, whether they are scientific laws, as in the example [2], or game rules, or moral rules, or civil laws, are always stated as universal generalizations. This is because they are intended to apply to many cases. The actual application of a rule or law is made by an argument that has as one of its premises the universal generalization stating the rule or law.

Fallacy of Hasty Generalization

An inductive argument like example [1] will be successful when it is a strong induction. That means that the inductive generalization in the conclusion must be supported by a sufficient number of particular cases cited in the premises. Argument [1] is a strong induction, for its general conclusion is supported by many hundreds of particular premises. Had the arguer drawn his inductive generalization from only a very few observed cases of Egyptian goose nesting behavior, then the induction would be much weaker and the general conclusion would not have been shown to be probably true.

This example illustrates a requirement for strong inductions: an inductive generalization will only be strongly supported by inductive premises if there are a sufficient number of cases of the right kind cited in the premises. If there are too few cases in the premises or if they are not the right kind of cases, then the inductive conclusion is not strongly supported and the induction is weak. To hold that a general conclusion is adequately supported by a weak induction is to commit the *fallacy of hasty generalization*. This logical error is so called because the arguer too hastily jumps to the general conclusion without waiting until he has sufficient evidence to strongly support it. Consider this example of inductive argument:

[3]   One of Master Albert's students, Scholar Jordan, obtained a bag of fig seeds that a traveler brought from Africa. He planted two of them and kept them in kitchen of the convent in Cologne. When neither of the seeds germinated, he drew the conclusion that no seed of the African fig will ever germinate in Germany.

Clearly, Scholar Jordan's argument [3] is an induction, for he attempts to draw a general conclusion on the basis of particular cases. Yet, it is a weak induction and fails to show that the inductive generalization in the conclusion is likely to be true. Two attempts to germinate seeds of a particular species in a foreign climate is insufficient to support the general claim that such seeds will never germinate in that climate. It may, of course, turn out to be true, but the evidence given in Scholar Jordan's argument does not show that it is probable because he commits the fallacy of hasty generalization. In order to construct a strong inductive argument, Scholar Jordan would have to make more trials and draw his conclusion from more cases.

Often cases of prejudice take the form of hasty generalization. Consider the following induction:

[4]   Sir Morgan was traveling from England to Rome. Upon his arrival in Rome, he greeted the first two Romans he encountered. Both of these men acted rudely toward Sir Morgan showing no respect for his rank and not even any common courtesy. On the basis of these two cases, Sir Morgan concluded that all Romans are rude.

Sir Morgan's argument [4] is a hasty generalization, for he draws a general conclusion about the behavior of thousands of Romans on the basis of just two cases. This is clearly insufficient to support his inductive generalization and his induction is very weak and, therefore, prejudicial. The fallacy of hasty generalization, then, is an error committed in inductive arguments when too few cases are given in support of an inductive conclusion. This is fallacious because such a procedure makes the induction too weak to be a reliable demonstration of the probability of the conclusion being true.

Fallacy of Sweeping Generalization

When applying a general rule or law to a particular case in argument, it is important to be sure that the application procedure is properly carried out. This involves two stages: first, the rule or law must be properly understood so that the arguer knows the proper kind of particular case to which the rule or law is intended to apply; second, the particular case must be carefully selected so that it is clear that it falls under the rule or law. Failure to do either of these things may result in the *fallacy of sweeping generalization*. This is the logical error of misapplying a rule or law to the wrong kind of particular case. Consider the following argument:

[5]   The creation of any artifact requires some pre-existing material from
            which the artifact will be fashioned.
        The created world is God's artifact.
        Therefore, the created world requires some pre-existing material from
            which God fashions the world.

The first premise of this argument [5] is a general rule about what is required for the creation of an artifact. The second premise applies this rule to God's creation of the world. On the basis of this application, a conclusion is drawn about the particular case cited in the second premise. On the face of it, this might seem to be a sound argument, but on closer inspection it is clear that this argument fails to distinguish between the way human beings create things and the way God creates things. In fact, the crucial difference here is directly relevant to understanding the meaning of the general rule stated in the first premise. God creates from nothing, but humans create from natural materials. Thus, the law of artifacts stated in the first premise concerns human artifacts and it has been misapplied to God's creation of the world. The arguer here has committed the fallacy of sweeping generalization, because he allows his general law to sweep in too many cases, including cases to which the rule was never meant to apply.

Exercise 42

Student: _____

For each of the following fallacious arguments, indicate whether it is deductive or inductive and identify the form of fallacy.

1.   Master Robert told of the case of a Bolognese surgeon who visited a Turkish military hospital in Dalmatia. Examining every patient and finding each to be very weak from wounds, he drew the general conclusion that all Turks are weak.

     ☐ This is a deductive argument.   ☐ This is an inductive argument.

     Fallacy name: _____

2.   Master Robert told of the case of a Bolognese surgeon who, knowing that both lacerations and bed sores were open wounds, concluded that the time taken to heal a laceration is the same as the time taken to heal a bed sore.

     ☐ This is a deductive argument.   ☐ This is an inductive argument.

     Fallacy name: _____

3.   Master Robert told of the case of a Bolognese surgeon who, knowing that any application of a stanching agent to a wound will retard blood flow to some degree, recommended his wounded patient eat the leaves of a certain plant known for its stanching effect. The surgeon was surprised when the wound continued to bleed despite the patient's ingestion of the leaves.

     ☐ This is a deductive argument.   ☐ This is an inductive argument.

     Fallacy name: _____

4.   Master Robert told of the case of a Bolognese surgeon who concluded that every amputation of a limb results in immediate death of the patient on the basis of the only two surgical amputations he had performed.

     ☐ This is a deductive argument.   ☐ This is an inductive argument.

     Fallacy name: _____

5.　Master Robert told of the case of a Bolognese surgeon who believed that every case of ingestion of hemlock extract must lead to immediate death on the evidence of the famous story of Socrates who died by hemlock poisoning.

☐ This is a deductive argument.　　☐ This is an inductive argument.

Fallacy name: _____

6.　Master Robert told of the case of a Bolognese surgeon who, upon learning that Parthians tend to be at least six feet tall, concluded that Parthian children are as tall as their parents.

☐ This is a deductive argument.　　☐ This is an inductive argument.

Fallacy name: _____

7.　Master Robert told of the case of a Bolognese surgeon who observed that one of his patients recovered from his wound after a discharge of discolored fluid from the wound site. The surgeon concluded that discharge of discolored fluid from the wound site is always a sign of immanent recovery.

☐ This is a deductive argument.　　☐ This is an inductive argument.

Fallacy name: _____

8.　Master Robert told of the case of a Bolognese surgeon who predicted the immanent recovery of his patient who had a large and deep laceration on his neck on analogy of the recovery of his patient who had a small laceration on his forearm.

☐ This is a deductive argument.　　☐ This is an inductive argument.

Fallacy name: _____

§18 Waiting for an Answer

Successful deductions are valid arguments. This means that when all the premises of such an argument are true, then the conclusion absolutely must be true. Generally speaking, valid arguments are a useful way to advance knowledge. Beginning with what is already known to be true and deriving a conclusion by means of a valid argument brings the arguer to new knowledge. The definition of validity, however, does not demand that all valid arguments advance knowledge. It is possible to construct a valid argument that does not articulate some new knowledge in the conclusion. Consider the following example:

[1]   Thunder is a rumbling sound in the atmosphere resulting from a discharge of lightning from atmospheric cloud formations.
        Therefore, the rumbling sound in the atmosphere called "thunder" is the result of a lightning discharge from clouds in the atmosphere.

Notice that in argument [1] the conclusion is actually the very same proposition as the premise from which it is drawn. The only difference between them is that they are stated in slightly different words. So, essentially the arguer is arguing that, because thunder is caused by lightning, it, therefore, is caused by lightning. Now, is this a valid argument? The answer is "yes" because the argument fits the definition of logical validity: an argument is valid when all the premises are true. Then the conclusion absolutely must be true. That is the case here. Assume that the premise *thunder is a rumbling sound in the atmosphere resulting from a discharge of lightning from clouds* is true. If this is true, then the conclusion, which says the very same thing, must be true. The conclusion of [1] could never be false when the premise of [1] is true. So, this argument is a valid argument.

Careful consideration of the nature of deductive arguments and the definition of argument validity reveals that it is valid to derive any proposition from itself. In fact, the safest possible deductive inference one can perform is to conclude that a proposition P is true on the basis that the proposition P is true, where P is any proposition whatsoever. Such an inference can never be invalid.

Begging the Question

While it certainly is true that deductively deriving a proposition from itself is technically valid, there still seems to be something wrong with an argument that does this. This is because there is a natural expectation that argument is not simply a process of giving reasons for a belief. As already mentioned, arguments are intended to advance knowledge. The whole point of constructing arguments is to be able to use them in ordinary life to show what is true on the assumption that it is not already known. In scientific research, the point of arguments is to reveal an explanation of what we know truly exists—that is, to provide a deeper insight and understanding into what we know by observation or some other means. One might already know that mammals reproduce sexually, but one wants to understand this better and to learn why mammals reproduce in this way and not in some other way. The way arguments are used, both in ordinary life as well as in scientific research, involves certain expectations about the function of arguments. A valid argument that simply derives a proposition from itself violates this expectation. One cannot learn something new from such an argument. Such arguments may be valid, but they are not useful for the purposes of ordinary life and scientific investigation.

When one encounters an argument in which the conclusion is simply the premise or one of the premises, one is likely to discard such an argument as useless. To produce such an argument as fulfilling the proper function of argument is to commit the *fallacy of begging the question*. When one begs the question one simply begins with a proposition as one of the premises and ends up in the conclusion with the very same proposition. One is, in a sense, simply going around in a circle—a vicious circle. Thus, this error is sometimes called the *fallacy of circular reasoning*. Sometimes it is obvious when this fallacy is committed, as in example [1]. Yet, it is not always immediately clear that an argument begs the question and one may have to analyze the argument carefully to spot the fallacy. Consider the following argument:

[2]   God exists because the Bible says so and the Bible is absolutely reliable
            because God inspired it.

This argument [2] for God's existence begs the question, but it may take some analysis to see this. In fact, the argument is a complex argument composed of two individual categorical syllogisms:

[3]   Whatever the Bible says is inspired by God who exists.
            Anything inspired by God who exists is true.
            Whatever the Bible says is true.

            Whatever the Bible says is true.
            That God exists is what the Bible says.
            Therefore, that God exists is true.

A diagram analysis of this complex argument [3] shows it to be valid, because each of the two categorical syllogisms of which it is composed is valid. The argument, however, clearly begs the question, because the final conclusion *that God exists is true* is already part of the premises. So, this argument comes down to concluding to the existence of God on the assumption that God exists, which is why God is able to guarantee the truth of the Bible.

An argument can be considered an answer to the question *is the conclusion true?* If one can give true reasons that necessitate the truth of the conclusion—that is, if one can prove the conclusion with a valid and sound argument—then the question is answered. If one attempts to answer the question by an argument that begs the question, then one has not effectively answered the question or simply answered it in a trivial and uninformative way. Therefore, the answer to the question *is the conclusion true?* still goes begging to be answered. This is why medieval university masters called this logical error "begging the question."

Exercise 43

Student: _____

Read the following dialogue and answer the questions that follow.

On the Size of Infinity

Because St. Stephen's Day always occurs in late December, it is usually a cold and raining day in Padua. So it was on that day in the year 1402 when Master Paolo of Lombardy, a professor of mathematics at the university, arrived home. His secretary met him at the front door with news of a visitor.

Secretary Guido:	Master, a Greek gentleman arrived one hour ago and is waiting for you in your study. Will you see him now?
Master Paolo:	Yes, I will see him immediately. And please ask Angelina to bring us some warm mulled wine. It is a cold day.
Secretary Guido:	Yes, Master.
Master Paolo:	[entering his study] Demetrios, my old friend! I thought that you were still at Constantinople. When did you arrive in Italy?
Demetrios of Nicaea:	My ship arrived in Venice two days ago. As soon as I could, I hired a donkey and made the trip here to Padua to see you. I have news of your old student Tito of Dalmatia.
Master Paolo:	Ah, yes, Tito. How is the boy? I have not seen him since he went to Constantinople to teach in the emperor's school two years ago. I have only received a few letters from him and none since last summer. Is he well? Does he still like his new job?
Demetrios of Nicaea:	As far as I know, he is in good health. Yet, I fear he has lost his position at the imperial school.
Master Paolo:	Lost his position! But how can that be? He is so bright and he was doing so well.
Demetrios of Nicaea:	It seems that he has lost the emperor's favor.
Master Paolo:	Please, Demetrios, be seated and tell me the story. Look, here comes the wine. Refresh yourself and tell me everything.
Demetrios of Nicaea:	Well it all began a year ago. As you know, the Emperor Michael is a fine mathematician and loves to discuss mathematical problems when he gets the time. About a year ago, he began to invite Tito to visit him often in the palace for intellectual discussions. They became interested in

245

problems of infinity and their discussions soon focused on this topic. The emperor claimed that there must exist infinities of different sizes. This seemed impossible to Tito and he denied this. For months they investigated and argued this question with great enthusiasm. Both the emperor and Tito agreed that, if all infinities are of the same size, then one infinite quantity cannot be contained within another infinite quantity. The emperor used this agreed upon premise to argue that all infinities are not of the same size. His argument went like this: Let us assume that all infinities are of the same size. Consider an infinite quantity such as time. Now, it is obvious that time as a whole is infinite, because every moment has a preceding moment and a succeeding moment. Take any one of these moments of time and divide it in half. Then one has two moments. Now, take either of these two moments and divide it in half and we have two smaller moments. Since any moment of time can be divided in half, it is obvious that this process of dividing moments can go on infinitely. But these infinitely divided moments of time are contained within the infinite extension of time. It follows from this that one infinite quantity of time can be contained within another infinite quantity of time. Given our agreed premise that, if all infinities are of the same size, then one infinite quantity cannot be contained within another infinite quantity, it follows that all infinities are not of the same size. But this contradicts the premise that all infinities are of the same size. Therefore, not all infinities are of the same size and some are greater than others.

Master Paolo: An impressive and valid argument. Yet, this could not have been the reason why the emperor dismissed Tito. What happened?

Demetrios of Nicaea: Well, Tito attempted to refute the emperor's argument with another argument of his own. He pointed out that he and the emperor agreed that an infinite quantity is an infinity of individual parts, such as parts of time or space. He added another premise that all infinities of parts are no greater or less than the number of the parts which is infinite. He then drew the conclusion that all infinities of part are infinities of an infinite number of parts.

Master Paolo: Good heavens! The Emperor accused him of a fallacy, I am sure.

Demetrios of Nicaea: Indeed he did. That is why he lost faith in Tito's intellectual abilities and, when Tito's appointment at the imperial school came up for renewal, the emperor gave the position to a different mathematician from Egypt.

Master Paolo: A sad story.

1. According to the story told by Demetrios of Nicaea, the Roman Emperor Michael Arithologos was interested in mathematics and invited the mathematician Tito of Dalmatia to visit him in his palace for intellectual discussions. In the course of these discussions, they became especially interested in a certain topic. What is this topic?

2.   Emperor Michael and Tito disagree about some important feature of infinity. About what do they disagree?

_____

_____

3.   Despite their disagreement, the Emperor and Tito do agree about something. What do they agree about?

_____

_____

4.   Emperor Michael presents an argument in support of his position on the nature of infinity. What is the conclusion of his argument?

Conclusion: _____

_____

5.   In his argument, the emperor sets out to disprove a certain proposition. What proposition is he attempting to disprove?

Premise: _____

_____

6.   In his argument, Emperor Michael uses a particular example of an infinity. What is his example?

☐   The infinity of God's power.

☐   The infinity of prime numbers.

☐   The infinity of temporal moments.

7.   In his argument, Emperor Michael says that it is obvious that time is infinite in extension. Why does the emperor believe this is true?

☐   Because God created time.

☐   Because every moment has a preceding and a succeeding moment.

☐   Because time is infinitely divisible.

8. In his argument, Emperor Michael says that it is obvious that the process of dividing moments of time in half can go on infinitely. Why does the emperor believe this is true?

    ☐   Because God created time.

    ☐   Because time is infinite in extension.

    ☐   Because every division of a moment of time results in two divisible moments.

9. In his argument, Emperor Michael derives a contradiction. What precisely is the contradiction?

    _____

    _____

10. What is the name for the form of Emperor Michael's argument?

    _____

11. Tito attempts to refute the emperor's argument with an argument of his own. What is Tito's argument?

    Premise 1: _____

    _____

    Premise 2: _____

    _____

    Conclusion: _____

    _____

12. Responding to Tito's attempted refutation, Emperor Michael accuses Tito of committing a fallacy. Is the Emperor correct?

    ☐   Yes. Tito begs the question.

    ☐   Yes. Tito equivocates on the term "infinity of parts."

    ☐   No. Tito has successfully refuted the Emperor with a valid dilemma.

§19 What is the Alternative?

A disjunctive proposition stating a set of alternatives may be true under two quite distinct circumstances. On the one hand, an either-or proposition can be considered as true when at least one of the alternatives is true. This leaves open the possibility of both alternatives being true. On the other hand, an either-or proposition can be considered as true when exactly one of the alternatives is true. This rules out the possibility of both alternatives being true. This means that disjunctions may be generally divided into two groups based on how the truth value of the disjunction is determined. Every disjunction falls into one of these two groups regardless of how complex it is—whether it is a dichotomy, a trichotomy, a tetrachotomy, and so on.

Exclusive Disjunction

Often when one uses a disjunction to state a set of alternatives, one has in mind alternatives that rule each other out. This kind of disjunction is true when exactly one of the alternatives is true. This is called *exclusive disjunction*, because the truth of one alternative excludes the truth of the other. Consider the following dichotomy:

> [1]   The captives are either dead or alive.

This is clearly an exclusive disjunction, because it is impossible that the captives are both dead and alive. One possibility being true rules out the other being true.

Exclusive disjunction can be a premise in any form of disjunctive argument. Suppose, for example, that the exclusive disjunction [1] is known to be true, as it obviously is. Suppose further that it is discovered that all the captives were executed by their captors so that it is true that *the captives are no longer alive*. It follows by disjunctive syllogism that *the captives are dead*:

> [2]   The captives are either dead or alive.
> The captives are not alive.
> Therefore, they are dead.

Argument [2] is clearly valid, as is any disjunctive syllogism. Intuition makes it clear that, given that only one of a dichotomous set of possibilities can be true and one is in fact false, then the other absolutely must be true.

Inclusive Disjunction

While some disjunctions state a mutually exclusive set of alternatives, not all do. It is possible to have a set of alternatives which can both be true at the same time. The disjunction stating such a set of alternatives will then be true if at least one of the alternatives is true and it will be true if both alternatives are true. This is called *inclusive disjunction*, because the truth of one of the alternatives does not exclude the truth of the other. Consider the following dichotomy:

[3]   Master John has either read Aristotle's book or a commentary on
            Aristotle's book.

This disjunction [3] is inclusive, because the master either read Aristotle's book or the master read a commentary on Aristotle's book or both.

Like exclusive disjunction, inclusive disjunction can be a premise in any form of disjunctive argument. Suppose, for example, that the inclusive disjunction [3] is known to be true. Suppose further that it is also known that the master has never read a commentary on Aristotle's book. It follows by disjunctive syllogism that he must have read Aristotle's book:

[4]   Master John has either read Aristotle's book or a commentary on
            Aristotle's book.
            He has not read a commentary on Aristotle's book.
            Therefore, he has read Aristotle's book itself.

Argument [4] is valid, as is any disjunctive syllogism. Intuition makes it clear that, given that a certain set of possibly inclusive dichotomous alternatives is true and that one of the alternatives is false, the truth of the other alternative is necessary.

Fallacy of False Dichotomy

Dichotomy is especially important in the various forms of disjunctive argument. This is because alternatives are often reduced to a set of two for convenience, especially in decision-making. When this is done, one must be careful to insure that the dichotomy is exhaustive—that is, that the two alternatives represent all the alternatives that exist. If the dichotomy is a set of exhaustive alternatives, then it is a *true dichotomy*. If there is at least one alternative beyond the two alternatives stated in the dichotomy, then it is a *false dichotomy*. The disjunction at [1] is a true dichotomy, because it is exhaustive. There are no other possibilities for the captives—they are dead and not alive or they are alive and not dead. Consider another dichotomy:

[5]   Scholar Stefanus is a student at either Oxford or Paris.

This disjunction [5] is a true dichotomy if these are the only possible places Scholar Stefanus may be studying. If it is also possible that he is studying at Padua, then this is a false dichotomy.

When a dichotomy is used as the premise of an argument, it must be a true dichotomy. If it is not, then the argument is either invalid or unsound or both. This kind of logical error is called the *fallacy of false dichotomy*. Consider, for example, the following argument:

[6]   The prince has two choices: to remain in the kingdom as a supporter of his father's claim to the throne or to leave the kingdom in rejection of his father's claim. In either case he will be a coward.

Argument [6] is a constructive dilemma that draws the conclusion that *the prince is a coward* from a dichotomy that the prince faces about what he will decide to do. Consider an analytical outline of this argument:

[7]   The prince either remains in the kingdom as a supporter of his father's claim to the throne or leaves the kingdom in rejection of his father's claim to the throne.
    If the prince remains in the kingdom as a supporter of his father's claim to the throne, then he is a coward.
    If the prince leaves the kingdom in rejection of this father's claim to the throne, then he is a coward.
    Therefore, the prince is a coward.

Argument [7], is a sound dilemma only if the dichotomy stated in the first premise is a true dichotomy—that is, the two alternatives represent all the alternatives open to the prince. If the dichotomous premise is a true dichotomy, then the argument is valid and sound, because both of the alternatives result in the same thing: the cowardice of the prince. If, however, the dichotomous premise is a false dichotomy, then there is at least one other alternative open to the prince—say, for example, that the prince remains in the kingdom and rejects his father's claim to the throne. This alternative does not necessarily result in the cowardice of the prince—indeed, it might take great courage to remain and oppose his father. Thus, the constructive dilemma is not a sound argument. If the dichotomy in the first premise of this argument [7] is a false dichotomy, then the arguer has committed the fallacy of false dichotomy making his argument unsound.

Exercise 44

Student: _____

Read the following dialogue and answer the questions that follow.

Evidence of Fallacies in Old Bologna

The chapter room of the Convent of Santa Macrina was unusually crowded on Pentecost Monday in the year 1233. Located in the university district of the old town of Bologna, the convent on this day attracted many law students who wished to hear a famous professor, Isaac of Nola, lecture on the *Codex Juris Romanorum* or Book of Roman Law. After the first of his series of lectures, which was devoted to the laws of evidence, Master Isaac agreed to take questions from the students in his audience.

Scholar Stefano:	Learned Master, it seems to me that the rules of evidence you have set forth in your lecture are unusually strict. I have in mind a criminal case. Consider, for example, the case of a person accused of battery against another. Now, according to you, the conviction for the crime of battery must rest on evidence of specific events that fit the definition of battery. Yet, cannot one argue in court that a certain person is guilty of battery on the grounds that battery is the crime of battering another and that a certain person commits battery when he batters another? Will you comment, Master?
Master Isaac:	One cannot argue in this way in court, unless he wishes to have his case dismissed by the magistrate.
Scholar Stefano:	Why, Master, would the magistrate dismiss a case argued in this way?
Master Isaac:	Because the argument is fallacious, young sir. The guilt of a man accused of battery cannot be properly established as a fact from the definition of what it is for such a man to be guilty of battery.
Scholar Hugo:	Thank you for your concise answer to Scholar Stefano, Master. I am most happy to have you point out the fallacy, for I have heard, once or twice, people who have argued like this about criminal cases. From my experience, I conclude that this is a common fallacy and that is committed in every criminal case that comes before a magistrate.
Master Isaac:	Are you not being too quick to draw your conclusion? Do you have sufficient evidence for such a generalization?
Scholar Giles:	Master, you must be amused at the poor quality of reasoning in this discussion. At the same time, you must be alarmed, for it is clear that the fallacious reasoning of those of us studying law at this university will result in our failing either our interim exams or our final exams. There

are no other possible results and, either way, we will not receive our law degrees.

Master Isaac: Young man, have you not fallaciously overlooked another possibility?

Scholar Giles: But, what other possibility . . .

Scholar Stefano: I heard of a case in the Civil Courts of Genoa, Master, where a lower magistrate's decision was reversed by the Duke's High Court upon appeal by the prosecutor. The case involved a certain nobleman who was accused of murdering a merchant in the streets on market day in a dispute over the price of fruit. The act was witnessed by very many people and the nobleman was known to have held a grudge against the merchant for many years. The magistrate acquitted the nobleman despite all the evidence against him. Upon appeal, the Duke's High Court ordered the nobleman retried and had the magistrate arrested for bribery. Please comment on this case, Master.

Scholar Hugo: Yes, Master, what is your learned opinion of the High Court's decision?

Master Isaac: The Duke's High Court acted wisely.

Scholar Stefano: How can you say that, Master? Certainly, the lower magistrate's judgment was justified.

Master Isaac: Explain, young sir, how you arrive at this conclusion.

Scholar Stefano: I consulted the archives of the Civil Court and I read the magistrate's decision. He reasoned from the fundamental truth that a man is noble when he performs noble, not criminal, deeds. The magistrate also pointed out that the fact that the accused was truly a nobleman—there seems to be no doubt of his noble birth. The magistrate then drew the conclusion that the accused could only do noble, not criminal, deeds. This was the basis of his decision for acquittal.

Master Isaac: If you study this judicial decision more carefully, you will find a fallacy. The High Court did well in reversing such an ill-founded decision.

Scholar Stefano: Well, I do not see any problem with the magistrate's decision . . .

Master Isaac: Young scholars, you are clearly not ready to study the laws of evidence. You must return to your study of logic and study the laws of good reasoning.

Master Isaac of Nola, a professor of law at the University of Bologna, is asked to comment on a hypothetical case of battery by Scholar Stefano. What is the argument given by Scholar Stefano upon which the master is asked to comment?

Premise 1: _____

_____

Premise 2: _____

_____

Conclusion: _____

_____

2. Master Isaac responds to Scholar Stefano's argument about the case of battery by pointing out that, were one to use such an argument in court, the case would be dismissed. Why does the master believe that the case would be dismissed?

☐   The case would be dismissed because of a lack of physical evidence.

☐   The case would be dismissed because of fallacious reasoning.

☐   The case would be dismissed because of a lack of factual evidence.

☐   The case would be dismissed because of prejudice against law students.

3. Master Isaac points out that a person accused of battery cannot be convicted of the crime on the basis of the definition of battery alone. What is the name for the error in Scholar Stefano's argument to which the master is referring?

Fallacy name: _____

4. Scholar Hugo says that he has heard some others commit the same error as Scholar Stefano and on the basis of his experience draws the conclusion that this error is committed in every criminal case. What form of argument is Scholar Hugo using to support this conclusion?

☐   Scholar Hugo's argument is a deductive argument.

☐   Scholar Hugo's argument is an inductive argument.

☐   Scholar Hugo's argument is an analogical argument.

5.   What is the form of Scholar Hugo's conclusion?

☐   Scholar Hugo's conclusion is a universal generalization.

☐   Scholar Hugo's conclusion is a universal particularization.

☐   Scholar Hugo's conclusion is an existential proposition.

☐   Scholar Hugo's conclusion is a negative proposition.

6.   Master Isaac accuses Scholar Hugo of committing a fallacy. What is the name of this fallacy?

Fallacy name: _____

7.   What is it about Scholar Hugo's argument that makes Master Isaac believe that this particular fallacy has been committed?

_____

_____

_____

_____

8.   Scholar Giles suggests that the master must be alarmed at the poor quality of reasoning used by his fellow law students. He explains his suggestion with an argument. What is Scholar Giles' argument?

Premise 1: _____

_____

Premise 2: _____

_____

Premise 3: _____

_____

Conclusion: _____

_____

9.   Master Isaac accuses Scholar Giles of a fallacy. What is the name of the fallacy?

       Fallacy name: _____

10.   Master Isaac suggests that Scholar Giles has overlooked another possibility. What
       alternative possibility might the master have in mind?

       _____

       _____

       _____

11.   Scholar Stefano cites a case heard in the Civil Courts of Genoa in which the
       magistrate's decision was reversed on appeal. Master Isaac claims that the Duke's High
       Court acted wisely in the case. What does the master mean by this?

       ☐   The High Court was right to reverse the lower court and order a retrial.

       ☐   The High Court was right to support the lower court's decision.

       ☐   The High Court was prudent to avoid the political implications.

12.   Scholar Stefano claims that the Genoese magistrate who originally ruled on the case was
       justified in his decision. He cites the argument given by the magistrate.   What is the
       magistrate's argument?

       Premise 1:   _____

       _____

       Premise 2:   _____

       _____

       Conclusion: _____

       _____

13.   Master Isaac indicates that there is a fallacy in the magistrate's argument. What is
       the name of the fallacy?

       Fallacy name: _____

§20 Personal Attack

The purpose of argument is to provide support for the truth of a conclusion. Arguments are capable of doing this because they are processes of giving reasons for beliefs. Arguments, however, cannot perform this function unless the subject matter of the reasons provided in the premises is relevant to the subject matter of the conclusion. Consider, for example, the following argument:

[1]   All Oxford masters lecture in Latin.
        Anyone who lectures in Latin must have an understanding of Latin
           grammar.
        Therefore, all scholars in Constantinople write in Greek.

This example [1] is an argument, because it is a process of giving reasons in support of a conclusion. It is, clearly, an unsuccessful argument, because the reasons given in the two premises have nothing to do with the subject matter of the conclusion. Were this argument to be a valid deduction or even a strong induction, the subject matter of the two premises would have to be relevant to the claim that *scholars in Constantinople write in Greek*. It is obvious, however, that the fact that Oxford masters lecture in Latin and know Latin grammar is completely irrelevant to the facts about the written language used by scholars in Constantinople. Were one to attempt to offer such an argument as providing good reasons for believing the conclusion, the arguer would be guilty of a *non sequitur fallacy*. The Latin phrase "non sequitur" means "it does not follow" and indicates the logical error of attempting to draw a conclusion that does not necessarily follow from the premises. Every invalid deduction, of course, is a non sequitur fallacy. The most extreme form of non sequitur fallacy would be an argument such as example [1] in which the premises not only fail to necessitate the conclusion, but are completely irrelevant to the conclusion.

Argumentum ad hominem

In argument there is a natural expectation that the premises are relevant to the subject matter of the conclusion. Any argument that violates this expectation is a non sequitur fallacy. Yet, there are many ways in which the subject matter of the premises can be irrelevant to the subject matter of the conclusion. Among the most common form of such fallacious argument is an argument in which the arguer attempts to show that his opponent's claim is false by personally attacking his opponent in some way and then pretending that he has logically defeated his opponent's position. This kind of argument of personal attack is called an *ad hominem fallacy*.

      The only proper way to show that one's opponent's claim is false is to show that it is based on fallacious reasoning or false premises. One cannot reasonably show that another person's beliefs are mistaken by showing that there is something wrong with the person himself. Any sort of argument aimed at showing that another person's beliefs or claims are false by attacking the other person in some personal way is an ad hominem fallacy. There three important forms of ad hominem attack.

Abusive ad hominem

One way in which an arguer might personally attack his opponent instead of attacking his argument or claim is to abuse his opponent's moral character. This is the kind of argument in which an arguer claims that another person's belief or claim is false because that other person is a morally bad person. A person's moral character, however, is logically irrelevant to the truth or falsity of his belief or claim. Evil people might, at least sometimes, speak the truth. This kind of ad hominem argument is called *abusive ad hominem* because the way in which the personal attack is made is by means of an abuse of an opponent's moral character. Consider the following example:

> [2] Scholar Marco argued that the magistrate's decision in the case is invalid and should be appealed on the grounds that this magistrate is known to be corrupt and bribed the duke to appoint him magistrate.

In argument [2], Scholar Marco is attempting to show by argument that the magistrate handed down a false and poorly reasoned judicial decision. The reasons he gives in support of this conclusion, however, are a non sequitur. Instead of analyzing the judicial decision and criticizing it, Scholar Marco attacks the magistrate's moral character by pointing out that the magistrate is corrupt and is guilty of bribery. The morality of the magistrate's actions, however, is irrelevant to whether or not his decision is a good one. Even if what Scholar Marco says about the magistrate is true, the judicial decision might still be valid and just.

  Abusive ad hominem is a common fallacy and an arguer must always be careful not to confuse the moral character of his opponent with the validity of his opponent's arguments or the truth of his opponent's claims.

Circumstantial ad hominem

Perhaps the most common form of ad hominem fallacy occurs when an arguer rejects another's argument or claim on the ground of some circumstance the other is in when he makes his argument or claim. The irrelevant personal circumstance can be of any kind. The circumstance may, for example, be the profit to the person whose argument or claim is being rejected or the condition of life of the person whose argument or claim is being rejected or some other personal circumstance. A person's personal circumstances, however, are logically irrelevant to the truth or falsity of his beliefs or claims or the validity of his arguments. Even if the arguer is right that his opponent is in the circumstances he claims, this does not show that his opponent must be wrong. This kind of ad hominem argument is called *circumstantial ad hominem* because the way in which the personal attack is made is by pointing to irrelevant circumstances. Consider the following example:

[3]   Bishop Albert's sermon about the sacred union of marriage and the divine command to care for one's family was clearly aimed at the prince who is known to neglect his wife and children. The prince responded to the bishop's admonition by writing a letter defending himself. In this letter he argued that the bishop was wrong to claim that family-neglect is evil, because the bishop is celibate and lives without a wife or children.

In example [3], the prince argues that the bishop's claim about the immorality of failing to care for one's family is false on the grounds that the bishop has no wife or children. This is a circumstantial ad hominem, because the bishop's mode of life is irrelevant to the truth of his claims about the sacredness of marriage and the duty to care for one's family. One does not have to have a family oneself to know that it is evil to neglect one's spouse and children.

Like abusive ad hominem, circumstantial ad hominem is a common fallacy. An arguer must always be careful not to confuse the personal circumstances of his opponent with the validity of his opponent's arguments or the truth of his opponent's claims.

Tu quoque

A common, but rather specialized, form of ad hominem fallacy is one in which moral or other advice is rejected as bad advice on the grounds that the advisor fails to follow his own advice. One who receives some advice and does not want to take it might attempt to justify his failure to follow the advice by arguing that the advice is not good advice. It is quite possible that one might develop a good argument showing that some advice is not good advice and should not be followed. Yet, if one argues against the advice solely on the grounds that the person giving the advice does not follow it himself, then one commits a *tu quoque fallacy*. The Latin phrase "tu quoque" means "you too" and is often used accusingly. Whether or not a person who gives advice follows that advice himself is logically irrelevant to the question of whether his advice is good advice and should be followed. Consider the following example:

[4]   Master Nicholas, a member of the faculty of medicine at the University of Toulouse for many years, told his students of a royal patient he once had who complained of chronic stomach ailments. Master Nicholas advised his patient to avoid rich meats such as beef and pork and eat only game and fish. Yet, his patient was fond of beef and pork and despised fish. He justified his failure to take Master Nicholas' advice by arguing that Master Nicholas himself eats beef and pork to some excess and, therefore, it was not unhealthy to eat such meats.

In this example [4], Master Nicholas' patient justifies his conclusion that eating beef and pork, even to excess, is healthy by the irrelevant premise that Master Nicholas does not follow his own advice. The fact that Master Nicholas does not follow the advice he gave to his royal patient does not, by itself, show that his advice is not good advice. The only way to show that it is not good advice is to analyze the advice itself and not simply look to whether the advisor takes the advice himself.

Tu quoque arguments are somewhat more specialized than abusive and circumstantial ad hominem arguments, because they always concern advice in one way or another. Yet, tu quoque is truly ad hominem, because it is a kind of personal attack that points to something irrelevant to the conclusion as a means of showing the conclusion to be true. An arguer must always be careful not to confuse the personal behavior of an advisor with respect to his own advice with the truth or falsity of the advice itself. It may very well be the case that an advisor may be under moral obligation to set a good example to those he advises by following his own good advice. Even if he does not, however, that alone does not demonstrate that his advice is false, bad, or should not be followed.

Exercise 45

Student: _____

Read the following dialogue and answer the questions that follow.

Who Gets the Last Word?

It was cold enough in Oxford that January of 1321 that university professors would lecture only if each student would bring some coal to keep the stove going throughout the class session. This is why Master Peter's usually drafty room was now quite warm with a good fire going in his tile stove. While most of his students were not much interested in the scheduled topic of the master's lecture, they were all happy to be out of the cold. Knowing this, the master took pity on his captive audience and decided to tell his students an interesting story. It would also be a good opportunity to put some logic into his students' heads.

Master Peter:	As you all know, I had planned to lecture on Aristotle's very difficult book on the soul. However, because you are all distracted by the cold weather and your attention is devoted to keeping warm, I will instead tell you an amusing story.
Scholar Paul:	Thank you, Master. This is most considerate of you. It would be most difficult today for us to focus our attention on the subtleties of Aristotle's account of the soul when all we really want to do is to get close to that warm stove.
Scholar Alwin:	Scholar Paul is quite right, Master, you are most considerate. Now, if you would also provide us with some of your fine stock of Falernian wine, our comfort would be complete.
Master Peter:	Perhaps a bit too complete! No, I think that wine would not improve your attention. Be content with the warm room and listen to my tale of a certain drunken man and his attempts at logical argument.
Scholar Giles:	We will do without wine, if we must, just so long as you do not put us out into that cold!
Master Peter:	Very well, then, attend! There was once a man named Bubos who claimed to be an expert stone mason. Yet, it is uncertain whether he really was as expert as he claimed for no one had ever seen the man lay one stone upon another. This Bubos, you see, spent most of his days sitting around the marketplace begging drinks from his friends with earnest promises to repay them as soon as he got work, which in Bubos' case meant never.
Scholar Paul:	I have a brother like that.

Master Peter:	Bubos had a wife named Xinia. People did not see much of her as she was very shy and kept to the house. She did not even go to the market to buy food, sending their only servant, an old lady who had long ago worked for Bubos' mother.
Scholar Alwin:	This is so far a very interesting story, but what does it have to do with logic?
Master Peter:	Be patient and attend! When in his cups,[1] Bubos would brag that he beat Xinia. At first people did not believe him, thinking him just a vulgar braggart. But he spoke of it so often that, after a while, people became rather disgusted. The people of the village began to avoid Bubos and he, in return, cursed them. Indeed, Bubos was becoming more and more of a public nuisance, loitering in the marketplace alternately cursing people and begging drinks from them.
Scholar Alwin:	I am sure that made him popular.
Master Peter:	Eventually, the village magistrate asked the local parish priest to speak to Bubos. If the priest could convince Bubos to reform his ways, then perhaps peace would return to the village. If not, then the magistrate would have no choice but to have Bubos arrested.
Scholar Paul:	Did the priest go to talk with Bubos?
Master Peter:	Indeed he did and they had quite a philosophical discussion! Hearing that the priest intended to confront him, Bubos decided to prepare for the discussion by improving his wits with drink. While the priest was saying Matins,[2] Bubos broke into the back of the church and stole the altar wine. By the time that the priest had finished the service and made his way to the marketplace, Bubos was thoroughly drunk.
Scholar Alwin:	That must have made for a lively discussion!
Master Peter:	The priest began by greeting Bubos in a friendly way and wishing him many blessings. Bubos' only reply was to belch loudly. The priest then decided to get right to the purpose of his visit. "Bubos, my friend," said the priest, "why do you sit here in the market place every day drinking too much and bragging of your disgusting behavior?" Bubos replied, "there is nothing disgusting about my behavior; it is perfectly justified." "Justified!" exclaimed the priest, "how can you claim that beating the innocent Xinia, who never raised her hand against anyone, is justified?" "Wife-beating is not only justified, Father, but it is beneficial to the wife," remarked Bubos. The priest said, "you are wrong, Bubos, and you well know it." He went on to explain, "violence against the innocent is contrary to human justice and an affront to God's law."
Scholar Paul:	What did Bubos say to that?

---

[1] when drunk.
[2] morning prayer

264

Master Peter:	Bubos verbally attacked the priest: "you cannot possibly know anything about the right and wrongs of wife-beating, Father. You are a priest and, as a priest, you live without a wife." The priest responded by pointing out Bubos' fallacy, but Bubos ignored this and continued: "and who are you, Father, to lecture me on right and wrong? You yourself often admit in your sermons that you, like all men, are a sinner. Well, given that you are a sinner, it follows that your conclusions about the sins of others must be false."
Scholar Giles:	This Bubos is not very logical.
Scholar Paul:	And he has a lot of gall to speak this way to a priest.
Scholar David:	So, what did the priest say to all that?
Master Peter:	The priest again pointed out Bubos' fallacy and again Bubos ignored this. Instead, the drunken man continued, "look, Father, there are only two possibilities: either I am right that beating my wife is perfectly justified or you are a sinner. You admit that you are a sinner. Therefore, beating my wife is perfectly justified. There, it is perfectly logical! I dare you to reject my argument."
Scholar Paul:	Did the priest reject Bubos' argument?
Master Peter:	Of course he did.
Scholar Alwin:	Well, it seems that wine had hardly improved Bubos' wits, unless he was trying to be funny.
Master Peter:	Oh no, Bubos took his arguments quite seriously.
Scholar Giles:	So, what happen next?
Master Peter:	It seems that Xinia had heard that the priest had gone to speak to her drunken husband and she was concerned enough for the priest's safety to leave the house and make her way to the market place. She intended to warn the priest to be careful of her violent husband.
Scholar Paul:	A good and brave woman.
Master Peter:	Seeing her approach, Bubos announced that he would demonstrate to the priest just how beneficial wife-beating can be and he picked up a heavy stone and flung it at Xinia. In his drunken state, however, Bubos' aim was very bad and he missed his intended target by a wide margin. Instead, the stone bounced off a sheep skin that was stretched tight over a large wooden frame to dry. The stone was propelled back toward Bubos, hitting him in the head and killing him.
Scholar Paul:	Remarkable!

Scholar David:	What did the priest do?
Master Peter:	The priest's only remark was that it seems that God had responded to Bubos' demonstration with a divine "syllogism" of His own.
Scholar Alwin:	In logic, as in life, God always has the last word.

1. Who is Bubos?

    ☐   The village magistrate.

    ☐   The village priest.

    ☐   The village drunk.

    ☐   The village idiot.

2. Who is Xinia?

    ☐   The village magistrate.

    ☐   The village priest.

    ☐   The shy wife of Bubos.

    ☐   The head of the stone-mason's guild.

3. According to Master Peter's story, why is it uncertain whether Bubos really was an expert stone mason?

    ☐   Because he was never observed to actually do any masonry work—or any work for that matter.

    ☐   Because the last building he worked on collapsed.

    ☐   Because Xinia locked up Bubos' masonry tools.

4. What is Bubos' attitude toward wife-beating?

    _____

    _____

    _____

5.   What is the priest's attitude toward wife-beating?

_____

_____

_____

6.   When the priest tells Bubos that he is wrong to beat his wife, Bubos personally attacks the priest with an argument. What is his argument?

Premise 1:   _____

_____

Premise 2:   _____

_____

Conclusion: _____

_____

7.   The priest accuses Bubos of committing a fallacy in this argument. What is the name of this fallacy?

Fallacy name: _____

8.   Given that the premises of Bubos' argument are both true, why is his conclusion fallaciously drawn—in other words, why does the priest believe that Bubos has committed the fallacy you named in number 7?

_____

_____

_____

_____

9.   Bubos claims that the priest has no right to lecture him on right and wrong and justifies this claim with an argument. What is the conclusion of Bubos' argument?

Conclusion: _____

_____

10.   What are the premises of Bubos' argument?

        Premise 1:   _____

        _____

        Premise 2:   _____

        _____

11.   Again, the priest accuses Bubos of committing a fallacy. What is the name of this
        fallacy?

        Fallacy name: _____

12.   Is the priest correct that Bubos has committed this fallacy in his second argument?

        ☐   Yes, whether or not the priest is a sinner is irrelevant to the truth of his
                admonitions against sin.

        ☐   No, the priest's bad example justifies other's sinfulness.

13.   When the priest points out Bubos' second fallacy, Bubos responds with yet another
        argument. What is this argument?

        Premise 1:   _____

        _____

        Premise 2:   _____

        _____

        Conclusion: _____

        _____

14.   What form of argument is Bubos using in his third argument?

        Argument name: _____

15. Is Bubos' third argument valid?

☐ Yes, it is valid.   ☐ No, it is invalid.

16. Is Bubos' third argument sound?

☐ Yes, it is sound.   ☐ No, it is unsound.

17. Why does the priest reject Bubos' third argument?

☐   Bubos' argument is an invalid deduction.

☐   While Bubos' argument is valid, it is unsound because the first premise is a false analogy.

☐   While Bubos' argument is valid, it is unsound because the first premise is a false dichotomy.

18. In reaction to the death of Bubos, the priest remarks that God responded to Bubos with a divine "syllogism." What does the priest mean by this?

☐   The priest is pointing out that God thinks in the way human beings do and therefore is subject to the laws of logic.

☐   The priest is claiming that God is taking vengeance on Bubos for living an immoral life and breaking the divine commandments.

☐   The priest is warning the villagers that they had better reform their lives or they will meet the same fate as Bubos.

☐   The priest is making an analogy between human reasoning and divine action. Because God is the creator of the universe, everything that takes place happens for the best because of God. Yet, God does not actually need to use syllogisms or other forms of argument to gain knowledge in the way human beings do, because God is the Perfect Being and knows everything without requiring a logical process proceeding from the known to knowledge of the unknown.

Appendix I
Schemata of Standard Deductive Forms

Valid Forms of the Categorical Syllogism

All F is G	All F is G	Some F is G	Some F is G
<u>All G is H</u>	<u>No G is H</u>	<u>All G is H</u>	<u>No G is H</u>
All F is H	No F is H	Some F is H	Some F is not-H

All F is G	All F is G	No F is G	All F is G
<u>All G is H</u>	<u>No G is H</u>	<u>All H is G</u>	<u>No H is G</u>
Some F is H	Some F is not-H	No F is H	No F is H

Some F is not-G	Some F is G	No F is G	All F is G
<u>All H is G</u>	<u>No H is G</u>	<u>All H is G</u>	<u>No H is G</u>
Some F is not-H	Some F is not-H	Some F is not-H	Some F is not-H

Some G is F	All G is F	Some G is F	All G is F
<u>All G is H</u>	<u>Some G is H</u>	<u>No G is H</u>	<u>Some G is not-H</u>
Some F is H	Some F is H	Some F is not-H	Some F is not-H

All G is F	All G is F	No G is F	All G is F
<u>All G is H</u>	<u>No G is H</u>	<u>All H is G</u>	<u>Some H is G</u>
Some F is H	Some F is not-H	No F is H	Some F is H

Some G is F	No G is F	All G is F	All G is F
<u>No H is G</u>	<u>All H is G</u>	<u>All H is G</u>	<u>No H is G</u>
Some F is not-H	Some F is not-H	Some F is H	Some F is not-H

Modus Ponens

If P then Q
<u>P</u>
Q

Modus Tollens

If P then Q
<u>not-Q</u>
not-P

Hypothetical Syllogism

If P then Q
<u>If Q then R</u>
If P then R

Disjunctive Syllogism

Either P or Q	Either P or Q
<u>not-P</u>	<u>not-Q</u>
Q	P

Conjunctive Syllogism

Not-both P and Q
P
not-Q

Not-both P and Q
Q
not-P

Constructive Dilemma

Either P or Q
If P then R
If Q then R
R

Destructive Dilemma

Either not-P or not-Q
If R then P
If R then Q
not-R

Reductio ad absurdum

not-P
[other premises]

↓

Both Q and not-Q
P

Appendix II
Catalogue of Common Fallacies

Affirming the consequent is the invalid deductive argument in which one premise is a conditional proposition and the other premise is the affirmation of the consequent of the conditional premise. The arguer then fallaciously concludes to the affirmation of the antecedent. For example: If Master William has read Boethius' book on hypothetical syllogisms, then he is familiar with conditional arguments. He is familiar with conditional arguments. Therefore, he must have read Boethius' book on hypothetical syllogisms. This fallacious form of argument should not be mistaken for the valid form modus ponens.

Argumentum ad baculum is the fallacious appeal to force or fear in place of reason in argument. For example: Everyone agrees with Master Henry, because those who do not are invited to sit at the back of the room furthest from the stove.

Argumentum ad ignorantiam is the fallacious appeal to ignorance in argument. For example: No one has ever proved that this book on minerals was not written by Aristotle, therefore he must have written it.

Argumentum ad hominem is a fallacious argument in which an opponent is personally attacked instead of his arguments or claims and the personal attack is claimed to have demonstrated the invalidity of the opponent's argument or the falsity of his claim. There are three categories of ad hominem argument:

> *Abusive ad hominem* is a fallacious argument in which the opponent's moral character is attacked instead of his argument or claim. For example: Master Alexander argues that God's existence can be proven by scientific reasoning, but we do not have to accept his argument because he rarely attends church services.

> *Circumstantial ad hominem* is a fallacious argument in which the opponent is personally attacked on account of his or her personal circumstances instead of his argument or claim. For example: Master William claims that he has constructed the best astrolabe at Oxford, but this claim is clearly false because he will become famous if the claim is accepted.

> *Tu quoque* is a fallacious argument in which advice is rejected on the grounds that the advisor does not follow his own advice. For example: Scholar Roger advised us to consult Master Robert for help in understanding these calculations of perspective. But we should not follow this advice because Scholar Roger himself did not seek Master Robert's help when he was struggling to learn the laws of perspective.

Argumentum ad ludificandum is the fallacious appeal to ridicule in place of reason in argument. For example: Anyone who spends hours studying conic sections begins to look like one. Therefore, such a person is a fool. (See also *argumentum ad rhonchum*.)

Argumentum ad misericordiam is the fallacious appeal to pity in place of reason in argument, especially moral or legal argument. For example: The Norman knights who robbed the villagers of their livestock were justified, because their pay from the king is in arrears.

Argumentum ad populum is the fallacious appeal to popular opinion in place of reason in argument. For example: Master Alan is the most popular lecturer on the theology faculty at Oxford. Therefore, his opinions must be true.

Argumentum ad rhonchum is the fallacious appeal to sneering in place of reason in argument. For example: Master Jordan's calculations about the position of the moon are obviously in error, because rhooooooch! (See also *argumentum ad ludificandum*.)

Begging the question is an argument in which the conclusion is assumed as one of the premises. For example: Scholar Geoffrey argued that God must exist because the Bible says so and God is the author of the Bible.

Circular reasoning is another name for the fallacy of *begging the question*.

Common cause is the fallacious presumption that two things are similar because one is the cause of the other when it is possible that the similarity is due to a third thing that caused them both. For example: It can only be that Scholar John learned algebra from Master Stefanus, because they both write their numbers in the same way.

Complex question is the fallacious presumption that there is a simple answer to a question which actually demands that another question be answered first. For example: Scholar Andrew asked Master Alexander whether they should continue their useless meetings.

Composition is the fallacious presumption that what is true of the part must also be true of the whole of which it is a part. For example: Scholar Bracho argued that the queen's gaudy necklace was very beautiful because it is composed of many individual crystals each of which is very beautiful.

Denying the antecedent is the invalid deductive argument in which one premise is a conditional proposition and the other premise is the negation of the antecedent of the conditional premise. The arguer then fallaciously concludes to the negation of the consequent. For example: If Master William has read Boethius' book on hypothetical syllogisms, then he is familiar with conditional arguments. He has not read Boethius's book on hypothetical syllogisms. Therefore, he is not familiar with conditional arguments. This fallacious form of argument should not be mistaken for the valid form modus tollens.

Derision is another name for the fallacy *argumentum ad ludificandum*. (See also *argumentum ad rhonchum*.)

Division is the fallacious presumption that what is true of the whole must also be true of each of the parts into which the whole can be divided. For example: Scholar Marco argued that, because the ship's hull is curved at each end, each individual piece of wood of which it is constructed must be curved at each end.

Equivocation is a fallacious argument in which the meaning of the terms or propositions composing it are not constant. For example: Walking down the narrow streets of the university district of Padua, Scholar Marco drew the attention of his companion Scholar Stefano to the two women above them leaning out of their second-story windows shouting across the street to each other. Scholar Marco remarked: "Those women will never agree because they are arguing from different premises."

False analogy is a fallacious comparison in argument in which what is known to be true of a well-known subject is concluded to be necessarily true of a lesser known subject on the basis of insufficient or irrelevant similarity of the two subjects. For example: Scholar Giles told us that, when he left home to come to Oxford to attend the university, his mother cried that he was too young to leave home and doing so at that time would result in his death, just as the bird that falls from the nest while still young surely dies.

False cause is the fallacious presumption that two events that happen close together in space and time must be related as cause and effect. For example: Just as Scholar John entered the rooms of his tutor Master Alexander, he began to sneeze. Clearly, Scholar John is allergic to his tutor.

False dichotomy is the fallacious presumption that a disjunction presents an exhaustive set of alternatives when it actually does not. For example: Master Odo told of the ancient Sicans who held the view that either one is a Sican or one is not civilized.

False dilemma is another name for the fallacy of *false dichotomy.*

Hasty generalization is a fallacious induction that draws an inductive generalization as a conclusion from insufficient inductive evidence. For example: On the day Scholar John first arrived in Oxford, he passed two masters on the street who were deep in a theological discussion. These were the first two masters he had ever seen. Greeting them and receiving no response, Scholar John drew the conclusion that all masters at Oxford ignore students.

Ignoratio elenchi is the fallacious presumption that a premise known to be true is relevant to and, therefore, supportive of a conclusion when it actually supports a different conclusion. For example: Master Odo told of a king who, when his enemies demanded half his kingdom or they would declare war, handed it over to them on the grounds that peace is preferable to war, thus encouraging his enemies to go to war to take the whole kingdom. (See also *non sequitur.*)

Non sequitur is a fallacious deductive argument in which the conclusion does not follow with necessity from the premises. All invalid deductive arguments are non sequitur fallacies and the most extreme form of non sequitur argument is one in which the premises are completely irrelevant in subject matter to the subject matter of the conclusion. For example: Master William has read Arabic books on constructing astronomical instruments and anyone who has read such books knows something about constructing an astrolabe. Therefore, Master William is a provocative lecturer. Clearly, Master William's knowledge of astrolabe construction gained from reading Arabic treatises on astronomical instruments is completely irrelevant to his talents as a lecturer. (See also *ignoratio elenchi*.)

Petitio principii is another name for the fallacy of *begging the question*.

Post hoc ergo propter hoc is another name for the fallacy of *false cause*.

Straw man is a fallacious argument offered in refutation of an opponent's position which is misrepresented as a different, much weaker position. The arguer then claims to have defeated the opponent's actual position. For example: Scholar John claims to have refuted Master Gerard's position that men are born with innate ideas of the good and the true, by asking an infant to express his innate ideas of the good and the true and getting no intelligible response.

Sweeping generalization is the fallacious misapplication of a general rule or law to a particular case in deductive argument. For example: After reading the story of the suicide of Alexias, Scholar Marco argued that Lysis clearly had no responsiblity for Alexias' death, even though he knew that Alexias was suicidal when Alexias asked him to return the sword Alexias had lent him. Scholar Marco reasoned that Lysis was simply following the perfectly true rule that everyone has a right to his own property.

Appendix III
Additional Exercise Sets

Additional Exercise Set A

1.   The Latin word *artes* means skills and the Latin word *scientia* means knowledge. Clearly, these ancient Latin words are the sources for our modern English words "arts" and "science." Compose a brief essay (two pages) explaining the relationship between the liberal arts and the sciences.

2.   Most modern universities have a college of arts and sciences. Using what you have learned about the seven liberal arts, compose a brief essay (two pages) explaining what is studied in a college of arts and sciences.

3.   Write a list of the seven liberal arts. Indicate which of these are language arts and which are mathematical arts. For each of the arts listed, write a paragraph indicating in a clear and precise way the specific skills represented by each art.

Additional Exercise Set B

1.   Compose an argument with two premises and write it in outline form. Your argument may be on any subject.

2.   Locate an argument in a book that you are reading for another class. Write out the argument in outline form.

3.   Write a list of five different words or phrases that are conclusion indicators.

4.   Write a list of five different words or phrases that are premise indicators.

Additional Exercise Set C

1.   Compose a brief essay (one page) explaining what a valid argument is. Give examples.

2.   Compose a brief essay (one page) explaining what a sound argument is. Give examples.

Additional Exercise Set D

1.   Select a paragraph from a book you are reading for another class. Identify the sentences in this paragraph that express propositions and those that express some other use of language.

2.   Write out five sentences expressing universal affirmative propositions on any subject you wish.

3.   Write out five sentences expressing universal negative propositions on any subject you wish.

4.   Write out five sentences expressing existential affirmative propositions on any subject you wish.

5.   Write out five sentences expressing existential negative propositions on any subject you wish.

6.   Write out five sentences expressing universal generalizations on any subject.

7.   Write out five sentences expressing universal particularizations on any subject.

Additional Exercise Set E

1.   Select a proposition from a book you are reading for another class. Draw a propositional diagram of that proposition.

2.   Compose a proposition of your own on any subject. Draw a propositional diagram of that proposition.

Additional Exercise Set F

1.   Compose two propositions having identical terms that are logically equivalent. Draw a set of propositional diagrams demonstrating the equivalence of your propositions.

2.   Compose two propositions having identical terms that are logically contradictory. Draw a set of propositional diagrams demonstrating the contradiction of your propositions.

Additional Exercise Set G

1.   Locate a categorical syllogism in a book you are reading for another class and outline it.

2.   Compose a categorical syllogism of your own on any subject.

Additional Exercise Set H

1.   Locate a categorical syllogism in a book you are reading for another class and use an argument diagram to determine its validity.

2.   Compose a categorical syllogism of your own on any subject. Use an argument diagram to determine its validity.

Additional Exercise Set I

1.   Locate an elliptically expressed categorical syllogism in a book you are reading for another class and use an argument diagram to determine its validity.

2.   Compose an elliptically expressed categorical syllogism of your own on any subject. Use an argument diagram to determine its validity.

Additional Exercise Set J

1.   Locate a soritical argument in a book you are reading for another class and use argument diagrams to determine its validity.

2.   Compose a lemmastic argument of your own on any subject. Use argument diagrams to determine its validity.

Additional Exercise Set K

1.   Locate a conjunction in a book you are reading for another class. Write out the simpler propositions of which it is composed.

2.   Locate a disjunction in a book you are reading for another class. Write out the simpler propositions of which it is composed.

3. Locate a conditional proposition in a book you are reading for another class. Write out the antecedent and consequent of which it is composed.

4. Compose a conjunction of your own on any subject. Write out the simpler propositions of which it is composed.

5. Compose a disjunction of your own on any subject. Write out the simpler propositions of which it is composed.

6. Compose a conditional proposition of your own on any subject. Write out the antecedent and consequent of which it is composed.

7. Compose a brief essay explaining the difference between categorical and conditional propositions. In your essay, include an explanation of why all simple propositions must be categorical, why conjunctions and disjunctions are categorical, and why conditionals must be complex propositions.

8. Compose six conditional propositions on different subjects. Make three of these factual conditionals and three counterfactual conditionals.

9. Compose five conditional propositions on different subjects. For each of your conditionals, use a different logical connective to indicate conditionality.

Additional Exercise Set L

1. Locate a disjunctive syllogism in a book you are reading for another class and outline the argument.

2. Compose a disjunctive syllogism of your own on any subject. Clearly outline the argument.

3. Locate a constructive dilemma in a book you are reading for another class and outline the argument.

4. Compose a constructive dilemma of your own on any subject. Clearly outline the argument.

5. Locate a destructive dilemma in a book you are reading for another class and outline the argument.

6. Compose a destructive dilemma of your own on any subject. Clearly outline the argument.

Additional Exercise Set M

1.   Locate a modus ponens in a book you are reading for another class and outline the argument.

2.   Compose a modus ponens of your own on any subject. Clearly outline the argument.

3.   Locate a modus tollens in a book you are reading for another class and outline the argument.

4.   Compose a modus tollens of your own on any subject. Clearly outline the argument.

5.   Locate a hypothetical syllogism in a book you are reading for another class and outline the argument.

6.   Compose a hypothetical syllogism of your own on any subject. Clearly outline the argument.

Additional Exercise Set N

1.   Compose a contradiction on any subject and write it out as the conjunction of a proposition and its negation.

2.   Compose a brief essay (one page) explaining what the Law of Contradiction is and why it must be true. Include an example in your essay.

3.   Compose a brief essay (one page) explaining why contradictions are impossible and absurd. Include in your essay an example of a contradiction.

4.   Compose a brief essay (one page) explaining what the Law of Excluded Middle is and why it must be true. Include an example in your essay.

5.   Compose a brief essay (two pages) explaining the difference between direct and indirect argument. Include examples of each type of argument.

6.   Locate a reductio ad absurdum argument in a book you are reading for another class and outline the argument.

7.   Compose a reductio ad absurdum argument of your own on any subject. Clearly outline the argument.

8.   Compose a brief essay (two pages) explaining how reductio ad absurdum argument depends on the truth of the Law of Contradiction and the Law of Excluded Middle.

Additional Exercise Set O

1.   Compose a brief essay (one page) explaining the difference between deductive and inductive argument.

2.   Compose three deductive arguments of different forms on any subject. Identify the forms of deduction in each case.

3.   Compose three inductive arguments of different forms on any subject. Identify the forms of induction in each case.

4.   Locate an example of induction by simple enumeration in a book you are reading for another class. Outline the argument.

5.   Locate an example of induction by method of agreement in a book you are reading for another class. Outline the argument.

6.   Locate an example of induction by method of difference in a book you are reading for another class. Outline the argument.

Additional Exercise Set P

1.   Compose a brief essay (one page) explaining what a fallacy is and the difference between formal and informal fallacies.

2.   Compose an invalid categorical syllogism on any subject and use a diagram analysis to show that it is invalid.

3.   Compose a simple conditional argument on any subject that is invalid because its non-conditional premise affirms the consequent.

4.   Compose a simple conditional argument on any subject that is invalid because its non-conditional premise denies (negates) the antecedent.

Additional Exercise Set Q

1. Compose a brief essay (one page) explaining what a univocal term is and give three examples of univocal terms expressed by differing term expressions.

2. Compose a brief essay (one page) explaining what an equivocal term is and give an example of a term expression that expresses two different terms.

3. Compose a brief essay (one page) explaining what an analogous term is and give an example of two term expressions that are analogous.

4. Compose a deductive argument of any form on any subject in which there is an equivocation on a term.

5. Compose an argument by analogy on any subject that contains a true analogy.

6. Compose an argument by analogy on any subject that contains a false analogy.

Additional Exercise Set R

1. Compose a brief essay (one page) explaining what inductive generalizations are and what role they play in inductive arguments.

2. Compose three universal generalizations that state rules or laws on any subject.

3. Compose your own example of an argument on any subject which commits the fallacy of hasty generalization.

4. Compose your own example of an argument on any subject which commits the fallacy of sweeping generalization.

Additional Exercise Set S

1. Compose a brief essay (one page) explaining why the fallacy of begging the question is also called the fallacy of circular reasoning.

2. Compose your own example of an argument on any subject that begs the question.

Additional Exercise Set T

1.   Compose your own example of an exclusive disjunction on any subject.

2.   Compose your own example of an inclusive disjunction on any subject.

3.   Compose an argument on any subject that commits the fallacy of false dichotomy.

Additional Exercise Set U

1.   Compose a brief essay (two pages) explaining why all invalid deductions are non sequitur fallacies. Give examples.

2.   Compose a brief essay (one page) explaining why ad hominem attacks are fallacious.

3.   Compose your own example of an argument on any subject that commits an abusive ad hominem fallacy.

4.   Compose your own example of an argument on any subject that commits a circumstantial ad hominem fallacy.

5.   Compose your own example of an argument on any subject that commits a tu quoque fallacy.

6.   Compose a brief essay (one page) explaining the difference between a tu quoque fallacy and the moral fault of failing to give good example.

Additional Exercise Set V

1.   Using the Catalogue of Common Fallacies in Appendix II, compose a brief essay (two pages) explaining why argumentum ad ludificandum, argumentum ad rhonchum, and the fallacy of derision are essentially the same fallacy. Give examples.

2.   Using the Catalogue of Common Fallacies in Appendix II, compose a brief essay (one page) explaining why argumentum ad ludificandum, argumentum ad rhonchum, and the fallacy of derision are fallacious.

3.   Compose your own example of an argument on any subject that commits the fallacy of derision.

Additional Exercise Set W

1.　Using the Catalogue of Common Fallacies in Appendix II, compose a brief essay (one page) explaining the fallacy of false cause. Give examples.

2.　Using the Catalogue of Common Fallacies in Appendix II, compose a brief essay (one page) explaining the fallacy of common cause. Give examples.

Additional Exercise Set X

1.　Using the Catalogue of Common Fallacies in Appendix II, compose a brief essay (one page) explaining the fallacy of composition. Give examples.

2.　Using the Catalogue of Common Fallacies in Appendix II, compose a brief essay (one page) explaining the fallacy of division. Give examples.

Additional Exercise Set Y

1.　Using the Catalogue of Common Fallacies in Appendix II, compose a brief essay (one page) explaining what a straw man argument is and why it is fallacious.

2.　Compose your own example of a straw man argument on any subject and indicate why it is fallacious.

Additional Exercise Set Z

1.　Using the Catalogue of Common Fallacies in Appendix II, compose a brief essay (one page) explaining what the complex question fallacy is and why it is fallacious.

2.　Compose your own example of a complex question on any subject and indicate why it is fallacious.

Glossary of Logical Terms

This glossary provides the definition of each of the logical terms used in this book for quick reference. More information on some of these terms is given in the Glossary of Latin Terms and the Catalogue of Common Fallacies in Appendix II.

abusive ad hominem : fallacious argument in which the opponent's moral character is attacked instead of his argument or claim.

ad baculum : fallacious appeal to force or fear in place of reason in argument.

ad hominem : fallacious argument in which an opponent is personally attacked instead of his arguments or claims where the personal attack is claimed to have demonstrated the invalidity of the opponent's argument or the falsity of his claim.

ad ignorantiam : fallacious appeal to ignorance in argument.

ad ludificandum : fallacious appeal to ridicule in place of reason in argument.

ad misericordiam : fallacious appeal to pity in place of reason in argument, especially in moral or legal argument.

ad populum : fallacious appeal to popular opinion in place of reason in argument.

ad rhonchum : fallacious appeal to sneering in place of reason in argument.

affirmation : a proposition with affirmative quality.

affirmation mark : a mark on a propositional or argument diagram indicating that a logically possible relation between the terms is affirmed.

affirmative quality : the characteristic of a proposition in which the predicate is affirmed of the subject.

affirming the consequent : invalid deductive argument in which one premise is a conditional proposition and the other premise is the affirmation of the consequent of the conditional premise. The arguer then fallaciously concludes to the affirmation of the antecedent.

analogical terms : terms that have meanings that are partly the same and partly different.

analogy : a comparison made in argument.

antecedent : the propositional part of a conditional proposition that states the condition or qualification of the consequent.

argument : the activity of giving reasons in support of a conclusion; esp. the process by which a knower proceeds in knowing from the known to the unknown.

argument diagram : a diagram displaying the logical form of a categorical syllogism.

argument to absurdity : another name for *reductio ad absurdum*.

Aristotle's square : a chart of the four basic types of categorical proposition showing their relationships with respect to contrariety, sub-contrariety, implication, and contradiction.

arithmetic : the art of recognizing and using discrete quantities (numbers).

art : skill or ability.

astronomy : the art of recognizing and describing continuous quantitative patterns traced by the regular movements of the heavenly bodies.

begging the question : fallacious argument in which the conclusion is assumed as one of the premises.

categorical proposition : a proposition stated without any conditions or qualifications.

categorical syllogism : a form of deductive argument with two premises and some distribution of exactly three distinct terms in the premises and conclusion.

circular reasoning : another name for the fallacy of *begging the question*.

circumstantial ad hominem : fallacious argument in which the opponent is personally attacked on account of his personal circumstances instead of his argument or claim.

common cause : fallacious presumption that two things are similar because one is the cause of the other when it is possible that the similarity is due to a third thing that caused them both.

complex argument : an argument composed of simpler arguments.

complex proposition : a proposition composed of simpler propositions linked together with some logical connective.

complex question : fallacious presumption that there is a simple answer to a question which actually demands that another question be answered first.

composition : fallacious presumption that what is true of the part must also be true of the whole of which it is a part.

conclusion : a proposition for which reasons are being given in an argument.

conclusion indicator : a word or phrase indicating the conclusion of an argument.

conditional proposition : a complex proposition composed of two simpler propositions one of which states the condition or qualification of the other.

conjunction : a complex proposition in which two or more simpler propositions are linked in a direct and unqualified way, usually with the logical connective "and."

conjunctive syllogism : a valid form of deduction in which the negation of a conjunction and the affirmation of one of the conjuncts are offered as reasons for the negation of the remaining conjunct.

consequent : the propositional part of a conditional proposition that states that for which the antecedent is the condition or qualification.

constructive dilemma : a valid form of deduction in which a disjunction and conditional propositions stating that each disjunct is a condition for the same result are offered as reasons for the affirmation of the result.

contradiction : the relationship between two propositions that always must have different truth values.

contrariety : the relation between two propositions that cannot be true at the same time, but may be false at the same time.

deduction : an argument that is intended to show that the premises necessitate the conclusion.

denial : a negative proposition.

denying the antecedent : an invalid deductive argument in which one premise is a conditional proposition and the other premise is the negation of the antecedent of the conditional premise. The arguer then fallaciously concludes to the negation of the consequent.

derision : another name for the fallacy of *argumentum ad ludificandum*.

destructive dilemma : a valid form of deduction in which a disjunction of negative alternatives and conditional propositions stating the same condition for the affirmation of the alternatives is offered as reasons for the negation of the condition.

dichotomy : a disjunction of two alternatives.

dilemma : a form of complex deduction in which a conclusion is drawn from a set of premises that includes a disjunction.

direct argument : a deductive argument in which the premises are intended to directly support the conclusion.

disjunction : a complex proposition in which two or more simpler propositions are linked in such a way that they are stated as alternatives to each other, usually with the logical connective "or."

disjunctive syllogism : a valid form of deduction in which a disjunctive premise and the negation of one of the disjuncts are given as reasons for the affirmation of the remaining disjunct.

distribution of terms : the arrangement of terms in the premises and conclusion of a categorical syllogism.

division : a fallacious presumption that what is true of the whole must also be true of each of the parts into which the whole can be divided.

elliptical argument : an expression of an argument with some part left unexpressed.

elliptical syllogism : an expression of a categorical syllogism with some part left unexpressed.

enthymeme : an elliptical categorical syllogism.

equivalence : the relationship between two propositions that always must have the same truth value.

equivocal terms : terms that have different meanings.

equivocation : fallacious ambiguity in argument where the meaning of the terms or propositions composing the argument is not kept constant.

existential quantity : the characteristic of a proposition in which the predicate term is affirmed or negated of the subject term in at least one, and maybe more, cases.

exclusion marks : marks on a propositional or argument diagram indicating that a logically possible relation between the terms is excluded.

exclusive disjunction : a disjunction in which the truth of one of the alternatives excludes the truth of the others.

fallacy : a logical error.

false analogy : fallacious comparison in argument in which what is known to be true of a well-known subject is concluded to be necessarily true of a lesser-known subject on the basis of insufficient or irrelevant similarity of the two subjects.

false cause : fallacious presumption that two events that happen close together in space and time must be related as cause and effect.

false dichotomy : fallacious presumption that a disjunction presents an exhaustive set of alternatives when it actually does not.

false dilemma : is another name for the fallacy of *false dichotomy*.

falsity : the property of a proposition that states what does not correspond to the way reality actually exists.

formal fallacy : a fallacious mistaking of an invalid deductive argument for a valid one.

genus : a kind of thing of which there may be more than one specific form.

geometry : the art of recognizing and using continuous quantities (figures).

grammar : the art of using the parts of language meaningfully.

hasty generalization : fallacious induction that draws an inductive generalization as a conclusion from insufficient inductive evidence.

hypothesis : a condition.

hypothetical proposition : another name for *conditional proposition*.

hypothetical syllogism : a valid form of deduction in which two conditional premises stating that one proposition is a condition for a second and the second a condition for a third are offered in support of the conclusion that the first proposition is a condition for the third.

ignoratio elenchi : fallacious presumption that a premise is relevant to and, therefore, supportive of a conclusion when it actually supports a different conclusion.

immediate inference : the drawing of a conclusion from a single premise in argument.

implication : the relationship between two propositions such that when the implying proposition is true, the implied proposition must be true.

inclusive disjunction : a disjunction in which the truth of one of the alternatives does not exclude the truth of the others.

indetermination mark : a mark on a propositional or argument diagram indicating the possible affirmation of more than one relation between two terms.

indirect argument : another name for *reductio ad absurdum*.

induction : an argument that is intended to show that the premises make the conclusion probable.

inductive evidence : the premises of an inductive argument.

inductive generalization : the universal generalization serving as the conclusion of an inductive argument.

inductive particularization : the universal particularizations serving as the premises of an inductive argument.

inference : the drawing of a conclusion from premises in argument.

informal fallacy : a logical error that is not limited to failure to recognize the invalid form of a deductive argument, but rather an error involving the meaning of the parts of an argument, the relevance of the premises to the conclusion, the interpretation of the scope or support of a generalization, the use of an argument, etc.

invalid argument : the logical relation in a deductive argument such that the conclusion may be false even when all the premises are true.

law : a universal generalization stating a law or rule and which is applied to a particular case in argument.

Law of Contradiction : a fundamental law of logic stating that it is impossible that anything should both be and not be at the same time and in the same respect.

Law of Excluded Middle : a fundamental law of logic stating that, for any proposition, either it or its negation, but not both, is true.

lemma : an auxiliary argument forming part of a complex argument.

lemmastic argument : a complex argument with lemmas.

liberal arts : the seven basic intellectual skills required for learning: grammar, logic, rhetoric, arithmetic, geometry, proportions, and astronomy.

logic : the art of recognizing and using the logical relationships between things that can be meaningfully articulated in language, esp. the art of recognizing, analyzing, and evaluating arguments and their parts.

logical form : the relation of the parts of a proposition or of an argument.

mediate inference : the drawing of a conclusion from more than one premise in argument.

method of agreement : an inductive argument in which a series of differing particular cases are offered in support of a general conclusion on the basis of a common element present in the differing cases.

method of difference : an inductive argument in which a series of differing particular cases are offered in support of a general conclusion on the basis of a presence or lack of some feature in the differing cases.

modus ponens : a valid form of deduction in which a conditional premise and the antecedent of the conditional are offered in support of the consequent of the conditional.

modus tollens : a valid form of deduction in which a conditional premise and the negation of the consequent of the conditional are offered in support of the negation of the antecedent of the conditional.

negation : a proposition with negative quality.

negative quality : the characteristic of a proposition in which the predicate term is denied of the subject term.

non sequitur : invalid deductive argument.

parts of an argument : the premises and conclusion of an argument.

parts of a proposition : the characteristics by means of which a proposition is able to state what is true or false of reality: subject term, predicate term, logical quality, logical quantity.

pentachotomy : a disjunction of five alternatives.

petitio principii : another name for the fallacy of *begging the question*.

post hoc ergo propter hoc : another name for the fallacy of *false cause*.

predicate term : the characteristic of a proposition that predicates something of the subject term.

premise : a proposition given in argument as a reason in support of a conclusion.

premise indicator : a word or phrase indicating a reason for a conclusion in an argument.

proportions : the art of recognizing and using the proportional relationships among discrete quantities (numbers).

proposition : a use of language that is capable of having truth value.

propositional diagram : a diagram showing the logical form of a proposition.

quality : the characteristic of a proposition that relates the subject and predicate terms with respect to affirmation or negation.

quantity : the characteristic of a proposition that relates the subject and predicate terms with respect to how much or how many.

reason : a proposition given in support of the truth of another proposition; the capacity by which human beings are able to know and deliberate.

reductio ad absurdum : a valid complex form of deduction in which a contradiction is validly derived from a proposition thereby disproving that proposition and proving its negation.

rhetoric : the art of using language effectively to accomplish various purposes.

rule : a universal generalization stating a law or rule and which is applied to a particular case in argument.

simple argument : an argument that is not composed of simpler arguments.

simple enumeration : an inductive argument in which a number of particular cases enumerated in the premises are offered in support of a general conclusion.

simple proposition : a proposition that is not composed of simpler propositions.

soritical argument : a complex categorical syllogism composed of a series of simple syllogisms in which the conclusion of one is used as the premise of the next and so on until a final conclusion is attained.

sound argument : a valid deductive argument with true premises.

species : a specific kind of thing; a specific form of a generic kind.

square of opposition : another name for *Aristotle's square*.

straw man : fallacious argument offered in refutation of an opponent's position which is misrepresented as a different, much weaker position.

strong induction : an inductive argument in which the premises give sufficient support to the probability of the conclusion being true.

subcontrariety : the relation between two propositions that cannot be false at the same time, but may be true at the same time.

subject term : the characteristic of a proposition that refers to a person or thing, a group of persons or things, or a species of persons or things.

sweeping generalization : fallacious misapplication of a general rule or law to a particular case in deductive argument.

syllogism : a deductive argument of some form; sometimes used as another name for *categorical syllogism*.

syllogistic chain : another name for *soritical argument*.

term : the characteristic of a proposition that conveys the subject matter of the proposition.

tetrachotomy : a disjunction of four alternatives.

trichotomy : a disjunction of three alternatives.

true analogy : an analogy in argument that derives a conclusion from a proper comparison in the premises.

truth : the property of a proposition that states what corresponds to the way reality actually exists.

truth value : the truth or falsity of a proposition.

tu quoque : fallacious argument in which advice is rejected on the grounds that the advisor does not follow his own advice.

universal generalization : a universal proposition with a subject term referring to a group or species.

universal particularization : a universal proposition with a subject term referring to an individual person or thing.

universal quantity : the characteristic of a proposition in which the predicate term is affirmed or negated of the subject term in all cases of the subject.

univocal terms : terms that have the same meaning.

unsound argument : a valid deductive argument with at least one false premise.

validity : the logical relation in deductive arguments such that, when all the premises are true, the conclusion absolutely must be true.

weak induction : an inductive argument in which the premises give insufficient support to the probability of the conclusion being true.

Glossary of Latin Terms

This glossary provides a translation of the Latin terms used in this book for quick reference. For definitions of these terms see the Glossary of Logical Terms and the Catalogue of Common Fallacies in Appendix II.

argumentum ad baculum : argument according to the stick

argumentum ad derisum : argument to derision

argumentum ad hominem : argument against the person

argumentum ad ignorantiam : argument to ignorance

argumentum ad ludificandum : argument to ridicule

argumentum ad misericordiam : argument to pity

argumentum ad populum : argument to the people

argumentum ad rhonchum : argument to sneering

artes : arts

ignoratio elenchi : ignorance of the refutation

modus ponendo ponens : the method of positing what is to be posited

modus tollendo tollens : the method of negating what is to be negated

non sequitur : it does not follow

petitio principii : postulation of the premise

post hoc ergo propter hoc : after this therefore because of this

reductio ad absurdum : reduction to absurdity

septem artes liberales : the seven liberal arts

tu quoque : you too